women's rites

a WATER book

water

Women's Alliance for Theology, Ethics and Ritual

women's rites

FEMINIST LITURGIES FOR LIFE'S JOURNEY

DIANN L. NEU

The Pilgrim Press
Cleveland

to Catherine Fei Min Hunt-Neu

BLESSED MAY YOU BE,

BELOVED DAUGHTER,

THROUGH YOUR

LIFE'S JOURNEY.

The Pilgrim Press, 700 Prospect Avenue, Cleveland, Ohio 44115-1100
pilgrimpress.com

For additional assistance in constructing liturgies, contact WATER, the Women's Alliance for Theology, Ethics and Ritual, 8035 13th Street, Silver Spring, MD (phone 301-589-2509; fax 301-589-3150; e-mail water@hers.com)

The author gratefully acknowledges permission to reprint "The Great Transparencies," and "Song: 'Now let us honor with violin and flute'" from *Collected Poems 1930–1993* by May Sarton. Copyright © 1993, 1988, 1984, 1980, 1974 by May Sarton. Used by permission of W. W. Norton & Company, Inc. Every effort has been made to trace copyrights on materials included in this publication. If any copyrighted material has been included without permission and due acknowledgement, proper credit will be inserted in future printings after notice has been received.

Printed in the United States of America on acid-free paper

08 07 06 05 04 03 5 4 3 2 1

Library of Congress Cataloging-in-Publication Data
Neu, Diann L., 1948–
Women's rites : feminist liturgies for life's journeys / Diann L. Neu.
p. cm.
Includes bibliographical references and index.
ISBN 0-8298-1515-5 (pbk. : alk. paper)
1. Feminist theology. 2. Liturgics. I. Title.

BT83.55 .N49—2002
264'.0082—dc21

2002042546
CIP

contents

PREFACE

Women worldwide are challenging old rituals and calling for liturgies that mark positively women's rites of passage. We are creating women's rites for life's journeys.[1] Needs unimagined in earlier centuries challenge existing liturgies and call for the creation of new ones. Examples include, among many others, involving children in the liturgy for a second marriage; anointing a woman with Alzheimer's disease; blessing divorced partners who want to be friends; memorializing persons who have died with HIV/AIDS or cancer; and affirming a woman called by her community to feminist ministry. These challenges and more can be met with additional resources beyond traditional liturgies.

New voices are calling for new rituals. Communities need liturgies to honor a woman's biological passages: menarche, menstruation, miscarriage, abortion, childbirth, menopause, and old age (called "croning"). Some women need rituals dealing with battering, sexual abuse, rape, trauma, and violence. Some families need ceremonies for coming out and holy unions. Women-church communities and feminist spirituality groups, groups from diverse cultures and religions, the lesbian/gay/bisexual/transgender/queer communities, and persons with disabilities are developing new rites that fill the spiritual, political, and justice needs of their members.

When Rabbi Debra Orenstein designed a class on "Introduction to Rabbinic Practice," she found no books for Jewish women's life cycle: birth, naming, Sabbath, marriage, mourning. In her words: "Learning about and from women's perspectives on lifecycle had been my first motivation. . . . I could not assign unwritten essays to my students."[2] So she edited the book *Lifecycles: Jewish Women on Life Passages & Personal Milestones*. I am writing this book for similar reasons from a Christian starting point, but I hope it is useful for others as a model of how to honor roots, challenge religions to be inclusive, and provide for unmet spiritual needs.

Many women and their communities worldwide are asking for feminist liturgies for women's rites of passage so that they will have resources to celebrate the life-changing moments in their lives and in the lives of their children. I share these liturgies, which were created in a North Atlantic context, with women of all cultures so that they can use them as models to stretch their imaginations to create the rites they need for their own contexts. I also present these liturgical texts so a feminist perspective of liturgical renewal can be documented.

As a liturgist and psychotherapist living in the Washington, D.C., area in the United States and working internationally through WATER, the Women's Alliance for Theology, Ethics and Ritual, in Silver Spring, Maryland, I seek to empower women to access the sacred through our own communities. As a middle-class, privileged, white, feminist, Catholic woman who grew up in Indiana and studied in Indiana, California, Mexico, Washington, D.C., and Germany, I try to weave diversity into the liturgies I craft. Nonetheless, I have not lived in poverty, although at one time I took a vow of poverty. As a woman of faith whose grandparents came from Catholic, Methodist, Lutheran, and Jewish backgrounds, I pay attention to the ecumenical and interfaith aspects of the liturgies I create. As an aunt who has a niece with disabilities, I value all women's bodies as imaging the Divine. As one who has been shaped by the positive and powerful spiritual and social justice traditions of the Catholic church, I challenge the Catholic church and all churches on social justice issues like including women and all marginalized peoples in the decision making. I worship with a women-church community in the Washington, D.C., area and coordinate the Women-Church Convergence, a coalition of thirty-one women's groups rooted in the Catholic tradition. I have listened to stories of other women's experiences as I have traveled to China, Africa, Cuba, Chile, Argentina, Uruguay, Brazil, Mexico, Nicaragua, Honduras, Germany, Switzerland, the Netherlands, England, Ireland, Sweden, Australia, Aotearoa (New Zealand), and Antigua. I have cohosted international groups and visiting scholars from these countries who have come to WATER. Exchanges with these women have helped me realize again and again the many ways that women from different contexts create liturgy.

The life cycle liturgies here are ones I designed with the WATER community, with a Washington, D.C., area women-church community called Sisters Against Sexism (SAS), with the Women-Church Convergence, and with women in the global community who have asked for my assistance. These women are feminists with roots in the Christian and Jewish traditions who find that the religions of their ancestors do not give them the spiritual nourishment they need. They are activists, academics, and ministers who seek to be part of a community that fosters egalitarian and democratic ways of being religious in the pursuit of a just society. Some are mothers who want to pass on a feminist faith to their children. Others are middle-aged women who are looking for more in life. Some are students who want to practice what they are studying. These women come from many walks of life. They are justice workers, community organizers, teachers, women's shelter workers, nurses, doctors, social workers, counselors, theologians, spiritual directors, Catholic nuns and former nuns, women ministers, and healers. Some of these women called me at WATER and asked me to work with them to create particular rites of passage. I, in turn, share these liturgies with you so that you and your community will have resources to help plan the rites you need.

I am well aware that many women around the globe have limited powers of ethical agency, fewer economic resources, and little leisure to engage in such liturgies as I present here. Some are trapped in cultural expectations and beliefs that have taken away their freedom. I hope that these liturgies and others like them can offer new possibilities for these women today or someday.

The feminist liturgies in this book, *Women's Rites: Feminist Liturgies for Life's Journey*, mark turning points in many women's journeys. They are based on my assumptions about phases of women's life journeys from my experience of working with women through WATER. The first two chapters introduce the topic. Chapter 1, "Blessing Women at Life-Changing Times," gives an overview of the need for women's rites from anthropological, psychological, and theological perspectives. It is an introduction to women's development, not an exhaustive treatise on the topic, but enough to give the general contours.

Chapter 2, "Designing Feminist Liturgies for Women's Life Passages," offers communities and individuals guidelines for creating women's life cycle liturgies. I suspect that this is a unique contribution of this book. I offer the format that I have developed during my thirty-plus years of liturgy planning. I hope it is useful.

Chapters 3 to 6 present the liturgical texts. Each begins with an introduction that focuses on women's experience, analyzes the current situation, critiques biblical and religious traditions, cites women's rites for life's journey globally, and presents five or six liturgies that honor women's life-changing times. Chapter 3, "Creating Community," documents six liturgies that honor women's relationships with family, friends, and community. Chapter 4, "Honoring Women's Blood Mysteries," presents six liturgies that validate a woman in her blood cycle from first menses and monthly menstruation to menopause and attaining wisdom. Chapter 5, "Making Reproductive Choices," offers five liturgies to support a woman as she makes choices for her reproductive life, from conception to abortion, birthing to adoption. Chapter 6, "Mourning Loved Ones," features five liturgies that help a woman make peace with relational losses, from ending a relationship to mourning a lost pregnancy, from the death of a loved one to honoring widowhood.

Chapter 7, "Women's Life Cycle Liturgies Worldwide," summarizes the book and shows how Christian and Jewish women who are creating women's rites for life's journey are claiming ritual authority. It ends with a call to go forth in the name of Wisdom Sophia, Shekinah, to celebrate feminist liturgies for life's journey to bless women at life-changing times.

I am grateful to WATER for providing me for over twenty years a place to live out my call to do feminist liturgical ministry. The WATER community has been invaluable in this work. Mary E. Hunt shared her keen theological reflection and sharp analysis of the texts. Carol Murdock Scinto provided precise editing and renewing insights. Cynthia Lapp offered suggestions for music and readings that were often just what was needed. Interns, visiting scholars, and international colleagues told me stories of the women's life cycle liturgies that they created and celebrated in their countries and cultural contexts. Carroll Saussy offered advice for putting it all together. The WATER Alliance worldwide has celebrated these liturgies and offered helpful feedback.

Thank you to the staff at Pilgrim Press for bringing this book to final form, especially Timothy Staveteig, the publisher, and Kris Firth for careful editing.

May these liturgies remind you that you are not alone in your life-changing transitions. May they give you and your community strength, courage, and creativity to plan the women's life cycle liturgies you need. And may you pass them on to the next generations.

NOTES

1. I speak in first person plural here and throughout this book because I am part of the movement of women who are creating women's rites for life's journeys.

2. Rabbi Debra Orenstein, ed. *Lifecycles: Jewish Women on Life Passages & Personal Milestones* (Woodstock, VT: Jewish Lights Publishing, 1994), xi. For a Christian book, see Marge Sears, *Life-Cycle Celebrations for Women* (Mystic, CT: Twenty-Third Publications, 1989).

one

BLESSING WOMEN AT LIFE-CHANGING TIMES

But remember. Make an effort to remember.
Or, failing that, invent.

Monique Wittig

Maria experiences her first menses. Her women-church[1] community wants to celebrate this special event with her and her mother. She agrees. It is time to create a liturgy to mark a girl's transition from developing girl to changing woman.

Susanna menstruates each month. She wants to mark this bodily change, to let go of the previous month and prepare for the forthcoming one. It is time to create a liturgy to honor a woman's sacred blood and bless her each month.

Hildegard is going through menopause. She desires to invite her family and friends to witness this turning point by celebrating a rite of passage. It is time to create a liturgy to mark a woman's change of life through menopause.

WOMEN'S LIFE JOURNEY

The menstrual matrix—menarche, menstruation, and menopause—encompasses a series of transformational processes unique to females. At menarche, girls begin to realize what it means to be a woman. During monthly menstruation, women experience bodily changes, which can include physical pain and emotional swings. By the time women reach menopause, they have gained wisdom from life's experiences. Grandmothers were marked by these passages; mothers have experienced these cycles; and daughters and their daughters will walk through these doors. According to the Cherokee, menstruating women perform a function of cleansing and gathering wisdom that benefits not only themselves, but also the whole nation.[2]

All women move from one life passage to the next from generation to generation, albeit in different contexts. Each woman's life journey mirrors the annual cycle of time, season to season, spring to winter. Birth leads to death to eternal life. Yet, each woman experiences her journey differently and anew, both because of her uniqueness and because she is shaped by class, race, gender, culture, economics, family, and religious background. Each woman relates to her body uniquely with varying degrees of angst, physical pain, and immobilization.

Life journey is a metaphor that is rooted in biology and conditioned by physical environment, cultural expectations, social norms, and religious expression. As females transition from infancy to childhood to adolescence and from adulthood to old age to death, they are marked by change, and they, in turn, change society. The well-being of societies depends on the ability to provide contexts within which the young, middle-aged, and old can find meaning and purpose in the cycles of their lives. Women's liturgies for life's journey offer women, families, and communities an opportunity for integrating themselves at life-changing times.

FINDINGS FROM ANTHROPOLOGY

In recent years, social and cultural anthropology has provided some theoretical tools for understanding a "rite of passage." Some liturgical theologians have used this research on rites of passage to explain better those Christian and Jewish rituals that mark life-changing times in the human life journey.[3]

"Rite of passage" is the term French anthropologist Arnold Van Gennep used to describe the experiences that mark life transitions, such as changes in social states; the experiences of birth, puberty, marriage, and death; crossing territorial boundaries; or adjusting to seasonal changes.[4] He argued that these passages are marked by a threefold structure. The first, a separation period, involves moving away from one's present position. The second, the liminal period, marks the transition time between two relatively fixed positions where a community communicates its myths, values, and new behaviors. Finally, the rites of reincorporation period facilitates the establishment of a new position for the subject. Van Gennep posited that, while some human transitions might stress one of these aspects more than another, the basic structure of separation, liminality, and reincorporation with its concomitant ritualization holds for all rites of passage.

Van Gennep's theory helps us understand the importance of rites of passage for the human life journey. His findings offer a beginning framework for feminist liturgies for life's journey. Yet, helpful as his schemes have been, feminist scholars have noted that he showed his bias regarding women's roles in society.[5] He stated that women's rites are more related to movement from an "asexual world" to a "sexual world," since "the social activity of a woman is much simpler than that of a man."[6] His androcentric approach renders women significant only in so far as they are involved in procreation. His research perpetuates the myth that male is the normative way of being human and female is derivative and secondary.

Victor Turner, a social anthropologist who died in 1983, furthered Van Gennep's work and explored in more detail the liminal period of this ritual schema.[7] He integrated Van Gennep's insights regarding liminality with his own interest in structure, antistructure, and communitas. Turner posited that the rhythm of status change in tribal societies is a passage from structure to antistructure (in the liminal period) and back to structure.[8] For him liminality is marked by the negative characteristics of being betwixt and between, ambiguous, neither one thing nor another, and by the positive attributes of movement toward growth, transformation, and reformulation, which foster deep bonding between liminars and the communication of the *sacra* (sacred). The norms, values, attitudes, and sentiments of a culture are communicated to the liminars at this time. Turner states that liminality is a time of creativity for the individual and for the society: the individual is reconfigured through the liminal experience and society, norms, and values can be reconfigured as well. In his later work Turner says that liminality is the "seedbed of cultural creativity in fact."[9]

Much of the literature on both women's and men's rites of passage to date uses the Van Gennep/Turner pattern of separation/liminality/reincorporation. While some authors hold on to these categories as given,[10] others make some changes in the threefold structure when speaking of women's ritual experience. Still others argue that the Van Gennep/Turner pattern fits men's rites of passage but is not appropriate to use to describe women's rites.

Working from a hermeneutics of suspicion, Catherine Vincie notes that "the androcentric bias operating in the field of anthropology has adversely affected the study of women's initiation rites primarily by ignoring women's ritual experiences or by judging them vis-a-vis men's rites. The first leads to women's invisibility; the second to their insignificance."[11]

Rita Gross, writing in 1980, was one of the first to show the religious significance of women's rites for women and for society as a whole. She analyzed the Aboriginal women's initiation in Australia and showed how it follows the threefold ritual pattern of rites of passage that she describes as withdrawal, seclusion, and return.[12] Her analysis suggests that while women's rites are different from men's because of women's physiological functions, their religious significance is the same: "membership in the sacred community, not exclusion from it."[13]

Carolyn Niethammer, writer and researcher of Native American life, argues that many Native American tribes follow the threefold pattern of initiation proposed by Van Gennep, although not all three elements are necessarily included. She uses Van Gennep's basic structure and changes the language to isolation, education, and festivity.[14] In a girl's initiation rite, during the isolation period, the young woman is kept away from normal family interaction. The period of education offers time to convey the values of womanhood as well as the behaviors expected of a young woman now. Festivity includes a joyful celebration of the maiden's change in status from a girl to a woman. Some rites are private; others include the entire village.

Anthropologist Claire Farrer is critical of applying the Van Gennep/Turner ritual scheme to women's rites. Having spent time with the Mescalero Apache, she prefers to speak of the girls' initiation rite of this tribe as a "rite of confirmation" and a "rite of intensification" rather than a rite of passage. She argues for using the term "cultural performance," in which the whole community is involved in expressing in ritual form its identity and the primary values and worldview it holds for itself, its members, and for others. Speaking of the girl's initiation rite, Farrer says,

> It is a rite of confirmation in that the main characters are already women—menstruation has made them so while the Ceremony publicly confirms the status of woman. It is a rite of intensification in that participants are viewed

> as having the potential of being better women for having experienced the good, holy, and proper and for having fully learned the vital importance of the woman's role: to become a mother and thereby perpetuate the people.[15]

The Van Gennep/Turner model for rites of passage (and its derivatives) is one that has informed the feminist liturgies for life's journey I present here. I name the threefold process as gathering, sharing, and celebrating within a liturgical context. The community *gathers*, separates (Van Gennep's word), and withdraws (Gross's word). They enter a liminal stage of *sharing* and creativity (Turner's word), to educate (Niethammer's word) the initiand and one another about the rite of passage they are celebrating. They *celebrate*, honor the passing to a new state in life with festivity (Niethammer's word), and reincorporate (Van Gennep's word) the initiand and the community into society and return to daily life. The women's rites I present here also reflect Claire Farrer's sense of "cultural performance." The community gathers to confirm the status of a woman and expresses in ritual form its identity and the values it holds.

Uncovering these anthropological findings on rites of passage leads me to ask: What kind of rites of passages do women need in the twenty-first century? To answer this question I turn to the social sciences for clues about women's life cycles.

RESEARCH FROM SOCIAL SCIENCES

Life stages was a theme for developmental psychologist Eric Erikson, who created a useful vision for life cycle passages. Although there are critiques of Erikson, particularly by women, his model of human life is widely used to explain human development.[16] He presented eight ages (more commonly called stages) of the social development of the person from infancy through advanced age, and the core struggle humans addressed in each season. Erikson's stages are epigenetic; that is, each stage is grounded in those that come before it and continues to develop in those to follow.

Each stage in Erikson's conception of the life cycle involves an individual's struggle between two conflicting tendencies that hopefully results in a basic strength. Three factors give rise to these crises: biology, cultural demands on the individual, and the individual's own ego (personality shaped from past decisions and predilections). If the crisis is resolved positively, the struggle gives birth to a strength or "virtue" that prepares the individual for the next crisis. A negative resolution leaves the needed personality strength poorly developed or nonexistent and puts one at risk in the next crisis. Although Erikson's crises are age-related, because the struggle continues throughout life, it is possible to resolve a psychosocial crisis at a later time, out of its ordinary developmental season. Sometimes this is more difficult, yet at other times, because the individual has developed other strengths, resolving the conflict is less difficult.

Erikson's stages follow and include the struggle between the two conflicting tendencies and the virtue that comes with the successful resolution of that conflict.

1. Infancy: basic trust versus mistrust (hope)
2. Early childhood: autonomy versus shame and doubt (will)
3. Play age: initiative versus guilt (purpose)
4. School age: industry versus inferiority (competence)
5. Adolescence: ego identity versus role confusion (fidelity)
6. Young adulthood: intimacy versus isolation (love)
7. Adulthood: generativity versus self-absorption and stagnation (care)
8. Old age: ego integrity versus despair (wisdom)

Erikson's theory helps us understand ordinary challenges of human life. For example, many people have at least one identity crisis. It also makes human development more predictable and helps us both appreciate life cycle processes and better understand their dilemmas. Erikson's theory offers a beginning framework for feminist liturgies for women's life journey.

Yet, helpful as Erikson's schemes have been for understanding aspects of aging, many feminists have noted that Erikson's developmental framework reflects the traditional, western, linear approach to development that appears to overlook the relational aspects. Women's seasons and stages have been studied and continue to be researched.[17] Carol Franz and Kathleen White contend that Erikson's theory is flawed because he did not listen to women's experience and the "interpersonal attachment" that women exhibit in relationships.[18] Still other theorists who subscribe to developmental processes challenge stage theory to take note of the vast differences among women and men within a culture and across cultures, races, and classes.[19]

Over the past several decades, feminist developmental theorists have exposed and critiqued the normativeness of the male perspective in cultures marked by unequal power relations according to gender. Carol Gilligan proposed that women and men simply develop differently. For her ground-breaking study of moral development, Gilligan interviewed an advantaged population of college-age women seeking abortions and concluded that women have a different voice.[20] She discovered that women relate differently than men and make moral choices based on relationships. She brought to general awareness the gender bias that permeates the theories of most developmentalists.

Object relations theorist Nancy Chodorow challenges some of the traditional gender constructions of identity.[21] Important as Chodorow's work is, it is flawed because she presumes full-time mothering, the nuclear family, and heterosexuality where women are still, by and large, the primary caregivers. She does not distinguish differing caregiving relations among women of color, lesbians, and working-class women.[22] Feminist liturgies for women's life journey reveal the diversity of women's voices and women's life cycles.

Mary Belenky, Blyhe Clinchy, Nancy Goldbeger, and Jill Tarule studied women in both formal and "invisible" colleges and discovered women's ways of knowing as unique.[23] From their research they named five ways in which women know. *Silence*, having no voice, is experiencing the self without the capacity to receive or generate knowledge. For silent women-knowers, to hear is to obey. *Received knowing*, the voice of others, is seeing knowledge as absolute and always in the possession of "authorities." For the received women-knowers, receiving ideas, not creating them, is important. *Subjective knowing*, the inner voice, is distrusting authority and understanding knowledge as personal and originating within one's self. For subjective women-knowers, truth is an intuitive reaction. *Procedural knowing*, the voice of reason, is perceiving knowledge as objective and relationally derived, though subject to multiple perspectives. For perceived women-knowers, knowing requires careful observation and analysis. *Constructed knowing*, integrating the voices, is understanding knowledge as built by the knower, acknowledging and taking responsibility for shaping knowledge. For constructed women-knowers, the knower must be put back into the known, in other words, these women reclaim the self by attempting to integrate knowledge that they feel intuitively with knowledge that they have learned from others. Feminist liturgies for women's life journey presented here pay attention to women's ways of knowing in personal reflection and community sharing.

Jeanne Stevenson-Moessner believes that invasion and abuse of any sort spiral through developmental stages with varying degrees of healing and scarring. "If we start our theory-building with violated bodies, traditional life span and developmental theories are not adequate for the implications and imprint of violence."[24] She believes that women's bodies are central to developmental theory. In fact, all human bodies—female and male—are central to developmental theories. Patricia Davis's research with adolescent girls shows that the real struggle is to find God in the midst of the horrors of violence. She offers that girls need adults who will listen to them, talk with them about the violence in their lives, help them wrestle with God, and protect them from ongoing violence.[25] The feminist liturgies for women's life journey presented here acknowledge that women have been abused.

Jean Baker Miller and her colleagues at the Stone Center for Developmental Research and Services at Wellesley College offer another model of women's development, which they call person-in-relation.[26] These researchers suggest that women's desire to define self in interrelationship and through human connection is a more holistic social model than the typically individualistic one. Their theory focuses on women's moving from attachment to continued connection as the goal of human growth, rather than on separation and independence. This model suggests that women live by relationship and care, and strive for the development of the total self in relationship with others.

Feminist psychologists at the Stone Center are shifting the models for women's development. They posit that women's growth occurs in connection, in the context of relationships. Therefore the goal for women is intimacy rather than independence.[27] They raise the question: What if intimacy and connection precede identity? This self-understanding of women implies that women seek to create and live in a world that is interdependent and interactional. Some would ask, might there be a middle ground for both women and men—a both/and approach that embraces the benefits of both independence and interdependence?

The person-in-relation model implies that throughout a woman's life cycle she matures by being in relationship with others. A girl child learns to relate to her own body and understand its power. A woman in early adulthood learns to be intimate in relationship and makes reproductive choices accordingly. Cross-cultural research reveals that a woman who is middle-aged and older enjoys her greatest power because many of the limitations that surrounded her in her youth are now removed.[28] As her menstrual blood ceases to flow, she feels fewer restrictions on her behavior concerning fertility. As a woman gains social, economic, and spiritual authority, she comes into her own prime. She becomes a wise woman and moves into leadership positions within her family, community, church or synagogue, and society that call her to share her wisdom. The feminist liturgies for women's life journey presented here are centered in women's relationships with self, other, and community.

After reviewing these theories from the social sciences, I am left with further questions. How do women's bodies, the vehicles through which women relate, image the Divine and resist the patriarchal reality of negative body images? What does feminist theology offer about revaluing female bodies as embodying sacred power?

INSIGHTS FROM FEMINIST THEOLOGIES

Women's bodies are at the heart of women's life cycle liturgies and at the center of kyriarchal[29] fear. The body is a site of resistance to and transformation of the patriarchal reality that demoralizes and desacralizes women's bodies. Feminist work begins with the premise that experience is embodied.

The theme of embodiment is central to feminist theology. Feminist theologians start with women's experience of body to reclaim the goodness of bodies, of femaleness, of sexuality, and of the earth. They speak of women imaging the Divine in our bodies, including bodily changes and processes that patriarchal, kyriarchal religions find difficult—menstruation, birth, sexual activity, menopause, aging.[30]

U.S. Catholic theologian Susan Ross notes that feminist theologies stress embodied thinking that is rooted in concrete experiences and oriented toward practical results. They promote an embodied morality that takes seriously both emotions and the contextual nature of the conception of body.[31]

British feminist theologians Lisa Isherwood and Elizabeth Stuart speak about the way "patriarchy has de-sacralized and demonized women's bodies" and the need for a paradigm shift to "revalue female bodies as embodiments of the sacred power of the universe."[32] Christine Gudorf reminds us that the body is synonymous with the self. She calls us to uncover the body-denying history of the traditions.[33]

German feminist theologian Elisabeth Moltmann-Wendel underscores the persistent body-psyche dualism in Christian theology, calling it "disembodied." She argues that Christianity has repressed and even profaned the human body and excluded and devalued all that is fleshy. She proposes a theology of embodiment that "seeks to open up a forgotten place that is important today, from which there can be theological thought and action: the human body."[34] U.S. feminist theologian Carter Heyward believes that the incarnation of God as embodied in the human Jesus is proof that the body is godly and holy.[35] U.S. feminist theologian Mary E. Hunt, writing about women's friendships, reminds us that

> virtually everything we do and who we are is mediated by our bodies. Whether we touch, mime, eat, cuddle, exercise, talk, play, make love, comfort, imbibe, relax, watch movies, massage, pray, sleep, or celebrate, virtually every relational act is a physical event, something that is influenced directly by our bodies. To call humans embodied beings borders on the redundant, but it must be stressed in feminist theology to make up for the centuries of disembodied writings that have shaped the Christian ethical tradition.[36]

Korean feminist theologian Chung Hyun-Kyung points out that "Asian women's epistemology is an *epistemology from the broken body*, a broken body longing for healing and wholeness."[37] Chinese feminist theologian Kwok Pui-lan notes that the language of the erotic, which is found in feminist theology and was first articulated by the black woman poet Audre Lourde, is virtually absent from the theologizing of nonwhite women who live elsewhere than the United States or Europe. She takes account that in places like Thailand and the Philippines the female body is still viewed as a body to be sold. "Flesh" constitutes the "flesh trade" and the "erotic" is defined as the power men have over women's bodies.[38]

African feminist theologian Elizabeth Amoah recounts:

> In many cultural and religious traditions the woman's body is conceived in such a way that the autonomy of her will and wishes is completely denied. She is seen as an object for unlimited access. It is not uncommon to find that in many cases of rape, the tendency is to blame the woman rather than the man. A particularly fashionable example is the reference to the so-called "provocative dress" of women as if this is a good excuse for violating their persons in cases of rape.[39]

U.S. ecofeminist theologians remind us that the same patriarchal traditions that have demoralized and desacralized women's bodies have sanctified the rape of both women and the earth. Carol Adams claims that the connection between nature and the body is a sacred source of divine revelation.[40] Sallie McFague notes that embodiment is what human beings have in common with all life on the planet. Bodies "may be the most intimate and the most universal way to understand reality."[41]

Delores Williams, U.S. womanist theologian, connects abuse of nature with racist violence against African American women during slavery in an essay, "Sin, Nature, and Black Women's

Bodies." She notes: "Very few people made the connection between America's contribution to the abuse and exploitation of the natural environment today with the dominating culture's historic abuse and exploitation of African American women's bodies in the nineteenth century."[42] She observes:

> Breaking the spirit of nature today through rape and violence done to the Earth, and breaking the spirit of nineteenth-century slave women through rape and violence, constitute crimes against nature and against the human spirit. Inasmuch as some Christianity has historically advocated that God gave man [sic] dominion over nature to use to his own advantage, it has not been difficult to create rationales to support this rape and violence. Christian slaveholders, believing they had ownership over the lower orders of nature (i.e., lower than themselves, who were the "highest" order of nature), assigned black men and women to the order of subhuman, on par with the lower animals. Thus these black people needed to be controlled.[43]

Nancy Eiesland analyzes the lived experiences of persons with disabilities[44] and challenges us to confront issues of difference in embodiment. She reminds us that persons with disabilities have been made into "the other," "the less than fully human," "the wicked," because their bodies symbolize the disorder that confronts the patriarchal order. She notes that the disabled God, with impaired hands and feet and a pierced side, demonstrates that "full personhood is fully compatible with the experience of disability."[45]

Feminist theologies are faced with yet additional issues of difference in women's bodies. The fact is most women's bodies have been exploited and abused either physically, sexually, or emotionally. At the same time, many women do not recognize the kind of abuse they have suffered in their homes, social networks, or workplaces. Our bodies carry this pain as we journey through life. Therefore the process of valuing our embodied selves is usually different. Embodiment must also acknowledge sociopolitical, economic, and cultural influences on the body, since marginalization and degrees of privilege affect how women differ in understanding ourselves as embodied. Social location expressed through gender, class, race, sexuality, and physical and mental abilities influences how we experience our bodies, our selves.

The feminist liturgies for women's life journey presented here reflect that we are our bodies. Marking women's bodily life transitions in liturgy helps us to be whole: to embody women as imaging a God-Who-Looks-Like-Us, to overturn the patriarchal dualism of pitting the soul against the body, and to reclaim the relationships between women and the Divine, women and one another, and women and the earth. One rightfully asks: What challenges do feminist theologies bring to the life cycle liturgies of Judaism and Christianity? How do Christian and Jewish liturgies celebrate and honor women's bodies?

CHALLENGES TO CHRISTIAN AND JEWISH LIFE CYCLE LITURGIES

Looking at Christian and Jewish liturgies, we find that they have overlooked blessing women during most transitional moments in our life journeys. In fact, patriarchy uses reversal as a way to profane women's bodies. Reversing the reversals is at the heart of feminist liturgies for women's life journeys.

The most obvious example of patriarchal reversal is the myth of a woman being born from the body of a man in Genesis 2. Women are the ones who give birth biologically, yet this myth reverses this life event by creating woman from man's side.

Reversal is evident in Christian and Jewish life passage rituals. For example, Christianity reverses the sacredness of birth in the sacrament of baptism by pouring water over the head of the child to welcome this life into the community. Yet it does not recognize as sacred the moment a woman's water breaks, the child's head crests, and this new life comes into the world. Women give physical birth, but clerics, who are usually males, perform the ritual of baptism. To the degree that Jewish liturgy celebrates birth, it is boys—not girls—who receive attention through the ritual of circumcision, *brit milah.*

Early Christianity had no rituals for adolescence because it was not a recognized part of the life cycle. Eventually western Christianity named confirmation the sacrament of coming of age in one's adult faith, yet it does not bless a girl when her blood flows for the first time and she comes of age and enters womanhood. The traditional rite of adolescence for a Jew is *bar mitzvah,* and since 1922, girls may now celebrate *bat mitzvah.*[46]

Of all the Christian liturgical rites, marriage shows the greatest diversity among different ecclesiastical traditions and geographical regions because of the local culture in which the church found itself. Most modern rites stress the equality of partners, female and male, yet in most cases, a man gives his daughter to another man. Ceremonies for same-sex partners are just coming into being, and ceremonies for divorce are rare. The classic Jewish wedding ceremony, *kiddushin,* implied that a woman was set aside as the man's sacred property. In Judaism, divorce is sanctioned as a way to end an unhappy marriage. It is mandated in cases of proven adultery.[47]

Christianity makes communion a sacrament and feeds people the body and blood of Christ, yet the Catholic and some Protestant traditions still do not recognize that women who give birth, breast-feed, and menstruate image the Divine Holy One and are called to ordination. The Jewish meal, on the other hand, is the women's domain as witnessed on *Shabbat,* each Friday evening when the woman of the house lights the candles to close the previous week and begin the Sabbath. The Catholic tradition of

Christianity ordains male, allegedly celibate men, yet holds that women do not image Jesus and therefore cannot be ordained and accepted into the decision-making circle of the church, the clergy.

From the days of the early church, Christianity has provided ritual care of the sick and dying. While all were called to corporal works of mercy (Matt. 25:31–46), only the priests could confer the sacrament. It is an ironic twist when in most cultures women are the healers. The office of deaconess (Rom. 16:1–2, 1 Tim. 3:11) for ministry with the sick was restored by many Protestant churches in the nineteenth century. Widowhood (1 Tim. 5:9–10) was a recognized ministry in the early church to provide prayer for the ailing and to visit and nurse sick women.[48] In Judaism, the religious *mitzvah* of visiting the sick is a personal religious duty.[49]

Christianity and Judaism both ritualize death by offering established methods for proper disposal of the body and for acceptable expressions of private and public grief. Funeral ritual is an act of honoring the dead, a time to attend to the psychological needs of the mourners and the pain of bereavement.

In summary, many traditional Christian and Jewish life cycle liturgies exclude women from sacred rituals because decision-making men fear women's power over life and, therefore, ritually claim it for themselves.[50] In an article in 1987, Christine Gudorf wrote about male sacramental power.

> Limitation of sacramental administration to men functions as a claim for men that they—not women—have exclusive power to create and sustain real life, spiritual life, through representing Jesus, the source of life. This claim implements a separation between ordinary natural life nurtured by women, and spiritual life nurtured by a male elite who serve as symbols for all men.[51]

The story is told of a priest who meets with a first communion class in his parish. He asks: "Who can tell us how many sacraments there are?" "I can, I can," shout most of the children. The priest calls on a young girl to answer his question. Full of herself, she responds, "Seven for boys, and six for girls." The priest is speechless. This young girl knows the truth and is not afraid to speak it out loud.

What girl children and women know is that gender makes a difference when it comes to the sacraments[52] and to liturgies for life's journey. In Protestant, Orthodox, Catholic, and Jewish worship, women and our life cycle needs have been pushed to the background of sacramental and liturgical celebrations throughout history. Some Protestant women have been ordained, but this does not insure that churches are meeting women's spiritual and liturgical needs. Some Orthodox women have brought feminism into their church. Some Catholic women, who have been working for over twenty-five years for women's ordination, are now claiming the public space of liturgy, remaining in the tradition,[53] and claiming, "We are church." In Reform, Reconstructionist, and Conservative Judaism, women have been ordained for over twenty years, yet this was the first stage in a long process as many now ask: "How might the Jewish community be enhanced if it fully incorporated women's experiences and talents?"[54]

Most churches and synagogues do not have liturgies that support and bless women during women's rites of passage. Why is this, one might ask? Marjorie Procter-Smith, U.S. Episcopalian feminist liturgist, offers a Christian critique: "The feminist liturgical movement has criticized the traditional form and content of all Christian life cycle rituals as being androcentric and designed to serve the interests of powerful men in the church and society."[55] Margaret Moers Wenig, U.S. rabbi and Jewish feminist liturgist, says of Judaism: "Some women are attempting to rectify the disembodied nature of most Reform worship by composing blessings for menarche, laments for rape, and rituals following miscarriage and abortion."[56]

Some cultures, like in Africa, have rites of passage rituals that are violent to women, such as the initiation ceremonies for girls that use female genital mutilation (which is against the law now) and the widowhood rites.[57] The needs of women and the oppression of women by patriarchal churches, synagogues, and societies worldwide are the social realities that give rise to women's new life cycle liturgical practices.

THE RISE OF FEMINIST LITURGIES

Women have participated in liturgies throughout history. Jewish women practiced gender-specific rituals in the domestic sphere, such as the separation of the dough, the lighting of the Sabbath candles, the ritual purity laws surrounding menstruation and birth, the maintenance of a kosher household, the cleansing of the home for the annual Passover meal, and the preparation of the dead for burial.[58] Jewish women were frequently present at synagogue worship,[59] and some were synagogue leaders and elders in their communities.[60] In the early Christian church, which was established out of Jewish roots, Christian women continued the ritual practices of Jewish women because this was what they knew. As women's worship styles have developed, they have been shaped by each woman's social location: geography, class, ethnicity, religious affiliation, age, marital status, sexual orientation, and historical time.

The earliest Christian liturgical communities were made up of women and men who were initiated into the community equally through baptism. Galatians 3:28 records this baptismal confession: "There is no longer Jew or Greek, there is no longer slave or free, there is no longer male and female; for all of you are one in Christ Jesus." In other words, the Christian community was inclusive, overcoming discrimination by race, economic status, and gender. The Christian community met in one another's homes, that is, in women's space. "The home, a domain traditionally associated with women, was the place where the *ekklesia* gathered."[61] Women created house churches and functioned as their ritual leaders.

By the fourth century, as Christianity became institutionalized, Christian women were gradually marginalized from the liturgical center and concomitantly women's liturgical practices were pushed to the margins of the church and became invisible. What happened to women's rituals between the fourth century and the twentieth century is yet to be uncovered by feminist scholars, if there is documentation available. We do know that the classical Liturgical Movement of the first half of the twentieth century, which emerged with the Second Vatican Council (1962–1965) and its Constitution on the Sacred Liturgy (1963) and also during the peak of the first wave of the Women's Movement, opened the door for contemporary feminist reconstructions of liturgical practices and concepts. The Women's Liturgical Movement emerged on the wings of the second wave of the feminist movement. By the end of the twentieth century groups of women were reclaiming ritual power for themselves and their communities.[62]

In the late 1960s and early 1970s, hundreds of thousands of feminist theologians, clergywomen, women rabbis, and laywomen started the women's spirituality movement in the United States that brought modern feminism into churches, synagogues, mosques, ashrams, and other religious communities worldwide. By the mid-1970s, feminist liturgical communities were growing in Europe, particularly in the Netherlands[63] and Germany.[64] By the 1980s, feminist liturgy groups were emerging in Latin America[65] and in Korea.[66] Now groups can be found on every continent.[67]

These feminist liturgical communities challenge women and men to rethink the basis of religious practice: interpretation of sacred texts, liturgical language and symbols, styles of leadership and relationships, decision-making processes, and liturgical texts.

Feminist liturgy developed gradually from the confluence of historical, political, secular, and religious awareness. It emerged in the United States from the struggles of the twentieth-century movements on behalf of oppressed people—civil rights, anti-Vietnam war, the women's movement, women's ordination, human rights, gay/lesbian/bisexual/transgender/queer rights, and reproductive choice. It emerged worldwide from these and similar movements unique to each country, such as the struggle for the reappearance of disappeared loved ones in Argentina. The feminist liturgical movement, countering historic male cooptation, asserts that women must shape liturgical traditions to remember women's own stories as well as those of other marginalized people.

Christian and Jewish feminists around the globe are creating women's rites of passage ceremonies to meet the spiritual needs of women and their communities. These rites are unique to each community, culture, and religion, yet there are some common global movements that significantly shaped feminist liturgical practices in the twentieth century. Four of these are the renewal of liturgical life, the networking of feminists of faith internationally, the global impact of the women's movement, and feminist activism in Christianity and Judaism.[68]

Liturgical renewal swept through Christianity and Judaism in the second half of the twentieth century at the same time as the second wave of the women's movement. Yet, for the most part, official liturgical reforms were implemented just before the profound cultural shifts that resulted from the women's movement. Thus, many women were dissatisfied with existing worship despite all the liturgical reforms because the liturgy did not address women's life cycle needs. Women protested worship within the churches and synagogues, and many women developed alternatives to existing liturgies, rituals, and ceremonies that they called agape services, bread-breaking ceremonies, and feminist liturgies. Miriam Therese Winter captures the angst of many Christian women:

I have sung songs that women have written,
But seldom in church on Sunday.
I have even prayed to my Mother God,
But not in the sacred rites.[69]

Sue Levi Elwell speaks of reclaiming Jewish women's oral tradition:

> For five thousand years, Jewish women have been told what words to say and when to say them, or, more often, when *not* to say them. *Kol isha erva,* the rabbinic dictum that a woman's voice is potentially sexually provocative and should therefore not be heard in public, has kept many women in silence. Too many of the words that *have* been spoken and sung by Jewish women have not been heard. Words of praise and petition, words of thanks and of pain, words of joy and of sadness have remained stifled in the mouths and hearts of Jewish women through the centuries. Jewish women are now in the process of establishing a new claim to language that is our birthright.[70]

Women began a liturgical exodus into a promised land that flowed with women's prayers, songs, readings, symbols, and feminist liturgies. "Feminists in exodus within the church" developed new communities, as Rosemary Radford Ruether described in *Women-Church: Theology and Practice of Feminist Liturgical Communities.*[71] Women-church communities,[72] re-imagining communities,[73] women's spirituality groups,[74] Rosh Hodesh groups,[75] and small intentional base communities[76] grew worldwide.

The networking of feminists of faith internationally ranged from confessional groups (the World Federation of Methodist Women and orders of Catholic sisters) to issue-centered networks (Women's Ordination Worldwide) to regions (the Circle of Concerned African Women Theologians) to conferences (Woman

Church Speaks, Chicago, 1983; Women-Church: Claiming Our Power, Cincinnati, 1987; Re-Imagining, Minneapolis, 1993; Women-Church: Weavers of Change, Albuquerque, 1995) to informal networking of women's communities and religions (Rosh Hodesh groups). Many of these networks were ecumenical and engaged in common activities like Women's World Day of Prayer and the Ecumenical Decade of Churches in Solidarity with Women. In North America, the Decade spawned the Re-Imagining Conference in Minneapolis in 1993 where the liturgies, particularly the Milk and Honey Ritual, became controversial for some churches, especially Presbyterians. Feminist liturgies were marking the churches and synagogues in a transnational way.

The global impact of the women's movement had a major impact on the liturgical, ecumenical, and interfaith movements. New reproductive technologies, changing sexual patterns, diversifying family patterns, increasing awareness of women's marginalization, and the pervasive violence against women are cultural shifts that soon affected women everywhere. Musimbi Kanyoro of Kenya reflects:

> For it is clear that this new spirituality which has broken into our lives, which is carried by the women's movement, will have to go through a period of searching, struggling and suffering until answers can be attempted to the questions, even those yet to be asked.[77]

International Women's Day, celebrated worldwide on March 8, and the United Nations Conferences (Mexico, 1975; Copenhagen, 1980; Nairobi, 1985; Beijing, 1995) focus the global nature of women's concerns. Women's lives have also been profoundly affected since the 1980s by the global political economy and information technologies. Global circulation connects women, quite literally, in seconds.

Feminist activism in Christianity and Judaism emerged from the renewal of worship life, the networking of feminists of faith internationally, and the global impact of the women's movement. Feminist theologizing rose from these developments. While all feminist theologies engage conflictually with traditional (Western) theology, male-dominated liberation theologies, and white-feminist theologies, there are unique aspects to each. African women engage in dialogue with African traditional religions, Islam, and Christianity, in search of their own voices, dignity, and wholeness.[78] Latin American women theologize in the midst of class consciousness and human rights violations.[79] Asian women develop their visions in conversation with diverse religious traditions.[80] Women of color in North Atlantic countries critique the prevailing white theologies out of their own community contexts such as mujerista[81] and womanist[82] theologies.

Within the confluence of these developments, liturgy has become a lightning rod for women's activism in the churches and synagogues. As Catherine Bell says, for many women, "the right to ritual" is "the symbolic equivalent of the right to vote and receive equal pay."[83]

FEMINIST LITURGY AT THE CROSSROADS

In the late 1960s and early 1970s, women in North America were celebrating "agapes," "bread-breaking ceremonies," and "women's prayer services." I was one of those women. Arlene Swidler edited *Sistercelebrations: Nine Worship Experiences* in 1974.[84] I wrote my thesis *Feminist Liturgies: Claiming Ourselves Church* in 1980 after surveying twenty-five Christian and Jewish women in the United States about their practices of women's rituals. By the 1980s, women and women's communities began creating, reproducing, and publishing "Sistercelebrations," "Feminist Liturgies," "Women-Church Celebrations," "Women's Prayer Services," "Rosh Hodesh Rituals," and "WomanPrayer." By the 1990s, feminist liturgical scholars were analyzing the feminist liturgical tradition and publishing books that describe the feminist liturgical movement that is inspiring women and challenging institutional religions. They document how women are claiming the authority to create, teach, and lead ceremonies on women's own terms. They assert that women must shape their liturgical traditions to remember women's stories as well as those of other marginalized people. A brief overview of some of these works will help put *Women's Rites: Feminist Liturgies for Life's Journey* in context.

Rosemary Radford Ruether in *Women-Church: Theology and Practice* (1985) presents the historical and theological understandings of church as a community of liberation from patriarchy and lays the ecclesial foundation for a feminist renewal movement. She offers practical guidelines for developing communities of worship and mutual support. She describes a complete revisioning of the sacramental fundamentals of baptism, eucharist, and the day-to-day practice of the Christian life. She provides women's liturgies for community formation, healing, rites of passage, life cycle, and seasonal celebrations.

She reports that women-church stands on two thresholds: looking forward to options in biblical and prebiblical faiths that were hinted at but probably never developed, and looking forward to new possibilities for liturgical and eucharistic celebrations. In Ruether's own words: "Women in contemporary churches are suffering from linguistic deprivation and eucharistic famine . . . This book takes steps to end that famine of the words of life and to begin to bake the new bread of life now."[85] She urges readers to do more than protest against the old. She challenges women, men, and children to begin to live the new humanity now by creating new communities that nurture their souls and support their beings.

Ruether's book was published after the 1983 conference, "From Generation to Generation: Woman Church Speaks," that was sponsored by a coalition of eight Catholic women's groups that later became known as the Women-Church Convergence.[86] Her book gives recognition to the movement that Elisabeth Schüssler Fiorenza called *ekklesia of women* and I named as women-church.[87] Rosemary Ruether describes the theology and documents liturgies that women's groups have celebrated. This book is an early invaluable source of the women-church movement.

WATER, the Women's Alliance for Theology, Ethics and Ritual, began publishing feminist liturgies through WATERworks Press in 1985. *Women-Church Celebrations: Feminist Liturgies for the Lenten Season* (1985) offered feminist and justice communities examples of liturgies that they could adapt for Lent and Holy Week. *WATERwheel,* the quarterly publication of WATER, first went to press in 1985 and has carried one of my feminist liturgies in each issue since that time to the present. We publish feminist liturgy books through WATERworks Press.[88]

Penina V. Adelman in *Miriam's Well: Rituals for Jewish Women Around the Year* (1986) compiles women-centered Jewish rituals based on Rosh Hodesh gatherings for all the months of the Jewish year. The collection integrates traditional rites and recent innovations by Jewish women in the United States and Israel.

Rosh Hodesh, the monthly holiday marking the new moon and signaling the start of a new month, is occasion for special praying and celebration in the synagogue. It has traditionally been identified with women through *midrash* and folklore as a time to rediscover the new moon as a source for monthly renewal. Penine Adelman presents the practice of new women's ritual marked in settings outside of the synagogue. In this context, the Jewish calendar is a vehicle for noting the monthly cycles of women's fertility and understanding the female aspects of the Divine. Each of the twelve months (and the thirteenth as well) bears a seasonal theme, a historical and biblical significance, and new meaning given to female ancestors. Penine Adelman notes:

> *Rosh Hodesh* groups appeal to all women who have felt disenfranchised from their heritage—orthodox and liberal women, lesbian and straight women, young and old women. *Rosh Hodesh* has become a sacred time for women. Separated from the usual mixed male and female society, women feel free to take on the task of reinterpreting and refining language, ritual, sacred symbol and story so that they can feel at one with their own authentic traditions.[89]

Celebrating Women (1986), a collection of prayer and worship material by women, was first published as a beautifully designed, low-budget photocopied pamphlet by Women in Theology and the Movement for the Ordination of Women in England. A much expanded edition was edited by Hannah Ward, Jennifer Wild, and Janet Morley in 1995. In the first edition there was a heavy focus on lamenting women's situation in the churches and society; therefore, the section "Out of the Depths" emerged. The later edition reflected this pain moving into constructive anger and clear-sighted analysis in the section "Breaking Through." The editors also added "Taste and See," which reveals women's sheer delight and praise of "Mother God," "Womanly God."

Marjorie Procter-Smith, in her book *In Her Own Rite: Constructing Feminist Liturgical Tradition* (1990), explores the common ground that exists between feminism and the liturgical movement. She identifies memory and imagination as twin foundations of liturgical events in a Christian context, and then applies them to women. She identifies language about people as well as language and images for the Divine as basic issues for the women's movement, then applies them to liturgy. She addresses the problem of using the Bible in feminist liturgy and preaching. She explores the feminist liturgical perspectives of the sacraments of baptism and eucharist and addresses the relationship between liturgy and life from a feminist perspective.

Procter-Smith assumes the full participation of women in liturgy; therefore, she leaves aside a discussion of women's ordination. She opens the door for future reflection on women's liturgical style. Missing in her construction of feminist liturgical tradition is the recovery of women's liturgical history, later done by Teresa Berger in *Women's Ways of Worship: Gender Analysis and Liturgical History* (1999).

Marjorie Procter-Smith's first book sets the stage for her second work, *Praying With Our Eyes Open: Engendering Feminist Liturgical Prayer* (1995),[90] in which she challenges women to pray consciously. She insists women must "disrupt processes of marginalization, claim the central prayers of the church as our prayers, and thereby transform them from the language of the rulers to the language of the whole people of God."[91] The goal of feminist liturgical prayer, according to Proctor-Smith, is resistance and transformation. Resistance to patterns of domination, including prayers of resistance, brings about transformation. It leads to the recreation of the church as communal and healthy.

In 1993 two edited volumes on women and ritual were published. *Women at Worship: Interpretations of North American Diversity,* edited by Marjorie Procter-Smith and Janet R. Walton, is a collection of fourteen essays that probe the meaning and the many expressions of contemporary feminist worship. The editors describe this book as a kaleidoscope, a kind of healing ritual, an introductory grammar to the learning of a new ritual language, and an invitation to the development of "resistance rituals" of all sorts, both within and without established religious traditions. In *Women and Religious Ritual,* edited by Lesley A. Northrop, fourteen women from a variety of religious, scholarly, and cultural backgrounds investigate the effects of religious ritual on women and how women are affecting religious ritual.

Two books have been published to date on women's life cycle ceremonies. Marge Sears published *Life-Cycle Celebrations for*

Women (1989), in which she describes liturgies for the cycles of women's bodies, such as "Celebration of Pregnancy," "Healing Ritual Following Stillbirth and Miscarriage," "Celebration at the Start of Menses," and "Celebration at the Onset of Menopause." Debra Orenstein edited *Lifecycles: Jewish Women on Life Passages & Personal Milestones* (1994) and two other similar volumes, bringing together over one hundred women to create the first comprehensive work on Jewish women's life cycle, including pregnancy, infertility, childbirth, welcoming children, adolescence, being single, invisible life passages, coming out, marriage, divorce, midlife, aging, death, and mourning.

While many communities of women are creating feminist liturgies and women's rituals, few publish their rituals and most do not document their work for the public. Miriam Theresa Winter, Adair Lumis, and Allison Stokes surveyed more than seven thousand women who belong to these groups in the United States. They conclude in *Defecting in Place* (1994) that women are celebrating their own liturgies, envisioning a more inclusive future, and empowering one another to challenge patriarchal religion, and they are in the process redefining church.

Prayers & Poems, Songs & Stories: Ecumenical Decade 1988–1998 Churches in Solidarity with Women, edited by Anna Karin Hammar and Anne-Marie Kappeli, was published in 1998 by the World Council of Churches. It appeared as an Easter newsletter to encourage women and churches to "make visible women's creativity in worship." This collection helped launch the Decade on Easter Sunday, on the Orthodox Sunday of the myrrh-bearing women (second Sunday after Orthodox Easter), Africa Women's Week, Asia Sunday, the International Women's Day (March 8), and a day celebrating a woman martyr or saint. *Of Rolling Waters and Roaring Wind: A Celebration of the Woman Song* (2000), edited by Lynda Katsuno-Ishii and Edna J. Orteza, is a similar collection. It compiles new materials that the Decade generated. These liturgical, spiritual, and artistic resources were written by women around the world who live in different social and cultural contexts and come from diverse church traditions.

Janet Walton, in *Feminist Liturgy: A Matter of Justice* (2000), treats four aspects of feminist liturgies: the historical context in which they develop; the tasks and principles that guide them; the possibilities they offer; and applications to institutional liturgies. She states: "feminist liturgies emerged from various communal and individual attempts to right what was wrong and make visible what had been hidden about God and about ourselves."[92] She reminds readers that feminist liturgies resist injustice and correct social imbalance. She believes that feminist liturgies seek to engage imagination, resist discrimination, summon wonder, receive blessing, and strengthen hope. In her closing chapter she applies what has been learned from feminist liturgies to weekly worship in institutional settings. This chapter is unique because she is among the first to apply the principles of feminist liturgy to institutional worship. More work is needed on this important point.

Making Liturgy: Creating Rituals for Worship and Life (2001), edited by Dorothea McEwan, Pat Pinsent, Ianthe Pratt, and Veronica Seddon, documents some of the liturgies from five women's communities in various parts of the United Kingdom: Catholic Women's Network (CWN), Catholic Women's Ordination, St. Joan's International Alliance, Wimbledon Experimental Liturgy Group, and Wherwell Liturgy Group. The first part of the book focuses on "making liturgy." The contributors started with the question "When women want to celebrate a particular event, be it a Eucharist or any other occasion which gives spiritual sustenance, what *process* is required to create a liturgy?"[93] They respond with introductory chapters on symbols, space, dance, inclusive language, creating liturgies for small and large groups, choosing music, and taking liturgy to the streets.

Dissident Daughters: Feminist Liturgies in a Global Context, edited by Teresa Berger, who is German born but living in the United States, maps the global struggle for women's rites. Women from fourteen communities in different parts of the world—Peru, Australia, the Netherlands, Korea, Canada, Chile, the United Kingdom, Iceland, Germany, Sweden, South Africa, Mozambique, the Philippines, and the United States—contribute from their own experience and social location. Each author profiles her community and describes a feminist liturgy the group has celebrated. This book reveals that feminist liturgies are changing the liturgical landscape worldwide. The similarities and differences in these works reveal how feminists are revisioning liturgy. I look forward to the day when generations of women can read feminist liturgy books written by Asian, Latin American, and African women, and I appreciate the materials already available.

These books and collections of feminist liturgies, and others like them, remember and imagine into history and tradition the collective identity of feminist liturgical communities. They record liturgical memory and imagination from generation to generation: whom we honor, whose stories we tell, what values we reinforce, what meanings we express, what transitions we mark, and what social roles we are expected to play.

These feminist liturgies, born of necessity, raise up the voices of women, making visible the faith life of people moving from oppression to liberation. They challenge and nurture feminists working to bless women at life-changing times. They support the healing and transformation of all relations. They provide feminist liturgical background that sets the context for *Women's Rites: Feminist Liturgies for Life's Journey.*

In summary, my attempt to bring a revisionist anthropological, social science, and feminist agenda to the table of feminist liturgical theology is a tentative effort at best. What I have found are pieces of data that support the need for feminist liturgies for women's rites of passage. My suspicion is that the next decades will provide more material in this area as women create such rites from their own contexts and write about them. In the meantime, I offer these liturgical texts to add to the cross-cultural conversation.

NOTES

1. Women-church is "a global, ecumenical movement made up of local feminist base communities of justice-seeking friends who engage in sacrament and solidarity," according to Mary E. Hunt in *Women-Church Sourcebook* by Diann L. Neu and Mary E. Hunt (Silver Spring, MD: WATERworks Press, 1993), 2.

2. Laura Owen, *Her Blood is Gold* (New York: HarperCollins, 1993), 46.

3. See Catherine Vincie, R.S.H.M., "Rethinking Initiation Rituals: Do Women and Men Do It the Same Way?" in *Proceedings from the National American Academy of Liturgy* (January 5–8, 1995), 145–70; David Power, *Unsearchable Riches* (New York: Pueblo, 1984), 91–92; Luis Maldonado and David Power, eds., *Liturgy and Human Passage*, Concilium 112 (New York: Seabury Press, 1979).

4. Arnold Van Gennep, *The Rites of Passage*, trans. Monika B. Vizedom and Gabrielle L. Caffee (Chicago: University of Chicago Press, 1960). Originally published in 1909 as *Les Rites de Passage*.

5. Vincie, "Rethinking Initiation Rituals," 149.

6. Van Gennep, *The Rites of Passage*, 67.

7. See Victor Turner, "Betwixt and Between: The Liminal Period in Rites of Passage," in *Forest of Symbols* (Ithaca: Cornell University Press, 1967), 93–111; "Liminal to Liminoid, in Play, Flow, and Ritual: An Essay in Comparative Symbology," in *The Anthropological Study of Human Place*, ed. Edward Norbeck (Rice University Studies, vol. 60, no. 3 (summer, 1974), 53–92; "Variations on a Theme of Liminality," in *Secular Ritual*, ed. Sally Falk

Moore and Barbara G. Myerhoff (Assen, the Netherlands: Van Gorcum, 1977), 36–52.

8. Victor Turner, *The Ritual Process: Structure and Anti-Structure* (Chicago: Aldine Publishing, 1969), 125.

9. Turner, "Liminal to Liminoid," 60.

10. See Louise Carus Mahdi et al., eds., *Betwixt and Between: Patterns of Masculine and Feminine Initiation* (Chicago: Open Court, 1987).

11. Vincie, "Rethinking Initiation Rituals," 148.

12. Rita M. Gross, "Menstruation and Childbirth as Ritual and Religious Experience among Native Australians," in *Unspoken Worlds: Women's Religious Lives in Non-Western Cultures,* ed. Nancy A. Falk and Rita M. Gross (San Francisco: Harper & Row, 1980), 280.

13. Ibid., 28.

14. Carolyn Niethammer, *Daughters of the Earth: The Lives and Legends of American Indian Women* (New York: Collier Books, 1977), 38–48.

15. Claire R. Farrer, "Singing for Life: The Mescalero Girls' Puberty Ceremony," in Mahdi et al., *Betwixt and Between,* 258–59.

16. Lawrence A. Hoffman uses Erikson in his *Introduction to Life Cycles in Jewish and Christian Worship* (Notre Dame, IN: University of Notre Dame Press, 1996), 7–10.

17. See Jeanne Stevenson-Moessner, ed., *In Her Own Time* (Minneapolis: Fortress Press, 2000), especially Elizabeth Liebert, SNJM, "Seasons and Stages: Models and Metaphors of Human Development," 19–44.

18. Carol Franz and Kathleen White, "Individuation and Attachment in Personality Development: Extending Erikson's Theory," in A. Stewart and M. Lykes, eds., *Gender and Personality: Current Perspectives on Theory and Research* (Durham, NC: Duke University Press, 1985), 268–95.

19. Stevenson-Moessner, *In Her Own Time.* Structural developmental theories of Jean Piaget, Lawrence Kohlberg, Carol

Gilligan, William Perry, Nancy Chodorow, Jane Loevinger, Mary Belenky et al., and Robert Kegan provide a necessary counterbalance to the prevailing theory of Erikson, which describes universal, invariant, linear, epigenetic, hierarchical developmental stages, and to the life span developmental theories.

20. Carol Gilligan, "In a Different Voice: Women's Conception of Self and Morality," *Harvard Review of Education* 47 (1977): 481–517.

21. For a further development of this thought, see Nancy Chodorow, *The Reproduction of Mothering: Psychoanalysis and the Sociology of Gender* (Berkeley: University of California Press, 1978).

22. See Pauline Bart, "Review of Chodorow's *The Reproduction of Mothering*," in Joyce Trebilcot, ed., *Mothering: Essays in Feminist Theory* (Totowa, NJ: Rowman & Aallanheld, 1983), 147–52.

23. Mary Belenky, Blyhe Clinchy, Nancy Goldbeger, and Jill Tarule, *Women's Ways of Knowing* (New York: Basic, 1986).

24. Stevenson-Moessner, "Incarnational Theology: Restructuring Developmental Theory," in Stevenson-Moessner, *In Her Own Time*, 14.

25. Patricia H. Davis, "Horror and the Development of Girls' Spiritual Voices," in Stevenson-Moessner, *In Her Own Time*, 113.

26. See Judith V. Jordan, Alexandra G. Kaplan, Jean Baker Miller, Irene P. Stiver, and Janet L. Surrey, *Women's Growth in Connection: Writings from the Stone Center* (New York: Guilford Press, 1991), 1–3.

27. Irene P. Stiver, "The Meanings of 'Dependency' in Female-Male Relationships," in Jordan et al., *Women's Growth in Connection*, 153. See Joann Wollski Conn, *Spirituality and Personal Maturity* (Mahwah, NJ: Paulist Press, 1989), for a helpful framework to understanding attachment and autonomy in psychospiritual maturity.

28. Judith K. Brown and Virginia Kerns, *In Her Prime*, 2d ed. (Chicago: University of Illinois Press, 1992).

29. See Elisabeth Schüssler Fiorenza, *But She Said* (Boston: Beacon Press, 1992), 7–8, where she describes "kyriarchy" as "a different understanding of patriarchy, one which does not limit it to the sex/gender system but conceptualizes it in terms of interlocking structures of domination."

30. See Lisa Isherwood and Elizabeth Stuart, *Introducing Body Theology* (Sheffield, England: Sheffield Academic Press, 1998).

31. Susan A. Ross, "Body," in *Dictionary of Feminist Theologies*, ed. Letty M. Russell and J. Shannon Clarkson (Louisville: Westminster John Knox Press, 1996), 32.

32. Isherwood and Stuart, *Introducing Body Theology*, 79–81.

33. Christine Gudorf, *Body, Sex and Pleasure* (Cleveland: Pilgrim Press, 1994).

34. Elisabeth Moltmann-Wendel, *I Am My Body: A Theology of Embodiment* (New York: Continuum, 1995), 103.

35. Carter Heyward, *Our Passion for Justice: Images of Power, Sexuality and Liberation* (Cleveland: Pilgrim Press, 1984), 137–47.

36. Mary E. Hunt, *Fierce Tenderness: A Feminist Theology of Friendship* (New York: Crossroad, 1994), 102.

37. Chung Hyun-Kyung, *Struggle to Be the Sun Again: Introducing Asian Women's Theology* (Maryknoll, NY: Orbis Books, 1990), 39.

38. Kwok Pui-lan, *Discovering the Bible in the Non-Biblical World* (Maryknoll, NY: Orbis Books, 1994), 63–76.

39. Elizabeth Amoah, "Violence and Women's Bodies in African Perspective," in *Women Resisting Violence: Spirituality for Life*, ed. Mary John Mananzan, Mercy Amba Oduyoye, Elsa Tamez, J. Shannon Clarkson, Mary C. Grey, and Letty M. Russell (Maryknoll, NY: Orbis Books, 1996), 80.

40. Carol Adams, ed., *Ecofeminism and the Sacred* (New York: Continuum, 1993).

41. Sallie McFague, *The Body of God: An Ecological Theology* (Minneapolis: Fortress Press, 1993), 18.

42. Delores Williams, "Sin, Nature, and Black Women's Bodies," in Adams, *Ecofeminism and the Sacred,* 24.

43. Ibid., 27–28.

44. People with disabilities describe themselves in a variety of ways, including "persons with disabilities," "physically challenged," and "differently abled." Nancy Eiesland uses "persons with disabilities"; therefore, I use it here. See Nancy Eiesland, *The Disabled God* (Nashville: Abingdon Press, 1994).

45. Ibid., 100.

46. Debra R. Blank, "Jewish Rites of Adolescence," in *Life Cyles in Jewish and Christian Worship,* ed. Paul F. Bradshaw and Lawrence A. Hoffman (Notre Dame, IN: University of Notre Dame Press, 1996), 99.

47. Lawrence A. Hoffman, "The Jewish Wedding Ceremony," in Bradshaw and Hoffman, *Life Cyles in Jewish and Christian Worship,* 147.

48. Karen B. Westerfield Tucker, "Christian Rituals Surrounding Sickness," in Bradshaw and Hoffman, *Life Cyles in Jewish and Christian Worship,* 157.

49. Stacy Laveson, "'Visiting the Sick' and the Deathbed Confession in Judaism," in Bradshaw and Hoffman, *Life Cyles in Jewish and Christian Worship,* 173.

50. Christine E. Gudorf, "The Power to Create: Sacraments and Men's Need to Birth," *Horizons* 14/2 (1987), 301.

51. Ibid., 297.

52. Susan A. Ross explores this in depth in *Extravagant Affections: A Feminist Sacramental Theology* (New York: Continuum, 1998).

53. See Miriam Therese Winter, Adair Lumis, and Alison Stokes, *Defecting in Place* (New York: Crossroad, 1995).

54. See Rabbi Debra Orenstein, ed., *Lifecycles: Jewish Women on Life Passages & Personal Milestones* (Woodstock, VT: Jewish Lights Publishing, 1994), x; and Margaret Moers Wenig, "Reform Jewish

Worship: How Shall We Speak of Torah, Israel, and God?" in *Women at Worship: Interpretations of North American Diversity*, ed. Marjorie Procter-Smith and Janet R. Walton (Louisville: Westminster John Knox Press, 1993), 31–42.

55. Marjorie Procter-Smith, "Contemporary Challenges to Christian Life-Cycle Ritual," in Bradshaw and Hoffman, *Life Cyles in Jewish and Christian Worship*, 240–61.

56. Wenig, "Reform Jewish Worship," 37.

57. Rebecca Yawa Ganusah, "Gendering Gospel and Culture," paper, 6 January 2001, Accra, Ghana; Rebecca Yawa Ganusah, "Widowhood Beliefs and Practices Among the Avatime of Ghana," in *Where God Reigns*, ed. Elizabeth Amoah (Accra, Ghana: Sam-Woode, 1997), 135–58.

58. See Teresa Berger, *Women's Ways of Worship: Gender Analysis and Liturgical History* (Collegeville, MN: Liturgical Press, 1999), 28.

59. See Ross S. Kraemer, *Her Share of the Blessings: Women's Religions among Pagans, Jews, and Christians in the Greco-Roman World* (New York: Oxford University Press, 1992).

60. See Bernadette J. Brooten, *Women Leaders in the Ancient Synagogue: Inscriptional Evidence and Background Issues*. Brown Judaic Studies 36 (Chico, CA: Scholars Press, 1982).

61. Margaret Y. MacDonald, *Early Christian Women and Pagan Opinion: The Power of the Hysterical Woman* (Cambridge, England: Cambridge University Press, 1984), 217.

62. I am indebted to Teresa Berger for a detailed account of the history of women at worship. See *Women's Ways of Worship*.

63. See Denise Dijk, "Developments in Feminist Liturgy in the Netherlands," *Studia Liturgica* 25 (1995): 120–28.

64. See Herta Leistner, ed., *Lass spüren deine Kraft: Feministische Liturgie*, (Gütersloh: Gütersloher Verlagshaus, 1997), 16–26.

65. WATER, though our Women Crossing Worlds Project, worked with women's groups in the Southern Cone from 1983 to the present.

66. See "Women Church of Korea," in *In God's Image* (June 1990), 56f.

67. See Teresa Berger, *Dissident Daughters* (Louisville: Westminster John Knox Press, 2001).

68. Ibid., 3–13.

69. Miriam Therese Winter, *WomanWord: A Feminist Lectionary and Psalter. Women of the New Testament* (New York: Crossroad, 1991), 266.

70. Sue Levi Elwell, "Reclaiming Jewish Women's Oral Tradition: Rosh Hodesh," in *Women at Worship: Interpretations of North American Diversity*, ed. Marjorie Procter-Smith and Janet R. Walton (Louisville: Westminster John Knox Press, 1993), 111–12.

71. Rosemary Radford Ruether, *Women-Church: Theology and Practice of Feminist Liturgical Communities* (San Francisco: Harper & Row, 1985), 67.

72. See Diann L. Neu and Mary E. Hunt, *Women-Church Sourcebook* (Silver Spring, MD: WATERworks Press, 1993).

73. See Nancy J. Berneking and Pamela Carter Joern, eds., *Re-Membering and Re-Imagining* (Cleveland: Pilgrim Press, 1995), 18–20. The fallout from the Presbyterian Church was of earthquake proportions. The Re-Imagining community has a newsletter and continues to offer yearly conferences. Re-Imagining, 122 W. Franklin Avenue, Room 7, Minneapolis, MN 55404-2435, 612-879-8036, www.reimagining.org, friends@reimagining.org.

74. See Winter, Lumis, and Stokes, *Defecting in Place;* and *The Ecumenical Review* (Geneva, Switzerland: World Council of Churches) vol. 53, no. 1 (January 2001): "On Being Church: Women's Voices and Visions."

75. See Elwell, "Reclaiming Jewish Women's Oral Traditions," 113.

76. See Bernand Lee and William D'Antonio, *The Catholic Experience of Small Christian Communities* (New York: Paulist Press,

2000); Call to Action Small Intentional Community directory; and the November 2001 taped interview with Bill D'Antonio and Diann Neu on "Small Worshipping Communities" for Faith Matters, an ecumenical radio show hosted by Maureen Fiedler, SL, of the Quixote Center in Mt. Rainier, Maryland.

77. Musimbi R. A. Kanyoro, "The Meaning of the Story: Theology as Experience," in J. S. Pobee, ed., *Culture, Women and Theology* (Delhi: ISPCK, 1994), 29.

78. See Mercy Amba Oduyoye, "Women and Ritual in Africa," in *The Will to Arise: Women, Tradition, and the Church in Africa*, ed. Mercy Amba Oduyoye and Musimbi R. A. Kanyoro (Maryknoll, NY: Orbis Books, 1992), 9–24.

79. See Ivone Gebara, *Levanta-te e anda: Alguns aspectos da caminhada da mulher na America Latina* (Sao Paulo: Edicoes Paulinas, 1989); Mary Judith Ress, Ute Siebert-Cuadra, and Lene Siorup, eds., *Del Cielo a la Tierra: Una Antolotia de Teologia Feminista* (Santiago, Chile: Sello Azul, 1994).

80. See Chung Hung-Kyung, *Struggle to Be the Sun Again: Introducing Asian Women's Theology* (Maryknoll: Orbis Books, 1990); Mary John Mananzan, ed., *Women and Religion: A Collection of Essays, Personal Histories, and Contextualized Liturgies*, 2d ed. (Manila: Institute of Women's Studies, St. Scholastica College, 1992).

81. See Ada Maria Isasi-Diaz, *Mujerista Theology* (Maryknoll, NY: Orbis Books, 1996).

82. See Katie Canon, *Katie's Cannon: Womanism and the Soul of the Black Community* (New York: Continuum, 1995); Emilie Townes, *A Troubling in My Soul: Womanist Perspectives on Evil and Suffering* (Maryknoll, NY: Orbis Books, 1993).

83. Catherine Bell, *Ritual: Perspectives and Dimensions* (New York: Oxford University Press, 1997), 238.

84. Arlene Swidler, ed., *Sistercelebrations: Nine Worship Experiences* (Philadelphia: Fortress Press, 1974).

85. Ruether, *Women-Church*, 4.

86. The eight groups were WATER (the Women's Alliance for Theology, Ethics and Ritual), Women's Ordination Conference (WOC), Quixote Center, National Coalition of American Nuns (NCAN), National Assembly of Religious Women (NARW), LAS HERMANAS, Institute of Women Today, and Chicago Catholic Women.

87. Elisabeth Schüssler Fiorenza, *Discipleship of Equals* (New York: Crossroad, 1993), 196.

88. See Diann Neu in the bibloigraphy for a list of the many liturgy books WATERworks Press has published.

89. Penina V. Adelman, *Miriam's Well: Rituals for Jewish Women Around the Year* (Fresh Meadows, NY: Biblio Press, 1986), 7.

90. Marjorie Procter-Smith, *Praying With Our Eyes Open: Engendering Feminist Liturgical Prayer* (Nashville: Abingdon Press, 1995).

91. Ibid., 13.

92. Janet Walton, *Feminist Liturgy: A Matter of Justice* (Collegeville, MN: Liturgical Press, 2000), 14.

93. Dorothea McEwan, Pat Pinsent, Ianthe Pratt, and Veronica Seddon, *Making Liturgy: Creating Rituals for Worship and Life* (Norwich, Norfolk, England: Canterbury Press, 2001), ix.

two

DESIGNING FEMINIST LITURGIES FOR WOMEN'S LIFE PASSAGES

Wisdom Sophia, be with me now.
Wisdom Sophia, be in my mind and in my thinking;
Wisdom Sophia, be in my heart and in my perceiving;
Wisdom Sophia, be in my mouth and in my speaking;
Wisdom Sophia, be in my hands and in my working;
Wisdom Sophia, be in my feet and in my walking;
Wisdom Sophia, be in my body and in my loving.
Wisdom Sophia, be with me all the days of my life, and beyond.
Wisdom Sophia, be with me now.

This prayer is one I pray often before I begin to create a feminist liturgy. Wisdom Sophia is the primary source of my inspiration for designing women's rites of passage. She has spoken to my heart and changed my prayer. She has become central in the liturgies of my community.

The Sophia figure and Wisdom practices have reemerged in contemporary theology and worship.[1] There is a newborn feminist interest in this ancient female figure from the Scriptures.[2] Divine Woman Wisdom continues her call for the liberation of all from patriarchal, kyriarchal power in society and in religious communities. She invites us to rearticulate symbols, images, and names of the Divine so that masculine God and Christ language is radically changed, and the Western cultural sex/gender system is radically reconstructed.

A PARABLE FOR FEMINIST LITURGISTS

Designing women's life cycle liturgies is like making a quilt. First the quilter gathers fabric in her house—old blouses and dresses, curtains that don't fit the windows anymore, baby dresses and worn jeans, her partner's shirts, clothes that friends have left and never reclaimed, old dish towels and sheets, material that she has been given from many countries. She makes a pattern. Then she reaches for her scissors. She cuts big pieces and little ones, long strips and short patches, perfectly square shapes and oddly cut ones. The old fabrics she has offer her new shapes and sizes. Parts of her life, of her lover's life, of her children's lives, parts of her house and parts of her friends' fabrics fall from her shears. Then she begins to arrange the patches into the pattern she has chosen and pin the fabric pieces to a backing cloth.

She discovers that she does not have enough pieces. The quilt will be too small, she thinks sadly. It just won't be big enough for her. She has another idea. She goes to buy new fabric so that she can cut bright strips and squares from it to continue her beautiful design. The woman hurries home, and gets out her scissors once again. She cuts more big pieces and little ones, long strips and short patches, perfectly square shapes and oddly cut ones. She takes the new pile of fragments, and begins to fit them in among the old pieces. Some look good together, others are harder to arrange. Finally the design looks just right.

But now she has a new worry. The quilt will be enormous. She realizes that she herself cannot do all the sewing to finish it. It would take more time than she has in her days, more time than is available in her weeks, her months, her life.

So she calls her friends. "Come and help me make a quilt," she says. They come. Some know just what to do. Others have never made a quilt before. Some call other friends, people who are strangers to her. They all bring needles. Those who are more experienced help the neophytes. Together they invent new ways to join the fabric. Some of them go out and bring back pieces of their lives. The quilt grows bigger and bigger. Babies sleep and play as their caresharers sew on the quilt. Children run and sing and learn their first stitches. Elders give advice and take their turn quilting.

Everyone sews and sews. The quilt grows larger and larger, brighter and bolder, more colorful and more diverse at every stitch. And the women look at the quilt that they are all making with their lives and they smile and smile, and rejoice in their hearts and are very glad.

Let those who have ears to hear, hear. Let those who have eyes to see, see. Let those who have hearts to feel, feel. Let those who have pieces to add, begin![3]

REVISIONING WOMEN'S LIFE CYCLE LITURGIES

This parable captures what is happening as feminists around the world reshape women's life cycle liturgies from their religious perspectives and in their own contexts. Women are gathering in diverse communities to create quilts, weavings, *arpilleras*, tie dyes, embroideries, blankets, serapes, and cloths of many colors. The liturgies these women craft address the spiritual needs of women at life-changing times from their own countries, cultures, clans, neighborhoods, and families. These women are revisioning culture and religion to integrate the old with the new. We are bringing feminist concerns to institutional religious services and prayers. We are reclaiming and redesigning traditional rituals and symbols. We are creating feminist liturgies to mark the turning points in women's life journeys. We are blessing women at life-changing times.

THE ART OF CREATING FEMINIST LITURGIES

Some people have a natural talent for creating liturgies, others have traditional training, and some have both. The art of creating feminist liturgies can be learned. Each individual, family, or community can create meaningful rites of passage to support one another in transition. Each can create out of one's own traditions and include the family of humanity and the Holy One (however one names the Divine). Each liturgy can be unique and reflect a particular context.

From my thirty years of liturgy planning in Catholic, ecumenical, interfaith, and cross-cultural settings, I have learned that to create liturgies you only need inspiration, time, thought, and resources. These guidelines may make your planning process more fruitful and/or give you courage to begin. This is the brainstorming method I use to begin planning. To illustrate this I will use Maria's liturgy, "From Developing Girl to Changing Woman: A Celebration of Menses," found in chapter 4 of this book.

Think of the particular liturgy that your community needs. An occasion will present itself. A person will ask for a blessing or ceremony for herself, a friend, or a family member. (For example, Maria experiences her first menses and she and her family want to celebrate her rite of passage with a liturgy.) Search with the individual or community members and talk about the need. (We need to create a liturgy to welcome Maria into womanhood, to honor menarche, and to proclaim our sacred power as women.) Write down the major theme (menses) and give the liturgy a tentative name if you can (Girls Becoming Women).

Focus the theme. Think of what you want this liturgy to say, why you are creating it, and what you want to happen to people during and after it. (Maria is a symbol of the passage to womanhood that each of us here and women of every culture experience. We want to bless Maria, honor menarche, and proclaim women's sacred power.)

Discover a symbol that will visibly carry the message of the liturgy. Symbols are key to successful liturgies. Reclaim symbols used by many traditions, such as oil, bread, salt, water, candles, and eggs. Try others, such as a variety of breads and drinks, shells, ribbons, fans, bells, chimes, mirrors, herbs, fruits, milk and honey, birdcage, or balloons. Choose one symbol or several. Keep it simple (egg, red candles, red fruits and drinks).

Identify readings, prayers, and blessings that make your message concrete. What do you want them to say? Whose words do you want to hear—scripture, poetry, excerpts by women from international and cross-cultural settings? Should these be mimed, danced, read chorally, spoken with many voices? Do you need to write new prayers, blessings, or stories? Be sure to use language that is inclusive of gender, ethnicity, class, age, abilities, and lifestyles. (We need to look for a reading on first menstruation.)

Select music that conveys your message. Identify songs, chants, and instrumental and taped music that support your theme. Note the mood and message to decide the appropriate place for each in your service. Use women's music whenever possible to educate others about it (in this example, Marsie Silvestro's "Let the Women Be There," Colleen Fulmer's "I Am Enough," and Carole Etzler's "Womanriver Flowing On."

Choose an environment that enhances the theme of the celebration. This could be outside near water, in a park or garden, in a special room, at someone's house, or in a church or chapel. (This liturgy takes place in Maria's home.) Arrange the seating in a circle around a circular table. Be attentive to color and its coordination with candles, cloths, symbols, and banners (red). Place the liturgical objects on the table or decide to bring them into the liturgy at an appropriate time. (In this liturgy we will do both.)

Share the leadership for various parts of the service with several people. The liturgy belongs to the community; therefore, it is not centered in one person. There is no main presider, rather various parts need to be initiated by different people. Decide who will lead each section. Give the leaders scripts and ideas to guide them in their parts, but encourage them to use their own words for introductions, blessings, and prayers. (In this example, leaders are Maria and her mother, her godmother, other girls, friends, and crones.)

Include body expression. Use postures and gestures to embody the message of the liturgy, such as movement to music, dance/choreography that includes hand motions or bowing, and warm embraces at the time of peace sharing. Use dramatic gestures when interacting with the symbols, for example, pour the water like a waterfall. In the course of the liturgy you may light a candle, wash your hands, break bread, drink from a cup, share herbs, plant bulbs, meditate on the colors of summer, or pray with your arms crossed in front of your chest swaying side to side. Be aware that many women's bodies carry pain from physical and emotional abuse. Ask permission to touch people. (In this liturgy, we light candles, bless our selves, eat, and drink.)

Involve children in the celebration. Invite children to be with the community at the beginning of the liturgy. Then after the readings gather them in another space to create the same symbol that focuses the liturgy. Have them return to the liturgy at a later time to share their symbols. (We want the young, not-yet-menstruating girls to light green candles and stay with us for the whole time.)

Be attentive to moments of transition in the liturgy. Check the transition times in the liturgy. When one part flows smoothly into the next the liturgy works. This is done best with both sounds and gestures appealing to the senses, not by announcement.

BRAINSTORMING GUIDE FOR CREATING WOMEN'S RITES

Use this guide to collect ideas for the rite of passage you are planning.

Focus the theme: (What do we need to liturgize?)
Environment: (How do we create a safe, sacred space that reflects the theme? Where?)
Symbol: (What symbol carries the message?)
Litanies/prayers: (What will we use? Do we need to write them?)
Readings/poems/stories/meditations: (Which ones will we use?)
Songs/chants: (Which will enhance the theme?)
Children's part: (What will the children do and when?)
Blessing the symbol: (How will we do this?)
Body expression: (How will we embody our message?)
Closing/sending forth: (How will we bring closure?)
Materials needed
Preparation
People for each part

DESIGNING THE LIFE CYCLE LITURGICAL STRUCTURE

When the previous brainstorming is complete, it is time to create the order of the liturgy. I have discovered the following to be an effective structure for a liturgy and offer it as a framework to help you and your community create the liturgies you need. To illustrate this, I will continue to use examples from Maria's liturgy, "From Developing Girl to Changing Woman: A Celebration of Menses."

Preparation

Create the space and ambience to reflect the message of the liturgy.

> *Buy a tambourine, red ribbons, a decorative egg, a ring, and herbs that will be given as gifts. Place a red candle, a green one, and a purple one in the center of a circle of chairs. Put a basket of red fruits and pitchers of red drinks along with them.*

Call to Gather

Welcome participants. Focus the liturgy, state why we are celebrating this theme, and invite people to gather.

> Welcome to this celebration for N. (*name of girl passing into womanhood*). We gather today to welcome you, N., to womanhood. You are a symbol of the passage to womanhood that each of us here and women of every culture experience. We gather today to honor menarche. We gather today to proclaim our sacred power as women.
>
> Our flow of blood represents our life-giving powers. As changing women, we celebrate the transmission of our fertility, our creativity, our spirit, and our intuition. As changing women, we dedicate the fertility of our life force to the next generations.

Naming the Circle

Invite participants to share their names, where they are from, and/or something that focuses the liturgy.

> Think of what the time of first menstruation means to you, what it did mean to you, or what it will mean to you. (*Pause*)
>
> Let us create our circle by speaking our names, sharing a word or phrase that comes to mind when thinking of menses, and giving a hand to the person on the right saying, "I am a woman" or "I will be a woman." (*Sharing, for example, "I am Diann. I honor women's sacred powers. I am a woman."*)

Music / Song / Chant

Be attentive to what mood you want to establish—quiet, festive, haunting, soothing. Music, songs, chants can be used in a variety of places in the liturgy.

The song "Womanriver Flowing On" by Carole Etzler was sung after the prayer and before the gift giving.

Prayer / Litany / Candle Lighting

Write or choose a prayer, litany, or candle lighting that could form a transition into the reading, be a general address to the Spirit for openness, or focus the theme of the liturgy.

> We light three candles today to express our experience as women. The red one is for those who are fertile, those who bleed each month. (*The young woman honored in the celebration lights the red candle.*)
>
> The purple is for the wise women who have passed beyond the biological capacity to give birth and have channeled their energies through their whole selves: mind, spirit, and body. (*A menopausal woman lights the purple candle.*)
>
> The green is for the young girls who will soon pass into womanhood. (*A young girl lights the green candle.*)

Readings

Choose one or two readings that will be central to the liturgy. These can be scripture passages, poems, excerpts from writings about women's rites of passage, or stories. If your group is scripture focused, you will want to choose a scriptural text from a feminist perspective. A sung or spoken refrain can be used to connect the readings and deepen the message.

I chose the reading "Marvelous Menstruating Moments" by Ntozake Shange from *Sassafrass, Cypress & Indigo*. The words were told by Indigo to her dolls as she made each and every one of them a personal menstruation pad of velvet.

Reflection

This is traditionally the homily, sermon, or preaching time. Since Wisdom Sophia speaks to everyone, the sharing is communal. Offer a few sentences that recap the message of the readings. Then pose one or two questions for reflection. Depending on the size of the group, form small groups, or share in the whole gathering.

> We women are rivers of life. Today we celebrate life as it is flowing on to another generation. Mother(s), what do you want to pass on to your daughter(s)? *(Pause)*
>
> Let this tambourine represent our voices and let these ribbons represent our blessings for N. *(the girl)*. As we pass the tambourine around the circle, shake it, attach a ribbon, and share what you want to pass on to N., who embodies the next generation of women. *(Sharing begins with the mother.)*

Song Refrain

If people are meeting in groups they need more than the spoken human voice to gather them back as a whole. Singing a song refrain that has already been a part of the service invites attention and brings closure to this section. (We repeated "Womanriver Flowing On.")

Presentation of the Symbols

Name the symbol, touch it, show it to the group, and say why you are using it.

> N., we have gifts for you to remind you of this special day.
>
> *(The mother gives her daughter a ring, saying:)*
>
> N., you traveled the road from nursing (or cuddling, if not the biological mother) in my arms as a baby to maturing into a young woman. I bless you for these and all the seasons of your life. Take this ring as a symbol of the passage well done.

(The godmother, or significant mentor, gives her godchild an egg, saying:)

N., womanhood means that you have the power to give birth. Use this awesome power maturely and lovingly. Protect yourself from dangerous pressures to misuse this power. I bless you for using your reproductive years wisely. Take this egg as a symbol of your reproductive powers.

(Another friend gives her the tambourine, saying:)

N., this tambourine represents our vision of womanhood. Treasure it and add to it your own wisdom. Keep your body sacred. Use it wisely. Preserve your reproductive power for the time when you are fully prepared to take responsibility for another life. We bless you for becoming the woman you will be.

(Another friend gives her herbs, saying:)

N., take these herbs for soothing cramps and calming irritations. Don't be angry with your body. When your body is in pain, listen to it and help it heal. I bless you for caring for your body.

Blessing the Symbol

Hold the symbol and/or invite participants to extend their hands toward it, then bless it. (*The symbols of fruit, wine, and drinks were then presented as follows:*)

Red is the color of women's life source. Red is the color of women's passion. Red is the color of women's creativity. We eat and drink food that is red today to remind us of women's life-giving energy. (*Women hold up the food and drink.*)

Blessed are you, Life-giving Holy Source, Wisdom Sophia, for ripening fruit on the vine and for weaving women's energies into a generational tapestry. Bless us as we eat and drink, remembering our life passages, and honoring women's sacred blood.

Interaction with the Symbol

Give directions about how to interact with the symbol. Specify how to pass the symbol: around the circle, one person offers it to others, stations/centers, several people start passing to different parts of the circle, groups of people come forward to drink water from the common well. Be specific so that people will feel comfortable.

Song

Use a song during or after the sharing of the symbol.

Sending Forth

Pay careful attention to the closure. When the liturgy ends abruptly, people can be left with an unresolved feeling. The Sending Forth gathers up the message of the liturgy and challenges people to go forth to act on it. I usually offer this challenging closure in three sentences or three parts.

> We have welcomed our sister and daughter, N., into womanhood. We have remembered our journeys to womanhood. We have praised women's powers.
>
> Let us open our circle now in song, remembering that we will be there for one another.

Greeting of Peace

I usually include a Greeting of Peace at the end of the liturgy to bring closure. People have created something together and want to bid farewell with hugs, hand shakes, warm greetings.

Song

Use a closing song that invites a spiral or circle dance so people can embrace, sway, and dance.

This is the general structure that I used for the following women's life cycle liturgies. May it help you create the women's life cycle liturgies you and your community need. May it guide you to trust your natural talents and/or stretch your traditional training. May it call forth your creativity and courage to put new pieces together to bless women, resist patriarchy, and transform societies.

NOTES

1. See Susan Cady, Hal Taussig, and Marian Ronan, *Wisdom's Feast: Sophia in Study and Celebration* (San Francisco: Harper and Row, 1989).

2. Ninna Edgardh Beckman, "Sophia: Symbol of Christian and Feminist Wisdom?" *Feminist Theology* 16 (1997), 32–54.

3. Diann L. Neu, "Women Revisioning Religious Rituals," in Leslie A. Northrop, ed. *Women and Religious Ritual* (Washington, DC: Pastoral Press, 1993), 156.

CREATING COMMUNITY

A "great cloud of witnesses" surrounds us and has preceded us throughout the centuries in the ekklesia of women.

Elisabeth Schüssler Fiorenza

Helped are those who love the lesbian, the gay, and the straight,
as they love the sun, the moon, and the stars.
None of their children, nor any of their ancestors,
nor any parts of themselves, shall be hidden from them.

Alice Walker

May you live ever after, Womanchild.
A life filled with laughter, Womanchild.
May the warm wind caress you, Womanchild.
May God smile, may she bless you, Womanchild.

Carole Etzler

Our souls proclaim the greatness of Wisdom Sophia,
Our spirits rejoice in Sophia our Liberator.

Luke 1:46

INTRODUCTION

Throughout her life's journey, each woman matures by being in relationship with family, friends, colleagues, and community. As mothers and grandmothers strive for the development of self in interrelationship and through human connection, so do their daughters and granddaughters. Each woman's growth occurs within the context of relationships. She creates and participates in a variety of communities for sustenance, support, and solidarity. Yet questions arise.

How can women, in this increasingly complex world, create the communities we need where children, women, and men of various races, religions, political convictions, classes, and cultures can peacefully and constructively live together? What kind of communities will provide the conditions of human development sufficient for the challenges of this century?

Traditional centers of community gathering have been transformed almost beyond recognition. In the North Atlantic world, many neighborhoods in large urban centers where everyone knew several generations of their neighbors' families have become suburbs where people rarely talk with one another. Churches are increasingly empty and individual psychotherapy is flourishing. Family meals have been replaced by fast food eaten in front of the TV. Neighborhood general stores have gone out of business and been taken over by corporate sprawling malls. In fact, many corporations have more money than some countries.

Some women and men are working to change spiritual and religious values regarding community. The feminist movement, both in its late nineteenth-century expressions and in its mid to late twentieth-century articulations, sparks women and men to rethink relationships and lifestyles, develop new structures of community, and search for more equitable styles of leadership. It encourages women to be protagonists of our lives, including religiosity, and to develop new beliefs and, above all, new ways to express what is deepest and most meaningful to us.

Feminist values of mutuality and equality are challenging and resisting patriarchal cultures, including religions, especially the Catholic and mainline Protestant churches, that define community for their members in heterosexual, male privileged ways. Marriage between a man and a woman is not the only acceptable lifestyle nor is the nuclear family the only recognized unit of community. Some women are choosing other women as lifelong companions, recognizing the value of friendships, and creating families of choice. Faith communities, answering the call of Wisdom Sophia, are laying hands on women and calling them to feminist ministry. Called by a Divine-One-Who-Looks-Like-Us, they model that women as well as men image God; they gather at her tables to break bread and do justice in her name. They proclaim: "We are church."

Wisdom Sophia, a feminist name for God that has roots in Wisdom literature, calls her people to create community. "Come and eat my bread, drink the wine I have prepared! Leave your folly and you will live. Walk in the ways of perception" (Prov. 9:6). Sophia is the Greek word of feminine gender for the English term "wisdom." Divine Sophia Wisdom reached her peak of power in the Hellenistic era, was limited in her divine status by Jewish monotheism, replaced in Christianity by Spirit, Jesus, and Mary, and erased from Christological tradition by church fathers. Recent feminist work has recovered Wisdom Sophia in the Hebrew Scriptures and Apocrypha, and rediscovered her great influence on early Christian circles.

Jewish Wisdom theology presents God as Divine Woman Wisdom who appears as God's own being in creative and saving involvement with the world. As Wisdom Sophia, God is present to the people of Israel. Woman Wisdom is a hidden treasure known only to God and the only one who knows God (Job 28), a street preacher and prophet (Prov. 1:8) who is with God during creation (Prov 8:22–31). She identifies her own words, actions, and gifts with those of God (Prov. 1:23; 8:6–9). She is a giver of life (Prov. 4:13), architect of her home, hostess and liturgist at her festive table (Prov. 9:1–6), the glory of God (Wisd. 7:25–26), mediator of creation (Wisd. 8:5–6). Wisdom shares the throne of God (Wisd. 9:3). She creates everything, makes all things new again and permeates the universe (Wisd. 7:23, 27; 8:1, 5). She appears on earth, lives among creation (Bar. 3:37), works in history to save her people. She is called sister, spouse, mother, beloved, hostess, liberator, justice-maker, and teacher. In her, the wisdom of women and the image of the Divine are united.

In early Christian writings Sophia seems to disappear, yet a deeper reading shows that a submerged theology of Wisdom Sophia permeates the Christian scriptures. Early Christian communities had access to and used early Jewish discoveries of Divine Wisdom to elaborate on the significance of Spirit, Jesus, and Mary. The complete unity between Sophia and the Spirit is expressed in Wisdom 7:22–23, 27, where Sophia assumes the functions of the Spirit. Spirit Sophia's universal presence is analogous to God's Spirit (Wisd. 7:24).

Early Jesus traditions interpreted the mission of Jesus as that of Divine Sophia: proclaiming Sophia-God as the God of the poor, the excluded, and all who suffer injustice. Just as Wisdom Sophia received everything from God, so Jesus received everything from God (Matt. 11:27a). Just as Wisdom is known only by God and is the only one who knows God, so Jesus has all wisdom (Matt. 11:27bc). Just as Divine Sophia gives her Wisdom as gift, so also Jesus reveals Wisdom to his chosen (Matt. 11:27d). Like Wisdom Sophia, Jesus speaks in the "I am" style, and with the symbolism of bread, wine, and water invites people to eat and drink. Like Wisdom Sophia, Jesus proclaims his message in the public square, is light and life of the world, calls people and makes them children and friends. Paul describes Jesus as "the Sophia of God" (1 Cor. 1:23–25; 2:6–8). Though s/he is the child and messenger of Sophia-God, Jesus-Sophia's Woman Wisdom presence is pushed aside partly by John's Logos-Son-male theology, by resistance to the Gnostic version of Christianity that embraced Sophia, by the rejection of female leadership in the churches, and by the growth of sexism and patriarchy in Christian communities. Female wisdom imagery passed to the figure of Mary of Nazareth, the mother of Jesus, who became known as the Throne of Wisdom.

Biblical women, named and unnamed, walked in the ways of Wisdom Sophia and used their gifts to transform the world. These foresisters who resisted and struggled for the liberation of their people are a source of authority for women who are creating communities in which they celebrate feminist liturgies. Eve and Lilith claimed their power by reaching for knowledge and found that it was good. Sarah, Hagar, Rebecca, Rachel, and Leah answered the call of Wisdom Sophia and put their faith in a covenant with the Holy One. Mary, a Galilean Jew and mother, listened, pondered, and knew that she had been chosen to give birth to Jesus, one who is the Powerful Liberator. Mary Magdalene, the foundation of Women-Church and the apostle to the apostles, shared with them the first news of the resurrection. Junia, Phoebe, Priscilla, Thecla, and other women leaders of the early house church movement were called to a discipleship of equals. These biblical women model feminist community and ministry for the women-church movement. They stand in a prophetic and subversive relation to kyriarchal religious institutions. Wisdom Sophia and the community of women resisters in the scriptures are the source of women-church's strength and authority.

A review of the literature shows that feminist communities are gathering in Wisdom Sophia's name on every continent of the world. Women-church communities,[1] Re-Imagining communities,[2] women's spirituality groups,[3] Rosh Hodesh groups,[4] and small intentional base communities[5] are emerging worldwide. These communities, feminist justice-seeking people who engage in sacrament and solidarity, are in exodus from patriarchal churches and synagogues and are claiming the center of the traditions. The social reality that gives rise to these communities is the oppression of women and marginalized peoples by the churches and synagogues, especially Catholic, Jewish, and mainline Protestant. Most religious traditions have members who resist the patriarchy of the tradition and create other forms of community.

Women around the world are creating communities and designing feminist liturgies for women's life journeys. Some have been meeting for years. The group to which I belong in the Washington, D.C., area has been meeting since 1979. Here are some groups from six continents with which WATER is in contact:

In Africa: The Circle of Concerned African Women Theologians in Accra, Ghana; Women-Church in South Africa; the Grail in Capetown, South Africa.

In Australia and the South Pacific: Women and Worship at Fitzroy Uniting Church in Melbourne; Women-Church in Sydney; Women's Resource Centre in Auckland, Aotearoa (New Zealand).

In Asia: Women-Church in Seoul, Korea; St. Scholastica's College in Manila, Philippines; Center for Feminist Theology and Ministry in Tokyo, Japan.

In Europe: The Catholic Women's Network and St. Hilda's Community in London, England; Oecumenische Vrouwensynoden in the Netherlands; Kvennakirkjan in Reykjavik, Iceland; Frauenstudien-und-bildungszentrum in Gelnhausen, Germany; Sofia-Massor in Stockholm, Sweden; Frauen Kirche in Lucern and Binningen, Switzerland; the Institute for Feminism and Religion in Dublin, Ireland.

In South America: Talitha Cumi in Lima, Peru; Con-spirando in Santiago, Chile; La Urdimbre de Aquehua in Buenos Aires, Argentina; Mujer Ahora in Montevideo, Uruguay; Mandragora in Sao Paulo, Brazil; Women at Matanzas Seminary in Matanzas, Cuba.

In North America: The Women's Centre at Brescia College in London, Ontario, Canada; the Catholic Network for Women's Equality in Toronto, Ontario, Canada; the Re-Imagining Community in Minneapolis, Minnesota; the Women-Church Convergence (a Catholic feminist network of thirty-one groups in the United States including 8th Day Center for Justice in Chicago, Illinois); A Critical Mass in San Francisco, California; Women-Eucharist in Boulder, Colorado; Chicago Women-Church in Chicago, Illinois; the Grail Women's Task Force in Loveland, Ohio; Greater Cincinnati Women-Church in Cincinnati, Ohio; Loretto Women's Network, Denver, Colorado; Massachusetts Women-Church in Boston, Massachusetts; San Francisco Bay Area Women-Church in San Francisco, California; Sisters Against Sexism in the Washington, D.C., area; Women-Church of Northern Virginia; Women's Ordination Conference in Fairfax, Virginia.

These communities and other women worldwide are listening to the needs of women in their own contexts and across international, cultural, racial, and economic boundaries. They are designing rites that create community. Here are two ceremonies from different continents and different contexts. The first story from Melbourne, Australia, describes a house blessing that is done in the name of Sophia. The second from Uppsala, Sweden, blesses a same-sex union.

Melbourne, Australia: House Blessing[6]

The context: Coralie Ling, minister of the Fitzroy Uniting Church, was asked to create a new house blessing for one of the members of her community. The church is in an inner city suburb. The worship community is made up of people who are attracted to the feminist, inclusive, lively, and justice-oriented nature of the liturgies and community. Coralie worked with Tricia, whose home was blessed, to create the rite.

The rite: Tricia welcomed her family and friends to the ceremony. A special friend blessed the light (a large candle), saying: "May Sophia who lights up the world bless this light and bring light to this home." Another friend held up a bowl of water, saying: "May Sophia who is the water of life bless this water and bring refreshment to this home."

The participants walked to each space of the house carrying sprigs of jasmine, honeysuckle, and rosemary. In each room they dipped the herbs in the water, and sprinkled the room while a reader proclaimed a Sophia verse from the Christian scriptures. For example, in the laundry and bathroom, she read: "Sophia delights in the creation of the seas, the waters and the fountains of the deep" (Prov. 8:27–30).

Another woman invoked Sophia, in similar fashion for each part: "Sophia bless this gate. May there be open paths for all who pass through it." In similar fashion they blessed the yard, veggetable garden, shed and worm bed, tree, front door and hallway, living room, and each room. One woman lit a candle in each room after it had been blessed and lit incense in the kitchen. The blessings included household pets also. After they had blessed each space, the gathered toasted Tricia and feasted with food and drink.

Reflection: While the liturgy does not address it specifically, it is important to remember that the seasons differ from country to country. Summer in the southern hemisphere is winter in the northern hemisphere. This liturgy reflects the growing practice of crafting a feminist liturgy, in this case, for a particular situation. It reveals the widespread use of naming the Holy One as Sophia. As women's homes are being used for house churches, the practice of house blessing is growing worldwide.

Uppsala, Sweden: Commitment Ceremony[7]

The context: Anna Karin Hammar and Ninna Beckman, priests of the Church of Sweden, an Evangelical-Lutheran Church, invited family and friends to bless their same-sex union on 27 December 2001 in the Cathedral of Uppsala. Since 1 January 1995 homosexual couples in Sweden can register their partnership in a civil act. The Swedish law equalizes heterosexual marriages and homosexual partnerships in all aspects except adoption, where a change of law is foreseen. The Church of Sweden, the largest church in the country with more than 80 percent of the Swedish population as members, offers homosexual church members the possibility to celebrate the gift of love and to affirm their partnership in a pastoral and liturgical rite affirming their love through prayer and blessings. There is not yet a fixed liturgy for this, but this means that there is instead great freedom for those who want to create something according to their own choice, as long as it is made in cooperation with the priest.

The rite: "The Gift of Love" liturgy of Anna Karin and Ninna began with witnesses reading the proclamation of the legal registration of partnership. Participants walked in procession and made five stops at different places in the cathedral:

The first stop, the Gift of Love: The gift of love was interpreted. The mutual vows were made public. The couple was blessed. Participants processed with candles while singing a hymn.

The second stop, the Gift of Prayer: Prayers were said at the tree of reconciliation using a candle holder symbolizing the world, which was inaugurated at the World Council Assembly in Uppsala in 1968. Prayers were offered for the couple, for the people of Palestine and Israel, Sudan, and Afghanistan. All processed to the song "Bells of Norwich," ringing a bell from Afghanistan and a bell from the United States in the prayer that "All shall be well again" with these two countries who were warring with one another at the time of this liturgy.

The third stop, the Gift of Hope: Readings from St. Julian of Norwich were proclaimed, while the participants stopped in front of a scene showing the Christmas crèche in wooden carvings. All sang a hymn on the theme of Julian that "all shall be well."

The fourth stop, the Gift of Tradition: In the chapel commemorating St. Bridget, readings from the Bible were shared: Song of Songs 4:9–10, 13 and John 15:11–17. The couple gave everyone a rose and the roses were carried in procession with bread and wine to the central altar.

The fifth stop, the Gift of Communion: The Rt. Rev. Christina Odenberg, the first woman bishop in the Church of Sweden, celebrated the mass in the presence of a large ecumenical community. The bishop spoke to the couple and blessed the community.

Reflection: This liturgy shows the growing acceptance of Holy Union Ceremonies within traditional church settings. Celebrating this rite in the cathedral symbolizes that same-sex love is central to the church in this context, the Church of Sweden. Their use of procession with five stops shows the long journey same-sex couples have been on before this love has been blessed by the church. Ringing bells "that all may be well" at the tree of reconciliation reflects that the love of two people does justice. It also offers a hopeful note that challenges other churches and religions to reconcile with gay/lesbian/bisexual/transgender/queer people.

Silver Spring, Maryland, USA: Creating Community

The context: I have been asked by many individuals and communities to design liturgies with them that they need to create community within their own context. Women's rites for life's journey are celebrated in a community context, and they create community among the gathered.

The rites: The liturgical texts are given here.

Reflection: The liturgies in this section mark the many ways some women are creating community and are nurtured by it. "We Are the Image of Wisdom Sophia" proclaims that women reflect the Divine as we journey through life. "Bless This House" introduces friends to a new living space, blesses the house by filling it with their warmth, laughter, memories, and prayers, and consecrates it as a house church. "Welcoming and Blessing a Child" initiates a new life into the community and gives thanks to those who have made it possible.

"Coming Out: Coming Home" gathers a circle of friends and family to show their love and support for a lesbian who has come out and is living out. "Ceremony of Holy Union and Commitment" marks the love two people have for one another (woman and woman, woman and man, or man and man) and their promise to love as equal partners, cherish and respect one another, nurture each other's personal and spiritual growth, create community together, and work for a more just society. "Laying on of Hands: Commissioning for Feminist Ministry" calls forth women from the community, blesses them, and sends them to break bread and do justice.

WE ARE THE IMAGE OF WISDOM SOPHIA[8]

Women image the Divine. The young, middle-aged, and crones mirror the beauty of Wisdom Sophia. Throughout her life journey, each reveals the Holy One. Each has wisdom to share with the others.

This liturgy honors the interconnection among women from generation to generation. It proclaims that women are saints. Use it for All Saint's Day, November 1, or any time your community needs to focus on the holiness of women.

Preparation

On the symbol table in the center of the room pour a mound of sand and add three large cowrie shells. Around the sand place baskets filled with different breads, nonalcoholic wine, a goblet, and a napkin. Intertwine these with blankets representing different cultures. Have a cowrie shell and sheet of music for each participant. Invite seven women to be bread blessers, and a dancer, young woman, middle-aged woman, and crone woman to interact with one another around the shells and readings.

Gathering Music: *(Play water sounds in the background.)*

Song: "Come and Seek the Ways of Wisdom," by Ruth Duck[9]

Come and seek the ways of Wisdom,
She who danced when earth was new.
Follow closely what she teaches,
For her words are right and true.
Wisdom clears the path to justice,
Showing us what love must do.

Listen to the voice of Wisdom,
Crying in the marketplace.
Hear the Word made flesh among us,

Full of glory, truth, and grace.
When the word takes root and ripens,
Peace and righteousness embrace.

Sister Wisdom, come, assist us;
Nurture all who seek rebirth.
Spirit-guide and close companion,
Bring to light our sacred worth.
Free us to become your people,
Holy friends of God and earth.

Call to Gather

(A dancer blesses the space and invites a young woman into the center. The young woman picks up a large cowrie shell, looks at it playfully, and puts it in the sand. She becomes a silhouette and watches the dancer, who beckons a middle-aged woman. This one looks at a shell, holds it in her hands, becomes a silhouette, and watches the dancer, who calls forth an elder crone. The crone takes a shell and holds it to her heart. The dancer blesses each woman and invites the three to embrace.)

(*One proclaims:*) Young, middle-aged, crone—each woman images the Divine. All are saints. (*Gesturing to the gathered, she repeats:*) Young, middle-aged, crone—we are images of Wisdom Sophia. We are saints. Welcome to this Women-Church liturgy, "We Are the Image of Wisdom Sophia."

During this season we remember the communion of saints, the ongoing relationship between the living and the dead. The communion of saints bonds us with the community of women, children, and men past, present, and future. The worlds of the living and the dead are very close at this time of the year.

Saints image God as we image God. Look around. Notice the faces among us. Turn to those around you and introduce yourself saying, "Hi! I'm Saint ________________ (*name*). I am an image of Wisdom Sophia." (*Introductions*)

Song: "When the Saints," traditional

Oh, when the saints go marching in,
Oh when the saints go marching in,
Oh, how I want to be in that number,
When the saints go marching in.

When women saints go dancing in . . .
We image God; Wisdom Sophia . . .

Invocation

Divine Imagination, Thoughtful God, Wisdom Sophia. You bring us together to celebrate that each of us is a gift of your sacred creativity. As we come into your community today we ask that you join us in the work of seeing sacredness in the faces to our left and right, in the eyes of those both like us and different. Join us in our discovery and in the joy it brings us in this holy moment as we celebrate your spirit in each of us. Amen. Blessed be. Let it be so.

Reading: A reading from our sister, Elisabeth Schüssler Fiorenza[10]

A liberating experience that the Catholic tradition provided for me as a woman is the teaching that everyone is called to sainthood. Even the vocation to the priesthood is superseded by the call to become a saint . . .

The "lives of the saints" provide a variety of role-models for Christian women. More importantly they teach that women, like men, have to follow their vocation from God, even if this means that they have to go up against the ingrained cultural mores and image of woman. Women, as well as men, are not defined by their biology and reproductive capabilities but by the call to discipleship and sainthood. The early Christians considered themselves as those who were called and elected by God, as the saints of God. This call broke through all limitations of religion, class, race, and gender.

Young woman (*to the crone*): Wise Grandmother, tell me, when do I image God? When do I look like Wisdom Sophia?

Crone: Let us respond to each phrase with the words, "You image Wisdom Sophia." When you are yourself . . .

All: You image Wisdom Sophia.

Crone: When you laugh with others . . .

All: You image Wisdom Sophia.

Crone: When you heal the injured . . .

All: You image Wisdom Sophia.

Crone: When you share your resources . . .

All: You image Wisdom Sophia.

Crone: When you march in protest . . .

All: You image Wisdom Sophia.

Crone: When you simplify your life . . .

All: You image Wisdom Sophia.

Crone: When you challenge the churches to do justice . . .

All: You image Wisdom Sophia.

Crone: Look into the face of the person next to you. When you are yourself, every day, in some way . . .

All: You image Wisdom Sophia.

Song: "Bless Sophia," by David Haas[11]

Bless Sophia,
Dream the vision,
Share the wisdom
Dwelling deep within.

Reading: A reading from our sister, Diana L. Hayes[12]

We are Hagar's daughters. We share in our sense of loss and abandonment yet we also share our knowledge of how to make it when times are difficult and the way is too dark to see. We have borne with us over the ocean the knowledge that enables us to continue to speak words of love, words of encouragement, words of empowerment . . .

We are Black women, tall, strong, bending but rarely breaking. We stand as beacons of hope and also as bearers of culture. We are not superwomen; we cry, we hurt, we grow weary in the struggle; nor are we mankillers, for they are our fathers, our husbands, our brothers, and our sons. We cry out with Fanny Lou Hammer: "I am sick and tired of being sick and tired." But having said that, we pick up our children, we shoulder our burdens, and we continue on. We seek love, a gentle hand, a loving heart, a sister-spirit to walk with through the storm.

Crone (*to the middle-aged woman*): Soul Sister, tell me, when do I image God? When do I look like Wisdom Sophia?

Middle-aged woman: When you stay in the struggle for liberation of all peoples . . .

All: You image Wisdom Sophia.

Middle-aged woman: When you share another's joy . . .

All: You image Wisdom Sophia.

Middle-aged woman: When you break bread and do justice . . .

All: You image Wisdom Sophia.

Middle-aged woman: When you teach those who have been rejected . . .

All: You image Wisdom Sophia.

Middle-aged woman: When you work for economic justice and social equity . . .

All: You image Wisdom Sophia.

Middle-aged woman: When you recognize that all creation is sacred . . .

All: You image Wisdom Sophia.

Middle-aged woman: When you confront patriarchy . . .

All: You image Wisdom Sophia.

Middle-aged woman: Look into the face of the person next to you. When you are yourself, every day, in some way . . .

All: You image Wisdom Sophia.

Song: "Bless Sophia," by David Haas

Bless Sophia,
Dream the vision,
Share the wisdom
Dwelling deep within.

Reading: A reading from our sister, Mary Hunt[13]

New images abound for a friendly divinity. Like the figure of justice: justice is no longer blindfolded. Justice stands with open arms and ample bosom ready to embrace and to nurture as necessary, to propel and encourage as appropriate. This is an image that women friends know and appreciate. The Pacha Mama, the Goddess of the earth in Latin America, is always connected with the harvest, the just production of the land tilled in right relations.

Middle-aged woman (*to the young woman*): Dear Friend, tell me, when do I image God? When do I look like Wisdom Sophia?

Young woman: When you light a candle . . .

All: You image Wisdom Sophia.

Young woman: When you hold someone who has been abused . . .

All: You image Wisdom Sophia.

Young woman: When you appreciate nature . . .

All: You image Wisdom Sophia.

Young woman: When you show compassion . . .

All: You image Wisdom Sophia.

Young woman: When you recognize yourself as an image of God . . .

All: You image Wisdom Sophia.

Young woman: When you risk being arrested for doing what is right . . .

All: You image Wisdom Sophia.

Young woman: When you make friends in all nations . . .

All: You image Wisdom Sophia.

Young woman: Look into the face of the person next to you. When you are yourself, every day, in some way . . .

All: You image Wisdom Sophia.

Song: "Bless Sophia," by David Haas

Bless Sophia,
Dream the vision,
Share the wisdom
Dwelling deep within.

Reflection

Look at the cowrie shell in your hand. Cowrie shells focus women's powers. They represent healing, fertility, rebirth, connection across cultures and generations, spirituality. Call to memory a woman who is holy, a saint, and an image of God, Wisdom Sophia, for you. This could be a woman who helped you at some point in your life; someone who shared her wisdom with you; your mother; your grandmother; your neighbor; one who noticed you needed a hug and embraced you. (*Pause*) Let this cowrie shell represent this woman. (*Pause*) How does she image the Holy? Describe her holy qualities. What stories about her will you tell the next generation of women? (*Pause*)

Now, turn to one or two people and share the name of this woman and one of her virtues that you admire. (*Sharing*)

Song: "Women's Voices, Women's Witness," by Manley Olson[14]

Women's voices, women's witness
Being faithful through the years.
Living lives of dedication,
Finding hope amid the tears.
God, you made us in your image,
From your womb you gave us life.
With this life we give you service.
Serve your people, show your grace.

Women's witness of the ages
Has persisted through the pain.
Tell the stories of our mothers,
Let us sing their songs again.
Women's voices of the future
Speak of visions yet unseen.
Tell the stories of our daughters
Filled with wonder, hope, and dreams.

Tell of visits to two women,
One a virgin, one grown old.
Yet to each there came a promise
Of a gift by God foretold.
Tell of one who shared her water,
Left replenished from the well.
Tell of women that first Easter
To whom Christ said: "Go and tell."

Celebrate the faith of Anna
And the loyalty of Ruth.

Stand with Noah and her sisters
Seeking justice, speaking truth.
Join with us in Sarah's laughter,
Raise your voice in Miriam's song.
Women's voices, women's witness,
Showing women they belong.

Litany of Women

Let us create a litany of women represented here. Proclaim the name of a woman whose memory has come to you during this liturgy. Let us hear a chorus of names. (*Naming*)

Song: "Women's Voices, Women's Witness," by Manley Olson[15]

When the bread and cup we're sharing,
When we hold a neighbor's hand,
Be like Martha in our service,
Be like Mary as we learn.
These our stories that surround us,
This our heritage to name.
Women's voices, women's witness:
We remember, we proclaim.

Eucharistic Prayer

(*Seven blessers come to the center and pray in turn.*)

First Blesser: Lift up your hearts.

All: We lift them up to God.

First Blesser: Let us give thanks to our gracious Mother God, Wisdom Sophia.

All: It is right to give her thanks and praise.

Second Blesser: Blessed are you, Loving and Challenging Friend, Wisdom Sophia,
With joy we give you thanks and praise for creating a diverse world

And for creating women in the image of God.
You call us to share your story,
So we join all women saints in singing your praises:

All: Holy Wisdom Sophia, we praise you, we thank you, we image you.

Third Blesser: Blessed are you, Womb of All Creation, Wisdom Sophia,
You create women in your image, the image of God.
From age to age you form women from your womb;
You breathe your breath of life into us.
And you call us to share your story,
So we join all women saints in singing your praises:

All: Holy Wisdom Sophia, we praise you, we thank you, we image you.

Fourth Blesser: Blessed are you, God of Our Mothers, Wisdom Sophia,
You call diverse women to participate in salvation history:
Eve, Lilith, Sarah, Hagar, Miriam, Naomi, and Ruth,
Mary, Mary Magdalene, Thecla, Phoebe, Hildegard of Bingen,
Sor Juana Inez de la Cruz, Sojourner Truth, and countless others,
And you call us to share their stories,
So we join all women saints in singing your praises:

All: Holy Wisdom Sophia, we praise you, we thank you, we image you.

Fifth Blesser: Blessed are you, Creator of all seasons and all peoples, Wisdom Sophia.
You call women by name
To be prophets, teachers, house church leaders, saints,
And to image your loving and challenging presence.
You call us to share their stories,
So we join all women saints in singing your praises:

All: Holy Wisdom Sophia, we praise you, we thank you, we image you.

Sixth Blesser: Blessed are you, Companion on the Journey, Wisdom Sophia.
You have built yourself a house,
You have hewn seven pillars,
You have prepared a rich banquet for us.
And you call us to share your story,
So we join all women saints in singing your praises:

All: Holy Wisdom Sophia, we praise you, we thank you, we image you.

(Each blesser picks up a basket of bread and drink and the seven pray together:)

All Blessers: Blessed are you, Holy Bakerwoman, Wisdom Sophia,
In your abundant love you welcome all to come and dine.
You proclaim from the rooftops,
"Come and eat my bread, drink the wine that I have drawn."
And you call us to share your story,
So we join all women saints in singing your praises:

All: Holy Wisdom Sophia, we praise you, we thank you, we image you.

All Blessers: Come, O Holy Sister Spirit, Wisdom Sophia, upon this bread and wine.
Come as the wind
and breathe your life anew into our weary bones.
Come as the rain and water our thirsty souls.
Come as the fire and purge us and our church
of sexism, racism, classism, heterosexism, and all evils.
You call us to share your story,
So we join all women saints in singing your praises:

All: Holy Wisdom Sophia, we praise you, we thank you, we image you.

Seventh Blesser: Come, Soul Sister, Wisdom Sophia,
And bring the new creation:
The breaking of bread,
The raising of the cup,
The doing of justice.
You call us to share your story,
So we join all women saints in singing your praises:

All: Holy Wisdom Sophia, we praise you, we thank you, we image you.

Seventh Blesser: Eat, drink, and partake of the banquet of life.
Receive the love, healing, and nourishment of Wisdom Sophia.

(*Blessers pass bread and goblets around the group.*)

Communion and Song: "This Day Is My Daily Bread," by Kathy Sherman[16]

(*Hummed as baskets and goblets are passed around, then sung with gestures.*)

This day is my daily bread, take it, bless it, break it, give it,
To all I meet this day.

Blessing of One Another

Look into the face of the person next to you and see a saint. Look around you at the communion of saints in which you are gathered right this moment. Saints are as common as shells on the shores of every continent. You are images of the Divine Imagination. Raise your hands in blessing over the heads of those saints around you. (*Pause*)

Divine Creator, Wisdom Sophia, we come from your sacred womb, your own image, born in love and supported by your very body, the earth. We ask that you bless us yet again, and continue to surprise us with the sacred in our own lives and in the lives of our sisters and brothers. May we bless others as we struggle and laugh, dance and stumble toward the new creation. Amen. Blessed be. Let it be so.

Sending Forth

Women saints, let us go forth with courage,
For we are the image of God.
Let us go forth in beauty,
For we are the image of God.
Let us go forth to recognize the face of the sacred in all living beings,
For we are the image of God.

Song: "Dance in the New Day," by Kathy Sherman[17]

Women go forth to proclaim your stories
Go with your visions and go with your dreams.
Women go quickly the night is waiting
For us to dance in the new day.

We gather around Holy Wisdom,
Trusting her warmth and her flame.
In her we are tender, fierce, loving and strong
As one we go forth in her name.

BLESS THIS HOUSE: A House Church Blessing

When people move into a new house, apartment, or living space, they want it to be filled with good spirits. They often have an open house or a house-warming party to introduce friends to their new place and bless their home by filling it with the warmth and laughter of friends.

In my childhood when my family moved to a new home, the priest came to bless our house. I remember thinking then of how this simple blessing connected my family with our parish church.

When I moved into a new home I wanted my friends to bless it as a women-church house. Women-church continues the tradition of the early Christian community by meeting in homes as house churches.

This house blessing was used for the blessing of my house. Variations on it have been used for the homes of other friends and colleagues. Use it to bless a new home, to mark a significant anniversary of a living space, or to bless a house as a house church.

Preparation

Invite friends to bring food for the meal. Gather incense, salt, a bowl of water, and a bough of evergreen. Ask certain people to bring a gift for a specific room of the house and ask them to say the blessing for that space.

Call to Gather

Welcome to this house blessing. N. and N. (*names of inhabitants*); thank you for inviting us to bless your new home. We gather to bless each room that you may each be blessed in your daily routines, be surrounded by the love of your family and friends, and live here in peace.

N. and N., we have a gift for your new home. (*Someone gives them the gift of chimes.*) Ring these chimes now to call the Spirits of Blessing into your new home.

(*The new owners ring chimes of welcome and say:*) Welcome to our new home. Welcome to our new house church. May this house be for all who enter a place of love and friendship, a place of healing and comfort, a place of wisdom and peace. Let us gather round as we plant sage, the herb of wisdom. (*Planting*)

Song: "Bless This House," by Helen Taylor, music by Mary Brahe[18]

Bless this house, [Sophia], we pray;
Make it safe by night and day;
Bless these walls so firm and stout,
Keeping want and trouble out.
Bless the roof and chimneys tall,
Let thy peace lie over all;
Bless this door, that it may prove
ever open to joy and love.

Bless the windows shining bright,
Letting in God's heav'nly light;
Bless the hearth a'blazing there,
with smoke ascending like a prayer;
Bless the folk who dwell within,
*Keep them loving and bless them with kin.
Bless us all that we may be
Fit, [Sophia], to dwell with thee;
Bless us all that one day we
May dwell, [Sophia], with thee.

(**line adapted*)

Blessing the Salt

(*The blesser pours salt into the hand of each person, and says:*) Salt symbolizes protection and healing. Let us create a circle of protection around this house. Circle the house, sprinkle a little bit of salt as you go, and offer a prayer of protection. Sprinkle salt by each door. (*Sprinkling*) Let us gather in the entranceway.

Prayer: adapted from Genesis 28:17, Psalm 84:1–2a

(*The owners sound the chimes to call all to prayer.*)

The following is adapted from the traditional opening prayer for the dedication of a church.[19] Please repeat each line after me:

How awesome is this place! (*Echo*)
This is none other than the House of Wisdom Sophia; (*Echo*)
This is the gate of heaven; (*Echo*)
And it shall be called the special place of Wisdom Sophia. (*Echo*)
How lovely is your dwelling place, O God of Hosts! (*Echo*)
My soul yearns and pines for the special place where Wisdom Sophia dwells. (*Echo*)

Song: "Walk Through These Doors," by Marsie Silvestro[20]

Grandmothers whose names we call
Ancient ones whose spirits have flown

Refrain: Walk through these doors with blessing
Walk through these doors with peace
Walk through these doors as holy ones
Enter the words we speak.

Children laughing in the day
Mothers crying in the night (*Refrain*)

Lovers dancing like a flame
Women standing strong and free (*Refrain*)

Reading: 1 Peter 2:4–9

Come to Christ, to that living stone, rejected by human beings but in God's sight chosen and precious; and like living stones by yourselves built into a spiritual house. . . . For it stands in scripture: "Behold, I am laying in Zion a stone, a cornerstone chosen and precious, and whoever believes in Christ will not be put to shame."

The honor, then, is for you who believe, but for those who do not believe, "The very stone which the builders rejected has become the head of the corner," and "A stone of stumbling, and a rock of offense" for they stumble because they disobey the word, as they were destined to do.

But you are a chosen race, a royal priesthood, a holy nation, [Wisdom Sophia's] own people, that you may declare the wonderful deeds of [her] who called you . . .

Blessings for Each Room

(Bless each room.)

Hostess: We will bless each room of the house in the following way. I will invite us into each room and sound the chimes. One among us will incense the room. We will pray a blessing. We will leave a symbol as a sign of this blessing. And finally we will asperge, that is, sprinkle the room with water. Let us move to the living room.

Blessing the Living Room

(Someone incenses the room.)

O Word Made Flesh, Wisdom Sophia, bless this living room. It is where we welcome friends, offer the warmth of our hearth, and share the many conversations that build our community. This is where we become strangers and aliens no longer, but members of the household of a family of choice and the community of women. We celebrate and bless that household of women-church, our sharing of stories and experiences, the times we reflect together on the Word of Wisdom Sophia, and the times that sharing passes over into warmth and welcoming of our fire and hearth. May you, N. and N., have many life-giving conversations here.

Let us say: Amen. Blessed be. Let it be so.

The stained glass windows are our symbol of blessing. (*Someone sprinkles them and the room with water.*)

Let us move to the bathroom.

Blessing the Bathroom

(*Someone incenses the room.*)

O Ever-cleansing Holy One, Wisdom Sophia, bless the bathroom(s) of this house and all those aspects of our lives that need cleansing and healing. We remember the times our mothers scrubbed away our mud and dirt when we were young, and we recall the spiritual cleaning of baptism as living water passed over us. Energize the waters here. Renew our spirits and relax our bodies. May we be cleansed of any unjust or unloving inclinations in our own lives, and may the community of women-church lend its hands to scrub away the mud and dirt of injustice and violence from our churches and our world. N. and N., may you be cleansed of all hurts that have been done to you; may you be blessed daily with energizing and healing water.

Let us all say together: Amen. Blessed be. Let it be so.

As a symbol of our blessing we leave this special soap. (*Someone sprinkles the room with water.*)

Let us move to the bedroom.

The Blessing of the Bedroom

(*Someone incenses the room.*)

O Loving One, Wisdom Sophia, bless the bedroom(s) of this house. We recall our need for rest and sleep as a source of new energy. This is a room to celebrate bodies and sexuality. We recall that our bodies have not always been celebrated by our religious tradition, but in the name of women-church, we bless them and the pleasure they give—and we name them holy. N. and N., we pray that your bedroom may bring you peaceful dreams, comfort to your body, and refreshment to your spirits. May you sleep with the angels here and feel the presence of Wisdom Sophia as you sleep and wake.

Let us all say: Amen. Blessed be. Let it be so.

As a symbol of our blessing we hang this picture. (*Someone sprinkles the room with water.*)

Let us move to the guest room.

Blessing the Guest Room (or wherever an overnight guest sleeps)

(*Someone incenses the room.*)

O Spirit of Hospitality, Wisdom Sophia, bless this guest room. We recall the special way in which Elizabeth greeted Mary and welcomed her into her home. May our hearts and our homes be especially welcoming of our friends and family, but may we also receive with gladness the stranger, the widow, the orphan, the alien, the homeless, the victim of discrimination. We pray a special blessing on the homes of women-church that have been a sanctuary to the undocumented, the persecuted, and the wanderer. We declare that space for hospitality in our hearts and our homes to be special and sacred space. N. and N., may you be blessed with life-giving guests.

Let us all say: Amen. Blessed be. Let it be so.

Our guest for tonight will sign and leave a guest book as our symbol of blessing. (*Someone sprinkles the room.*)

Let us move to the study.

Blessing the Study (or whatever nook contains study material)

(*Someone incenses the room.*)

O Curious Holy One, Wisdom Sophia, bless this study. Bless our intellects, our fresh ideas, and our creativity. We recall that rooms such as this often house books and tapes with the stories of our women-church traditions: the lives of women saints, the insights of women mystics, the works of feminist theologians, and our feminist liturgical texts. We celebrate that rich tradition and we pray that our lives, our work and our legacy to the next generations may help the women-church tradition to grow and flourish. N. and N., may you continue to be productive and creative in your work.

Let us all say: Amen. Blessed be. Let it be so.

We leave books here as symbols of our blessing. (*Someone sprinkles the room.*)

Let us move to the kitchen.

Blessing the Kitchen

(*Someone incenses the room.*)

O Nourishing One, Wisdom Sophia, bless this kitchen where food is prepared with great and loving care. We know this room in a special way since generations of women before us have been the food-gatherers and food-makers of our world. We bless the culinary creativity where many bare their souls and share their secrets as they peel and cut and dice and strain and heat and pour.

As we do, we are painfully aware that this room meant isolation and aloneness for many of our foremothers. For too many, it was a place of social segregation. But we also know that many women have worked together in the kitchens of our world. We pray an end to the aloneness and segregation of women's traditional work, while we bless and celebrate the community women have created in the kitchens of the world. N. and N., may you continue to nourish your bodies and your spirits and those of your family and friends.

Let us say: Amen. Blessed be. Let it be so.

We leave herbs here as our symbols of blessing. (*Someone sprinkles the room with water.*)

Let us move to the garden (porch or deck).

Blessing the Garden (Porch or Deck)

(*Someone incenses the area.*)

O Holy Spirit, Wisdom Sophia, bless this garden where we connect with nature. It is here that many a woman talks with the flowers, waters the herbs, connects with the natural world, shares stories with her neighbors, and sips tea to reflect on the day's events. It is here that we touch the healing powers of nature, listen to the birds, gaze at the trees, and watch life come and go. And so we celebrate and bless the gardens of women-church that make this house a "house of prayer" that has no walls, no limits, no boundaries—only an openness to the world and the vistas beyond. N. and N., may this garden connect you to the global community.

Let us say: Amen. Blessed be. Let it be so.

We leave this chair as a blessing. (*Someone sprinkles the garden with water.*)

Let us move to the dining room.

Blessing the Dining Room

(*Someone incenses the room.*)

O Holy One of Thanksgiving, Wisdom Sophia, bless this dining room, the gathering place where we share both nourishment and community. It is here that we share together the meals that have been handed down to us by our families, our friends, and our religious tradition. It is here that we bless and break the bread, and bless and share the wine that has been left to us by Jesus and his friends—both women and men—who have celebrated this meal of thanksgiving for centuries.

And so we extend our hands, palms up, and bless this our bread and wine as a community called to a royal priesthood, a discipleship of equals. We bless as well the food that we brought to share as nourishment for our bodies. And in so doing, we remember the great women who worshipped in spirit and in truth in centuries of house churches: Mary, Mary of Magdala, Lydia,

Prisca, Justa, Junia, Phoebe, and the thousands whose names we will never know. It is their legacy we claim and pass on tonight as we bless and celebrate this sacred space and sacred meal. N. and N., may you continue to share many sacred meals here.

With hands joined we say: Amen. Blessed be. Let it be so.

Our food and candles are our symbols of blessing. (*Someone sprinkles water around the room.*)

Song: "Song of Community," by Carolyn McDade[21]

We'll weave a love that greens sure as spring,
Then deepens in summer to the fall autumn brings
Resting still in winter to spiral again
Together my friends we'll weave on, we'll weave on.

A love that heals friend, that bends friend,
That rising and turning then yields friend,
Like mountain to rain or frost in the spring
Or darkness that turns with the dawn
It's by turning, turning, turning my friend,
By turning that love moves on.

Blessing of Peace

N. and N., as we have blessed your house, so we bless you. Our love continues to move on as we come together as a community and as we move away from this place to create community with others. N. and N., may you continue to be blessed. Let us bless one another with hugs before we share in the feast that we have prepared. (*Hugging*)

Sending Forth

Let us go forth to share our meal and then to return to our homes.

N. and N., may you continue to be blessed as you come home.
May we each find pleasure, comfort, and peace in our homes.
May we share our homes with family, friends, and community.

Song: "We're Coming Home," by Carolyn McDade[22]

Refrain:
We're coming home to the spirit in our souls.
We're coming home and the healing makes us whole.
Like rivers running to the sea,
We're coming home, we're coming home.

As the day is woven into night,
As the darkness lives within the light,
As we open vision to new sight,
We're coming home, we're coming home.

(*Refrain*)

Bearing words new unto each day,
Speaking bold where only silence lay
As we dare to rise and lead the way,
We're coming home, we're coming home.

(*Refrain*)

To create a world of joy and peace
Where the power of justice does release
Love abounding, wars forever cease,
We're coming home, we're coming home.

(*Refrain*)

Sharing the Meal

WELCOMING AND BLESSING A CHILD

Welcoming a child into the community is an age-old custom. When a child is born (or adopted), the parent(s) want to present her or him to family, friends, and usually a religious community. There is a universal impulse to celebrate a new life and to give thanks to those who have made it possible. Some Christian traditions welcome a child and baptize at the same time. Others welcome, then baptize later. Some bless the child. This liturgy can be adapted for any of these traditions. It is designed for a home celebration, yet it is easily adapted to a church or other special place.

Preparation

Center a table in a circle of chairs and place on it a pitcher and a bowl of water. Gather symbolic gifts for the child, such as those listed in this liturgy: a garment, candle, oil, and seedling tree. Have materials available for the children and adults to make cards for the child when they arrive. If you wish, invite family or friends to be godparents. This liturgy is written for a girl child whose parents are both present for the naming. If the child is a boy, and/or one parent is present, adapt accordingly.

Gathering Music

(Play lullabies as people arrive. Invite the children to draw pictures for the child to be honored and the adults to make cards for the child.)

Welcome

(*The parents welcome the guests.*)

Thank you for joining us today to welcome (and baptize) N. We are so glad that you are here for this sacred and joyous occasion. You have supported us from conception through pregnancy to birth [*for adoption:* You have supported us through our adoption process], and now we present our child to this community. We stand in awe before this miracle of life.

Most of you know each other; some are just meeting. You are an important community for us and for N. We value that community and the love and support you each contribute to it. We want you to meet each other, so speak your name and say, briefly, how you are connected to our family. (*Introductions and sharing*)

Call to Gather

(*A representative of the community speaks.*)

Today we welcome this new child into our circle of family and friends. Most cultures and religious traditions welcome and name a new person with a ceremony. We gather to promise our support and friendship to N. and N. (*names of the child and the parents*). We gather to participate in the universal impulse to celebrate a new life. We gather to initiate this child into our community.

This is the day Wisdom Sophia, the Creator of All Life,
has made for us.
Let us rejoice and be glad in it.
Let there be feasting and laughter.
Let there be presents and sharing of wishes.

For to us a child is born.
To us an heir is given.
May this child be wonderful and wise, a maker of peace.
Blessed is she who comes in the name of Wisdom Sophia.

Song: "Sing of a Blessing," by Miriam Therese Winter[23]

During the song the parents will present N. to each of us. Gently greet and bless this precious child. (*Parents walk around the circle and pause in front of each person.*)

Sing, we sing of a blessing (*Echo twice*)
A blessing of love. (*Echo*)
A blessing among us. (*Echo*)
Love will increase. (*Echo*)
A blessing of peace. (*Echo*)

Share now, share in a blessing. (*Echo twice*)
A blessing of love. (*Echo*)
A blessing of joy. (*Echo*)
Love will increase. (*Echo*)
A blessing of peace. (*Echo*)

Rise up, rise for a blessing. (*Echo twice*)
A blessing of love. (*Echo*)
Now and forever. (*Echo*)
Love will increase. (*Echo*)
A blessing of peace. (*Echo*)

Remembering the Ancestors

(*A family member prays:*) Let us pray, remembering our ancestors, in a litany of presence. Our response is "Be with us today and always."

All you who have cared for children: loved them, cuddled them, fed them, changed their diapers, raised them to be just and compassionate,

Response: Be with us today and always.

Family member: Ancestors of N.'s bloodline (*name specific ones, if known*),

Response: Be with us today and always.

Family member: Creators of the home of N. (*name the immediate household: birth-givers, caretakers, siblings . . .*),

Response: Be with us today and always.

Family member: All who have cared for planet Earth to make it safe and healthy for the next generations,

Response: Be with us today and always.

Family member: In the company of the Beloved Creator, Wisdom Sophia, who makes us in her Divine Image, we promise to care for children from generation to generation. Amen. Blessed be. Let us make it so.

Testifying to the Birth [Adoption] and Naming

(*A friend asks the questions.*)

N. and N., what name have you given your child? Tell us the story of her birth [adoption] and naming? (*The parents describe N.'s birth [adoption process] and state what and why they named the child.*)

Blessing the Birth Mother [for adoption]

(*The parents offer the blessing.*)

Birth mother of N. (*the child's birth name, if known*), we are grateful to you for entrusting N. (*the child*) to us. We empathize with the sacrifice you made and the sadness you must feel. We wish you peace.

Wisdom Sophia, Source of All Life,
Bring peace to N.'s birth mother.

Blessing the Parents

(*A representative of the community blesses the parents.*)

N. and N., we thank you for making the choice to bring new life into your family, our community, and the world. Receive now a blessing in thanksgiving for you and your life.

Be praised, Creator of All Life, Wisdom Sophia,
For N. and N. (*parents' names*) who gave birth to [adopted] this child.
Surround them with love, energy, and healing powers.

Affirming the Godparents

(*If this is part of your tradition, the parents ask:*)

N. and N. (*names of godparents*), as representatives of our families and our community, will you support N. (*baby's name*) and call her to be most fully herself?

(*Godparents respond:*) We will.

Affirming the Community Connection

Each of you has a significant role to play in N.'s life as mentors, educators, caregivers, community advisors, listeners, and playmates. The Chinese believe our lives are inextricably bound—tied and connected with the red thread of life through history and through the future. Will you support N. and call her to be most fully herself?

(*All gathered respond:*) We will.

Renunciation and Affirmations [for Baptism]

Leader: N. and N. (*parents*), what do you ask of our church for N. (*the child*)?

Parents: Baptism.

Leader: You have asked to have N. baptized into a church that is filled with contradictions, yet it is one that is your tradition. As N. journeys in faith, may she be surrounded by the best of the tradition and learn to work to change what is unjust. As parents and friends let us help N. by declaring our faith.

Do you reject the evils of sexism, racism, classism, heterosexism, and all the isms that keep people divided?

Parents: We do.

Leader: Do you reject the abuse of the earth?

Parents: We do.

Leader: Do you believe in a God of many names: Wisdom Sophia, Holy Spirit, Jesus, Mother and Father, Comforter, Lover, Life-giving One, Liberator?

Parents: We do.

Receiving the Garment

(*The blesser touches the garment and says*): Pour out your Spirit, Wisdom Sophia, upon this garment.

(*She gives N. the garment.*)

N., this garment is a symbol that you are part of our community of justice-seeking friends. Receive this garment as an outward sign of your dignity. May you and others respect your body always. May this cloth remind you of this special day.

Receiving the Light

(*The blesser lights the candle and says*): Pour out your Spirit, Wisdom Sophia, upon this flame.

(*She gives N. the light.*)

N., receive this light of Wisdom Sophia. May you keep the flame of faith alive in your heart. May you spark peace and justice for all.

Blessing the Water

(*A representative blesses with water.*)

As the water breaks in the mother's womb, as the water broke in your mother's womb to welcome you into the world, so we use water today to welcome you, N., into this community of family and friends. Water connects you with your ancestors and all of humanity.

(*The blesser takes the bowl of water, breathes on it, and says:*)

In the beginning, the Spirit brooded over the waters.

Before there were rivers, seas, and springs, Wisdom Sophia was present.

In the watered garden, Eve knew bliss.

Through the waters of the flood, women kept faith.

By the waters of the sea, Miriam danced her people to a promised land.

In the water of the womb, all life finds its course.

In the waters of the wells, women find hope and carry it to whole towns.

In Galilee, in Canaan, in Babylon, in Africa and Asia and Latin America, in every part of the world, women have carried water.

Jesus, Sophia's Child and Miriam's Prophet, used water to welcome his followers into a community of justice-seekers.

(*The blesser touches the water and says:*) Pour now your Spirit, Wisdom Sophia, upon this water.

(*The parents and godparents dip their hands in the water, touch the child, and say:*) Pour out your Spirit, Wisdom Sophia, upon N.:

The spirit of love and joy,
The spirit of wisdom and understanding,
The spirit of right judgement and courage,
The spirit of knowledge and reverence.
Pour out your Spirit, Wisdom Sophia, upon N.

Receiving the Oil

(*The blesser touches the oil and says:*) Pour out your Spirit, Wisdom Sophia, upon this oil.

(*Representatives of the community take some oil in their hands, touch the child, and say:*) We anoint you, N., with the oil of gladness in the name of Sophia Spirit. As Christ was anointed priest and prophet, may you minister as Wisdom Sophia calls you. May she strengthen you with her power and bring you happiness forever and ever and always.

Receiving Gifts from the Community

This is a time for sharing wishes, hopes, and dreams for N. What do we wish for N.? (*Following are some of the gifts that one community shared.*)

(*N. is given pictures the children have drawn. Invite the children to present them.*)

N., receive these pictures of our wishes for you on this day.

(N. is given the cards participants have written. Invite them to speak aloud their wishes.)

N., receive our dreams and hopes for you this day.

(N. is given a seedling tree.)

N., receive this tree as a symbol of the ways you will grow and change.

Reading: "Little Girl Child," by Gwen Benjamin[24]

Little girl child Newborn,
God's image Reborn,
Enfolded in your mother's gentle arms,
Nestling.
For you, her body was broken,
Her blood was shed,
God's grace.
You feel her heart beat close to yours,
God's grace.
You feel her heart beat close to yours,
God's pulse.
Little girl child I greet you.
Soft whisper of Divine Sophia
You were there from the beginning of time.
I have known you forever.
Gentle, people-loving spirit
Seeking others on the road,
Inviting them to dinner.
Image of God's goodness.

Brave defiant Lilith,
Taking tea with God,
Dancing and celebrating with God.
Nascent Earth Mother,
The seeds of life already within you,

Co-creator with God,
Your blood to shed—not to maim in war,
But to cleanse, purify, create.
Little girl child I celebrate you.

Will you know violence in this man's world?
Will your gentle sexuality be allowed to blossom?
Will you know the joy of mutuality?
Little girl child I fear for you.

O God who brought us to birth,
Who loves and nurtures us as a mother,
Enfold this little one in your strong gentle arms.
She is your daughter, your sister, your lover.
Weave her life with strong fine thread.

Little daughter, granddaughter, sister, friend,
I love you.

Song: "Womanchild," by Carole Etzler[25]

Can you hear the wind singing,
Womanchild, Womanchild.
As to life you come springing, Womanchild. (*Repeat*)
With the strength of an eagle
May you soar to the sun.
With the grace of the willow
May you dance, may you run.
May the earth find you growing, Womanchild (*Repeat*)
And may love guard your going, Womanchild.

And the world you inherit, Womanchild (*Repeat*)
May you joyfully share it, Womanchild (*Repeat*)
For you are the sister of each one living there
Of the beasts in the forests,
Of the birds in the air.

May you love and defend them, Womanchild (*Repeat*)
May you always befriend them, Womanchild.

May you live ever after, Womanchild (*Repeat*)
A life filled with laughter, Womanchild (*Repeat*)
May you climb to the mountains,
May you sail o'er the sea,
May you run through the meadow,
May you always be free.
May the warm wind caress you, Womanchild (*Repeat*)
May God smile, may she bless you, Womanchild.

Greeting of Peace

Filled with awe and wonder at the delicacy of new life, let us bless one another with peace. (*Hugging*)

Final Blessing

May we bring joy to those who love us, as we grow to love in return.

May our spirits enlarge in a life of goodness and joy.

May we model for future generations deep respect for all humanity.

Eating Together

Let our party continue with food and feasting. (*All share a dinner, dessert, or symbolic food together.*)

COMING OUT: Coming Home

A rite of Coming Out needs to be celebrated in every country corner and city center of the world, because lesbian women, gay men, bisexual, and transgender people (sometimes called queer) live everywhere. Coming out is both a one-time event and a lifetime process. Once someone says out loud to herself or to someone else that she is lesbian, she is always choosing to tell her story again and again and again. Living as an openly queer person in this historical time means going against heterosexual norms and often encountering people who just don't understand. Yet, ironically, coming out—and living out—means coming home. It says, "I am who I am."

This liturgy celebrates coming out and being out. It is written as a lesbian coming out, but can easily be changed for a gay male, bisexual, transgender, or queer coming out, or a joint lesbian and gay coming out. Use it as a model for the one you or friends need to celebrate.

Preparation

Buy a lavender candle, wind chimes, water pitcher, and basket that will be given as gifts to the person coming out. Gather a bowl for the water, an evergreen branch to sprinkle water, a loaf of bread, a glass of wine, and a glass of juice. Place these on a central altar table that is covered with a special cloth.

Naming the Circle

We are here to celebrate N.'s (*name of person*) coming out and living out. Congratulations, N., for knowing yourself and for telling others who you are.

Let us create our circle of support by each in turn speaking our names, acknowledging our support of N., and giving a hand to the person next to us as a sign of that support. (*Sharing*)

N., feel the love and support of this circle of friends and family. (*Raise the joined hands*) Remember it when times are tough, and some days they will be. We love you. We sing our support.

Song: "Good For the World," by Holly Near and Jeff Langley[26]

Good for the world for coming out (*Sing three times*)
When we come out it's good for the world.

Good for the world for opening doors . . .
Good for the world for telling the truth . . .
Good for the world for sharing support . . .

Blessing the Four Elements

Let us bless the four elements of the universe—fire, air, water, and earth—for they have called home to the world our friend N.

(*Four blessers, in turn, bless four elements.*)

Blesser of Fire: South

(*The blesser walks to the center-south and lights a candle on the altar.*)

Source of Fire,
O Searing Flame,
Wisdom Sophia,
Fill N.'s heart and all our hearts with a spark of passion.
Empower us and every lesbian, gay, bisexual, and transgender person with courage
To emerge from cocoons of hibernation and isolation.
Release our imaginations from their hiding places.
Guiding Light,
Fire of Justice,
One Who Brings Us Home.
Amen. Blessed be. Let it be so.

Blesser of Air: East

(The blesser walks to the center-east and plays the chimes on the altar.)

Source of Air,
O Whispering Wind,
Wisdom Sophia,
Fill N.'s lungs and all our lungs with the breath of healing.
Blow away the staleness.
Bring freshness into our lives.
Gentle Breeze,
Rustling Sound,
One Who Brings Us Home.
Amen. Blessed be. Let it be so.

Blesser of Water: West

(The blesser walks to the center-west, pours water into the bowl, and sprinkles participants with the evergreen branch.)

Source of Water,
Ever-bubbling Spring,
Wisdom Sophia,
Fill N.'s being and all our beings with emotions that flow freely.
Wash away the hurts and pains of all oppressed people.
Quench our thirst for spiritual and sexual connection.
Ocean Womb,
Wellspring of Life,
One Who Brings Us Home.
Amen. Blessed be. Let it be so.

Blesser of Earth: North

(The blesser walks to the center-north and places a basket of bread on the altar.)

Source of Earth,
Mother of Our Being,
Wisdom Sophia,
Fill N.'s body and all our bodies with courage for loving one another.
Cradle and protect us as we discover our real selves.

Enlighten us with dreams, visions, and inner wisdom.
Sacred Ground,
Fertile Soil,
One Who Brings Us Home.
Amen. Blessed be. Let it be so.

Chant: "The Earth, the Air, the Fire, the Water," source unknown[27]

The earth, the air, the fire, the water
Return, return, return, return (*Repeat*).
I-A, I-A, I-A, I-A, I-O, I-O, I-O, I-O (*Repeat*).

Reading: "Invisible for Too Long" by Diann Neu

Reader: For a very long time I have wanted to reach out to you in solidarity, to work with you to transform injustice . . .
. . . But I have been invisible for too long.

Response: Come out, come out, wherever you are!

Reader: I work next to you in so many places. I am the doctor who comforted your dying mother. I am the teacher of your nine-year-old daughter. I am the therapist who helped you free yourself . . .
. . . But I have been invisible for too long.

Response: Come out, come out, wherever you are!

Reader: I stand beside you in so many places. I am the minister who marched next to you as we advocated for a woman's right to choose. I am the nun by your side at the women's shelter where you volunteer. I am the social worker at the mental health center who works with your sister . . .
. . . But I have been invisible for too long.

Response: Come out, come out, wherever you are!

Reader: I am your invisible sister, your invisible brother. I have been invisible for too long. I yearn to be known for who I am. As you come out, you give me courage.
. . . I yearn to be visible.

Response: Come out, come out, wherever you are!

Telling the Story of Coming Out

N., you have listened to this call. You have chosen to be visible. Tell us your story of coming out. (*The person who is coming out and living out shares her story with the participants.*)

Honoring the Person

Thank you, N., for trusting us enough to share your life with us. We respect you. We honor you. We support and affirm you. (*Participants respond by sharing words of support and affirmation.*)

We would like to honor you with a few mementos.

N., this candle (*hold the one from the altar*) symbolizes your passion for truth. When you burn it, and every candle, reignite this spark. (*Give her the candle.*)

N., these chimes (*play them*) symbolize the unique melody that is yours. When you play them, remember your powerful story. (*Give her the chimes.*)

N., this water pitcher (*hold the one from the altar*) symbolizes the deep well that you are. When you pour water from it, feel your pains and hurts wash away. (*Give her the water pitcher.*)

N., this basket of bread (*hold the one from the altar*) symbolizes the nourishment that you are to us and to others you meet. When you use this basket, visualize the many ways you fill others with your love. (*Give her the basket.*)

(*Speak other words and give other gifts as you choose.*)

Litany of Thanksgiving

Leader: Gracious and Loving Wisdom Sophia, we praise you for creating N. a lesbian. We praise you for creating us, your lesbian, gay, bisexual, transgender, queer, and heterosexual people.

For bringing us out of our closets and into full life,

Response: We praise you.

Leader: For embracing us with your love and care,

Response: We praise you.

Leader: For giving us a company of friends and a family of choice,

Response: We praise you.

Leader: For teaching us that our gender and our sexuality are gifts for the community,

Response: We praise you.

Leader: For strengthening us to cope with misunderstanding, fear, and hatred,

Response: We praise you.

Leader: For helping us break through the heterosexism and homohatred in ourselves, our families and friends, our culture and society, our churches and synagogues,

Response: We praise you.

Leader: For enlightening us with dreams of holy impatience,

Response: We praise you.

(Add others.)

Leader: Gracious and Loving Wisdom Sophia, we praise you for creating N. a lesbian. We praise you for creating us your people.

Blessing the Bread

(The person who has come out holds the bread and prays:) Blessed are you, Holy Lover, Wisdom Sophia, for nourishing us and bringing us home.

Blessing the Fruit of the Vine

(A close friend holds glasses of wine and juice and prays:) Blessed are you, Gracious Source, Wisdom Sophia, for quenching our thirst and bringing us home.

Blessing the Festive Meal

(Another friend extends her hands over the food and prays:) Blessed are you, Nourishing Mother, Wisdom Sophia, for giving us friends to feed our hunger and bring us home.

Song: "We're Coming Home," by Carolyn McDade[28]

Refrain:
We're coming home to the spirit in our souls.
We're coming home and the healing makes us whole.
Like rivers running to the sea,
We're coming home, we're coming home.

As the day is woven into night,
As the darkness lives within the light,
As we open vision to new sight,
We're coming home, we're coming home.

(*Refrain*)

Bearing words new unto each day,
Speaking bold where only silence lay
As we dare to rise and lead the way,
We're coming home, we're coming home.

(*Refrain*)

To create a world of joy and peace
Where the power of justice does release
Love abounding, wars forever cease,
We're coming home, we're coming home.

(*Refrain*)

Greeting of Peace

Today, N. has come out and come home. We have each come home. Filled with the spirit of this resting-place, let us embrace one another in love. (*Greeting*)

Sharing a Festive Meal

Let us share our festive meal. (*Eating, drinking, and dancing*)

CEREMONY OF HOLY UNION AND COMMITMENT

When two people find one another as lifetime companions, they usually want to gather family, friends, and colleagues to celebrate their good fortune. For some women, their life partner is a man, for others it is a woman. The theme of a wedding and a commitment ceremony is the same. Two people promise publicly to love as equal partners, cherish and respect one another, nurture each other's personal and spiritual growth, create community together, and work for a more just society. Some ask, "Do we need a commitment ceremony at all?" Lesbians and gay men often question, "Since secular and religious law in most countries provides us no legal standing, what validity is there in a commitment ceremony? Would we be mimicking heterosexual weddings by choosing to have a liturgy of our own?" Most couples, straight and lesbian, ask, "What power does communal affirmation have for us?"

This liturgy has been adapted for holy unions, for commitment ceremonies, and for weddings. Use it as a model to design the partnership liturgy you want and need.

Preparation

Choose a setting that matches your values and lifestyle, one that will accommodate your guests. Couples have chosen community centers, gardens, backyard settings, churches, homes, parks, a private room in a restaurant or hotel, outside by the sea or riverbank. Set the chairs in a semicircle. Place a table in the front and cover it with a meaningful cloth. Put candles, flowers, rings, bread, wine, and cups on it. This is a time to use family heirlooms and symbols that can have sentiment for you in the future.

Processional

(When the guests have arrived, the processional music begins. Pachelbel's Canon, *Handel's* Pasacaile, *or Clarke's* Trumpet Voluntary *work well for this entrance. Those who have a part in the ceremony usually process in first, followed by the couple. Some couples prefer to walk in together. Others choose to enter arm in arm with their parents. Some walk in with their children.)*

Welcome

(One of the partners, or a person they designate, welcomes those gathered using words similar to the following:)

We want to welcome all of you and thank you for joining us today. We are so happy you are here to share in our joy. You are the people in our lives who have helped us arrive at this place on our respective paths. You have helped us to be who we are and to create the relationship we are so delighted to have. Each of you has made some difference in our lives. If it were not for you we would not be who we are now or where we are now.

Introductions

(The other partner, or a designated person, continues:)

We want you to know one another. You come from different parts of our lives, so a lot of you have not met, although most of you have heard about each other. Take a couple of minutes right now and introduce yourself to anyone who is sitting near you. Tell them your name, where you are from, and how you know us. *(Sharing)*

Song: "We Are a Wheel," words by Hildegard of Bingen, music by Betty Wendelborn[29]

We are a wheel, a circle of life;
We are a wheel, a circle of power;
We are a wheel, a circle of love;
Circling the world this sacred hour.

Call to Gather

This sacred hour we are gathered as a community of friends and family to witness the love and commitment N. and N. have created from the union of their own individual lives. We gather to give thanks for their love and for the new life it has created. Their love for one another, for each of us here, and for the broader community shows that love makes a difference in the world. Proclaiming that love publicly takes an act of courage. Thank you, N. and N., for inviting us to witness your love.

Our presence here for and with you, N. and N., is a sign of our support, of our love, and of our commitment to you as a couple. Our coming together today in the context of this liturgy is a declaration that love is powerful and transforming, that human companionship and love are precious values. We come together, not to mark the start of a relationship, but to recognize a bond that already exists. This union is one expression of the many varieties of loves in this room.

The ceremony today will include three readings, the rite of marriage, an exchange of vows and rings, a eucharist, and a blessing. Feel the power of love this day, know of love's presence as we share with N. and N. Let us ask the Holy One to bless us.

Opening Prayer

God of Love, Spirit of Commitment, Wisdom Sophia,
Thank you for this day!

Bless this occasion that brings us together to celebrate with N. and N. as they join their lives.

Bless what we do and say here to reflect our deepest selves and our sense of the sacredness of life.

Bless all creation through this sign of your love shown in N. and N.'s lives.

God of Love, Spirit of Commitment, Wisdom Sophia,
Thank you for this day!

Reading 1

The story of Ruth and Naomi reminds us of love's qualities. A reading from the book of Ruth 1:16–18.

But Ruth said, "Do not press me to leave you or to turn back from following you! Where you go, I will go; where you lodge, I will lodge; your people will be my people, and your God my God. Where you die, I will die—there will I be buried. May God do thus and so to me, and more as well, if even death parts me from you!"

When Naomi saw she was determined to go with her, she said no more to her.

This is the word of the God of Love.

Response: Thanks be to God.

Song: "Make Wide the Circle," by Rae E. Whitney[30]

Make wide the circle,
*Let all our sisters in!
In ever-widening circles
Let love and peace begin!

Refrain:
Love! Peace! Let us begin.
Love! Peace! Let us begin. Oh,
Love! Peace! Let us begin.
Love! Peace! Let us begin.

*Let one another in!
*Let family and friends in!

*(*lines adapted)*

Reading 2

A reading from 1 Corinthians 13:1–13.

If I speak in human tongues or the tongues of angels, but have not love, I am a noisy gong or a clanging cymbal. And if I have prophetic powers, and understand all mysteries and all knowledge, and if I have all faith, so as to remove mountains, but have not love, I am nothing. If I give away all I have, and if I deliver my body to be burned, but have not love, I gain nothing.

Love is patient and kind; love is not jealous or boastful; it is not arrogant or rude. Love does not insist on its own way; it is not irritable or resentful; it does not rejoice at wrong, but rejoices in the right. Love bears all things, believes all things, hopes all things, endures all things.

Love never ends; as for prophecies, they will pass away; as for tongues, they will cease; as for knowledge, it will pass away. For our knowledge is imperfect and our prophecy is imperfect; but when the perfect comes, the imperfect will pass away. When I was a child, I spoke like a child, I thought like a child, I reasoned like a child; when I became an adult, I gave up childish ways. For now we see in a mirror dimly, but then face to face. Now I know in part; then I shall understand fully, even as I have been fully understood. So faith, hope, love abide, these three; but the greatest of these is love.

This is the word of Love.

Response: Thanks be to God.

Song: "Make Wide the Circle," by Rae E. Whitney

Make wide the circle,
*Let all our lovers in!
In ever-widening circles
Let love and peace begin!

Refrain:
Love! Peace! Let us begin.
Love! Peace! Let us begin. Oh,
Love! Peace! Let us begin.
Love! Peace! Let us begin.

*Let all the children in!
*Let all the city in!

(**lines adapted*)

Reading 3

A reading of the Beatitudes. (*Choose a version of Matthew 5:1–10 you are familiar with, or a contemporary adaptation of it, such as "The Gospel According to Shug," from* The Temple of My Familiar *by Alice Walker.*[31])

Song: "Make Wide the Circle," by Rae E. Whitney

Make wide the circle,
*Let all our neighbors in!
In ever-widening circles
Let love and peace begin!

Refrain:
Love! Peace! Let us begin.
Love! Peace! Let us begin. Oh,
Love! Peace! Let us begin.
Love! Peace! Let us begin.

*Let all cultures and races in!
*Let the whole world in!

(**lines adapted*)

Words of Reflection: "What's Love Got to Do with It?" by Mary E. Hunt

(Mary wrote these words for the commitment ceremony of Margaret Sequeira and Donna Jones.)

Good day to all of you, and warm wishes to you, N. and N., on this festive occasion. On behalf of all of us gathered, let me thank you two for inviting us to share in the goodness of your love. Thank you especially for giving us this opportunity not only to support you in your commitments to one another, but also for the chance to meet people from many facets of your lives, and in so doing to be enriched by what I think of as your love seeking community. That is what makes this day different from every other day. You have decided to mark time in a new way from this day forward, dividing your lives into the time before you proclaimed your love and the time after, in what I, speaking for all of us gathered, hope will be many happy, healthy years.

Thank you for inviting me to express a few thoughts on this special occasion, thoughts which, borrowing boldly from Tina Turner, I have focused around a central question for all of us, "What's Love Got to Do With It?" In all the hoopla of the parties this weekend, and especially in all of the debate which surrounds same-sex marriages, I worry that love may be moved off center stage just when it deserves a solo. Or, that in overusing the word we might miss its power completely.

Getting married is a gutsy thing to do today. Standing before the people you most want to think well of you and promising to keep at this relationship through thick and thin is risky business, human frailty being what it is. I admire you as I catalogue just how frail I am, indeed how frail most of us are, in this regard. But love insists.

In your case, commitment is made even more difficult by loving at a time when the President of the United States [Clinton] doesn't believe in such things for women like us, and can't seem to keep his prejudices to himself. I know you don't need his approval, but it is hard for some people to understand what we're about here today when the President doesn't get it and is ready to sign our rights away before we receive them. Between that attitude and the outcry of the Religious Right, it is amazing that you and other lesbian, gay, bisexual, and transgender friends have the courage to trust your love, live it out, and more so in this climate, to entrust it to the rest of us. Good for you!

Your efforts are thwarted too by so-called Christian churches, the churches of which you are both a part whose doors are all but closed to you today. History alone will judge those churches that disgrace themselves by offering blessings to animals for the feast of St. Francis but withhold their sacraments from same-sex couples who seek nothing more than to call attention, religious attention, to their love as heterosexual people have done for millennia. I know you don't need institutional approval, but it is important that you know that the People of God are with you today in the persons of your family and friends, despite the recalcitrance of the kyriarchies. Given such behaviors, it is a wonder that you want to celebrate your love in the context of a religious community. But you do, and so we are here from a range of backgrounds to offer you our religious support.

Your love and your choice to celebrate it in this way is even controversial in the larger community of lesbian and gay people. No less a theological expert than comedienne Kate Clinton speaks of events like today as cases of "mad vow disease." There may be days down the road when you will think she was right—I must have been mad to do it—but I think that something far more powerful is at play here for which we who are privileged to participate as witnesses can only express our gratitude. That something is love. The answer to Tina Turner's question, "What's love got to do with it?" is everything.

Love is what brought you together for reasons you'll never fully understand and no one has a right to expect you to explain. Love is why you bother to work out the little things, like whose turn it is to do the dishes, and the big things, like whether and when to choose children. Love is the excuse for giving each other extra time in a day when there just isn't another minute. Love is the reason why you've decided to enter into one another's families when you each have a family of your own. There is no other good explanation for such things, and love will have to do, and it does just fine.

Love is not a political matter at base, nor only a private one. Rather, love is the very essence of ourselves in community, which some like you have found and touched and hope to deepen together. You have been lucky in love because many people long all their lives for what you have in such abundance today. Guard it, but above all enjoy it to the max. It may not happen again. Love is like that.

Given this very unique but quite abundant experience called love, it is no wonder that love is the name of God, of the Divine, of Sophia. And her nickname is love and his middle name is love, and its confirmation name is love because there is no other better way to describe what is so palpable this important day when you put us in touch with something so precious. The insights of Alice Walker and Ruth that we have just heard, these sacred texts by two other loving, justice-seeking women, the music, prayers, and vow sharing that make up this ceremony are vivid testimony to the presence of the Divine in all things, and above all, in love. Likewise, our sharing of bread and wine reminds us that love is always very concrete, and that it has consequences that shape the world. It is for this that we can only be grateful for love, just grateful.

Thank you for standing before us today, giving love two beautiful faces, so that we may see it in ourselves, in one another and in our God forever. That's what love has to do with it, all of it. Amen. Blessed be. Alleluia.

Sharing Memories/Reflections/Blessings

Love is revealed to us through the beautiful faces of N. and N. What memories do you have of their love? Let us share these memories now. (*Sharing*)

Rite of Partnership

We read in the book of Corinthians that "faith, hope, and love abide, but the greatest of these is love." We as a community are here to witness the love of N. and N. Come forward, N. and N., to speak your vows to one another.

Vows of N. and N.

(*N. and N. face each other, join hands, and repeat in turn:*)

I take you, N., to be my partner // and I promise you these things: // I will be faithful to you and honest with you // I will respect you, trust you // help you, listen to you, // and care for you. //

I will share my life with you // in plenty and in want, // in sickness and in health, // I will support you and encourage you // to share your gifts with family and friends and with the larger community to which we belong.

Family Vows

Leader: Families of N. and N., please come forward and form a circle around them. The vows N. and N. have made affect not just each of them but everyone around them. Their union is not just of two individuals but of two families and two communities. We ask now if N. and N.'s families will promise to come together as one and support N. and N. as they build a life together. We also ask N. and N. to commit to their families to continue to grow in love and support their families as they build their lives.

(*To the families:*)

Families, will you support, celebrate, and witness N. and N.'s relationship? Will you forgive and ask for forgiveness when there is hurt and misunderstanding? Will you strive with them as they strive to live together in mutuality and love, as they work toward making their dreams a reality?

Response: We will.

Leader (to N. and N.): N. and N., will you support and celebrate with your families who have loved you, cared for you, and let you go? Will you forgive and ask for forgiveness when there is hurt and misunderstanding? Will you strive for deeper understanding, love, and mutuality with your families?

Response: We will.

Community Vows

Leader: All gathered here, you have come from diverse parts of N. and N.'s lives. You are friends from childhood, college, work, and church, but you all have in common your relationship with each of them. You have been brought together today as one community and are asked to witness, support, and celebrate the commitment N. and N. have made.

(*To the community:*)

This community of N. and N., will you support, celebrate, and witness N. and N.'s relationship? Will you forgive and ask for forgiveness when there is hurt and misunderstanding? Will you strive with them as they strive to live together in mutuality and love, as they work toward making their dreams a reality?

Response: We will.

Leader (to N. and N.): N. and N., this is your community, which over the years has grown and will continue to evolve throughout your lives. Do you promise to support and celebrate with your community? Will you forgive and ask forgiveness when there is hurt and misunderstanding? Will you be a source of love and strength to them?

Response: We will.

Exchange of Rings

Leader: In partnership ceremonies, the giving and receiving of rings is not simply a perfunctory act—not simply the giving of a piece of jewelry. Rather, rings are a visible sign of the sealing of a promise, an announcement that can be seen for all the days and years to come.

N. and N., rings are made of precious substances and symbolize the treasure that your relationship holds. Fashioned to be worn as a circle, they are a sign of love that is a continuous, strengthening tie. N. and N., as you give and receive rings, may you be attentive to the bond of love that is ever deepening between you.

Response *(The couple exchanges rings, and repeats in turn)*: **N., I give you this ring as a sign of my love for you, // as a symbol of the communities to which we belong, // and as a reminder of the vows and promises we have made here today.**

Pronouncement of Holy Union

(*Said by all, in unison:*)

We speak for the circle, for the Spirit of love in each heart gathered around us, seen and unseen. With the power of life invested in us, we pronounce you joined together as partners in life, love, and spiritual integrity.

Blessing the Bread

(*One partner blesses the bread.*)

Come, extend your hands toward the bread and wine.

Blessed are you, Gracious and Loving Holy One, Wisdom Sophia, for this eucharistic love feast. You call us to the banquet table. We take, bless, break, and eat this bread in thanksgiving for the love we have known, in thanksgiving for the love we have received, in thanksgiving for the love we have given and will give. May our love increase.

Blessing the Wine

(*The other partner blesses the wine.*)

Blessed are you, Holy One of Joy, Wisdom Sophia, for creating this fruit of the vine. Young wine reminds us of new love; aged wine, growing richer and fuller, symbolizes long-lasting love. We give thanks for this fruit of the vine and recall the lasting love of beloved partners and dear friends. May our love increase.

Communion

(The couple passes the bread and wine around the circle for all to eat and drink.)

Song: "Bring the Feast to Ev'ry Hillside," by Joan Prefontaine[32]

Bring the feast to ev'ry hillside
Where the hungry people wait.
Loaves and fishes multiplying:
Common miracles create!
While some choose to keep their table
Where a wealthy few can dine,
Let us praise a wider venture:
Moving banquets, bread and wine.

Bring the feast to ev'ry hideout
Where the poor and thirsty dwell,
Cries of pain and desperation,
Cardboard shelters, prison cells.
Where there is no grass to rest on,
Where the earth's been paved and torn,
Let us spread communal tables
Till injustice is outworn.

Who will love deserted spaces?
Who will share a stranger's cup?
Who will bless those no one blesses?
Who will speak and dare stand up?
O Creator, Life Sustainer,
Spark of hope in young and old,
Help us spread and move the table
Where we often fear to go.

Dancing at inclusive tables,
Gay and straight together sing.
Join with us to strengthen, nurture,
Let our justice-voices ring!
Bread that knows no gendered language,
Grapes of solidarity;
Sisters, brothers, join the Love Feast,
Dance to shape community.

Closing Blessing

Leader: Let us ask the God of Love, Wisdom Sophia, to bless and keep N. and N. in her care. I invite each of us to respond "Blessed be" to the following blessing.

N. and N., may your lives together be joyful and content, and may your love be as bright as the stars, as warm as the sun, as accepting as the ocean, and as enduring as the mountains.

Response: Blessed be.

Leader: May you respect, have patience with, and delight in your cultural, spiritual, and personal differences.

Response: Blessed be.

Leader: May you remember that your love, like planet Earth, when nurtured, fertilized, and watered can withstand the most treacherous storms. May you let the roots of your relationship be planted into the solid ground of love so that in the dry season you may drink deeply from its source.

Response: Blessed be.

Leader: May your heart hear more than words—listening to each other's silences and exploring each other's processes. May you have the courage to not always agree but always understand.

Response: Blessed be.

Leader: May your love for each other pull you beyond yourselves into the hearts and lives of all those calling for justice, dignity, and love.

Response: Blessed be.

Leader: May you be blessed with wisdom to find the path upon which you both may walk, and with clear vision to keep sight of the grace that surrounds you.

Response: Blessed be.

Leader: May you continue to make your love clearly and truly a reflection of the infinite love that embraces us all.

Response: Blessed be.

Leader: And may you, N. and N., be blessed in the name of the Holy One, Wisdom Sophia, who loves us into being, the Beloved who is the way of love, and the Spirit whose burning love sets us free. Amen. Blessed be. Let it be so.

Sending Forth

With this blessing, this part of our celebration is concluded. Let us go forth in the name of the God of Love, filled with the power of love revealed through N. and N.

May we each treasure love this day.

May we give thanks for those we have loved and for those who have loved us.

May love increase so that violence and injustice may cease.

Amen. Blessed be. Let it be so.

Recessional

(*The music of Handel's* Water Music Suite *begins to play. N. and N. walk out, followed by their party and the guests.*)

Reception

LAYING ON OF HANDS:

Commissioning for Feminist Ministry

Throughout church history, individuals have been called forth for ministry. A laying on of hands symbolizes this commissioning. In this liturgy the community calls forth feminists for feminist ministry. A version of this ceremony was written for and celebrated at the 20th Anniversary of the Women's Ordination Conference.

Use this liturgy as a model to commission feminist ministers in your parish, your congregation, or your organization.

Preparation

Invite people to lead various parts of the liturgy and, as appropriate, to speak in different languages.

Call to Gather

Leader One: Filled with the power and the visions,
the challenges and the commitments
of the Discipleship of Equals,
Let us lay hands on one another and commission one another
for feminist ministry.

Response (in different languages): Let us lay hands on one another and commission one another for feminist ministry.

Reading: "A Magnificat for Today," adapted from the Gospel of Luke 1:46–55

Song: "Blessed Is She," by Colleen Fulmer[33]

Blessed is she, who believes
That the promise made her by our God
Would be fulfilled, would be fulfilled.

We, women and men who are Church,
Our souls proclaim the greatness of God.
We magnify the presence of Wisdom Sophia.
Our spirits rejoice in Wisdom Sophia our Liberator.
For she has looked with favor on us
And the time has come for us to claim our heritage.
Yes, from this day forward all generations will call us blessed.

Song: "Blessed Is She," by Colleen Fulmer

Blessed is she, who believes
That the promise made her by our God
Would be fulfilled, would be fulfilled.

For great things have been done through us
And those who went before us.
Holy is our name.
We have shown mercy and strength as women, from age to age.
We have gathered our courage and steadfastness
And moved to heal the brokenhearted with tenderness and care.
We have called forth truth and created a new shape for living
what we believe to be just.
Yes, we have been hungry and have filled each other with
good things.
For we have kept our promises and journeyed and struggled
in the hope of our dreams . . .
touching and healing . . .
laughing and crying . . .
questioning and loving . . .

Yes, indeed, by our living and our faithfulness,
By our passions and our courage,
All generations from this day forth will be blessed.

Song: "Blessed Is She," by Colleen Fulmer

Blessed is she, who believes
That the promise made her by our God
Would be fulfilled, would be fulfilled.

Presentation of Ministers and Request for Laying on of Hands

Leader One: Spirit of Life and of Power,
time and again throughout history
you call forth your ministers from the community
and send them to do works of justice:
to feed hungry souls,
to give drink to thirsty ones,
to free captives.
Come, Ruah, Wisdom Sophia, Fulfiller of Promises,
Bless us, your feminist ministers,
to do your works of justice.

In a moment, we will ask you to raise your hands as you want to be called forth from and blessed by this community for your particular feminist ministry in the Discipleship of Equals. In a moment, we will ask for you to raise your hands for as many blessings as you wish, and we will respond with a blessing. Those around you will lay hands on you. (*Pause*)

(*Dancers bring cloths into aisles and wave, move, dance, billow them in blessing.*)

Music: (A musician plays and hums "Blessing Song," by Marsie Silvestro[34])

A healer: Raise your hands if you want a laying on of hands for healing ministry—for people, broken communities, our ecosystem, hospital and hospice work, mental health providers, spiritual directors, ecologists, and gardeners.

Lay your hands, if you can, on a person near you whose hands are raised or extend your hands in blessing. (*Pause*)

Let us bless these hands for the ministry of healing. Please respond:

All: Bless these hands.

A politician: Raise your hands if you want a laying on of hands for political ministry: justice-making, grass-roots organizing, women's health advocacy, global connecting, affordable housing.

Lay your hands, if you can, on a person near you whose hands are raised or extend your hands in blessing. (*Pause*)

Let us bless these hands for the ministry of politics.

All: Bless these hands.

A feminist educator: Raise your hands if you want a laying on of hands for feminist educational ministry: teaching, mentoring, feminist media and values, writing, feminist/womanist/mujerista/Minjung theologies.

Lay your hands on, or extend your hands, and bless these hands for the ministry of feminist education.

All: Bless these hands.

An artist: Raise your hands if you want a laying on of hands for ministry through the arts: dance, performance, visual arts, music.

Lay your hands on, or extend your hands, and bless these hands for ministry through the arts.

All: Bless these hands.

A liturgist: Raise your hands if you want a laying on of hands for liturgical ministry: creating feminist liturgies, preaching, praying, healing, celebrating eucharist, liturgical arts, and dance.

Lay your hands on, or extend your hands, and bless these hands for liturgical ministry.

All: Bless these hands.

A faith-sharer: Raise your hands if you want a laying on of hands for faith-sharing ministry: creating feminist family values, feminist faith-sharing with children, working to overcome domestic violence.

Lay your hands on, or extend your hands, and bless these hands for the ministry of feminist faith-sharing.

All: Bless these hands.

A leader: Raise your hands if you want a laying on of hands for leadership ministry: community leadership, fund raising, pastoral leadership, elected office, team leadership in sports.

Lay your hands on, or extend your hands, and bless these hands for leadership ministry.

All: Bless these hands.

An activist: Raise your hands if you want a laying on of hands for activist ministry: lobbying Congress and bishops, ending world hunger, organizing farmworkers, demanding a halt to destructive nuclear proliferation, marching and protesting for whatever issues call for justice.

Lay your hands on, or extend your hands, and bless these hands for activist ministry.

All: Bless these hands.

A disciple: Raise your hands if you want a laying on of hands for the ministry of creating a Discipleship of Equals. We hope that all hands will be up.

Lay your hands on, or extend your hands, and bless these hands for the ministry of creating a Discipleship of Equals.

All: Bless these hands.

Song: "Blessing Song," by Marsie Silvestro[35]

Bless you my sister, bless you on your way.
You have roads to roam before you're home
and winds to speak your name.
So go gently my sister, let courage be your song.
You have words to say in your own way,
And stars to light your night.
And if ever you grow weary
And your heart song has no refrain
Just remember that we'll be waiting to raise you up again.

And we'll bless you our sister,
Bless you on your way
And we'll welcome home all the life you've known,
and softly speak your name.
Oh we'll welcome home all the self you own,
and softly speak your name.

Prayer of Empowerment for the Struggle

Leader One: Please respond to each section of this prayer of empowerment for the struggle with the words: "For feminist ministry we thank you."

Ruah, Wisdom Sophia, Filler of Promises,
Bless these hands to do your works of justice.
We call out to you, Wisdom Sophia, in these troubled times
As your church is caught in the struggle to recognize feminist ministry.
Yet we remember how you guided your people of old
By calling Miriam to dance her people into a promised land.
We remember how you called the apostolic women: Justa, the Syro-Phoenician woman; Junia, a woman imprisoned; Phoebe, a presider of a local church; Prisca, a minister who supported her-

self, and Mary Magdalene, the first to proclaim Jesus' resurrection to her brothers.

Let us respond:

All: For feminist ministry we thank you.

Leader Two: For all ages, you have given your Church feminist ministers: apostles, prophets, martyrs, carers for the sick, preachers, healers, teachers.

Each according to the gifts received and the needs of your people.

Let us respond:

All: For feminist ministry we thank you.

Leader Three: Turning from these memories,

We look anew to the wonder of our own time:

We see in a new Pentecost the recognition of new ministries.

We hear the many voices raised in teaching, prophesying, praying, and praising;

And we see the many hands stretched out to heal, to lift up, to comfort, and to sustain,

Carrying each other's burdens and upholding a global community.

Let us respond:

All: For feminist ministry we thank you.

Leader One: Encouraged by this faith and hope,

We turn to you, Wisdom Sophia.

We ask you to bless us, your feminist ministers, who, in the cry of the people and in the word of the community, have received the call to feminist ministry.

We ask you, Wisdom Sophia, to pour out your Spirit upon us,

That we may have the gifts of wisdom and understanding,

See visions, dream dreams, break bread, do justice.

Let us respond with these words: Pour out your Spirit upon us, Wisdom Sophia.

All: Pour out your Spirit upon us, Wisdom Sophia.

Leader Two: When the bread is not enough,
When our hope is dim,
When our energies are frazzled,
Refresh us with your Spirit, Wisdom Sophia.
May we, your feminist ministers, become a Discipleship of Equals.
May we be blessed by your grace, Wisdom Sophia.
May we be supported and cherished by our communities.
Let us respond:

All: Pour out your Spirit upon us, Wisdom Sophia.

Leader Three: Pour forth your Spirit, Wisdom Sophia,
on your people with whom we minister.
Pour forth your Spirit even on the kyriarchal Church
That the whole People of God may benefit from feminist ministries.
Pour forth your Spirit on our families and friends
That they may offer us loving care, understanding, and support.
Let us respond:

All: Pour out your Spirit upon us, Wisdom Sophia.

Greeting of Peace

Leader One: Blessed and filled with the power of Wisdom Sophia,
Let us greet one another with hugs and embraces of peace
For our journey in the twenty-first century. (*Greetings*)

Sending Forth

Leader Two: Discipleship of Equals,
We leave here commissioned as feminist ministers
For today and well into the twenty-first century.

Leader Three: Sisters and brothers of the global community,
Let us turn and face the doors,
And go out together to the ends of the earth.

Leader One: Sisters and brothers,
Join each other, hand in hand,
As we carry on.

Song: "Sister, Carry On," by Carolyn McDade[36]

Sister, carry on, (*Repeat*)
It may be rocky and it may be rough,
But sister, carry on.

Sister, don't lose the dream, (*Repeat*)
Don't sell out for no short time gain
Sister, don't lose the dream.

Sister, we share the way (*Repeat*)
Heart to heart and hand to hand
Sister, we share the way.

NOTES

1. See Diann L. Neu and Mary E. Hunt, *Women-Church Sourcebook* (Silver Spring, MD: WATERworks Press, 1993). Women-Church Convergence, 2572 Argile, Chicago, IL, 773-784-2498, www.women-churchconvergence.org.

2. The first Re-Imagining conference took place in Minneapolis, Minnesota, in 1993. (See note 73 in chapter 1.)

3. See Miriam Therese Winter, Adair Lumis, and Alison Stokes, *Defecting in Place* (New York: Crossroad, 1995); and *The Ecumenical Review* (Geneva, Switzerland: World Council of Churches) vol. 53, no. 1 (January 2001): "On Being Church: Women's Voices and Visions."

4. See Sue Levi Elwell, "Reclaiming Jewish Women's Oral Tradition: Rosh Hodesh," in *Women at Worship: Interpretations of North American Diversity*, ed. Marjorie Procter-Smith and Janet R. Walton (Louisville: Westminster John Knox Press, 1993), 113.

5. See Bernand Lee and William D'Antonio, *The Catholic Experience of Small Christian Communities* (New York: Paulist Press, 2000); Call to Action Small Intentional Community directory; and the November 2001 taped interview with Bill D'Antonio and Diann Neu on "Small Worshipping Communities" for Faith Matters, an ecumenical radio show hosted by Maureen Fiedler, SL, of the Quixote Center in Mt. Rainier, Maryland.

6. Coralie Ling, "Creative Rituals: Celebrating Women's Experiences in an Australian Feminist Context" (D.Min. diss., San Francisco Theological Seminary, 1998), 203–6.

7. Anna Karin Hammar, e-mail to Diann L. Neu, 16 March 2002.

8. This liturgy was planned with members of the Women-Church Convergence, Diann Neu, Rose Mary Meyer, Sheila Dierks, Darlene Noeson, and Joanne Cullen, and celebrated at the 1998 Call to Action Conference in Milwaukee, Wisconsin.

9. Ruth Duck, "Come and Seek the Ways of Wisdom," music "Madelin" by Donna Kasbohm, *Bring the Feast* (Cleveland: Pilgrim Press, 1997), 10. Used by permission.

10. Elisabeth Schüssler Fiorenza, *Discipleship of Equals: A Critical Feminist Ekklesialogy of Liberation* (New York: Crossroad, 1993), 95–96.

11. David Haas, "Bless Sophia," Hawaiian chant, *Bring the Feast* (Cleveland: Pilgrim Press, 1997), 3. Used by permission.

12. Diana L. Hayes, *Hagar's Daughters: Womanist Ways of Being in the World* (New York/Mahwah: Paulist Press, 1996), 60–61.

13. Mary Hunt, *Fierce Tenderness: A Feminist Theology of Friendship* (New York: Crossroad, 1994), 166.

14. Manley Olson, "Women's Voices, Women's Witness," music "Holy Manna" by William Moore, 1825; *Bring the Feast* (Cleveland: Pilgrim Press, 1997), 48. Used by permission.

15. Ibid.

16. Kathy Sherman, CSJ, "This Day Is My Daily Bread," lyrics and music, *Singing My Soul* © 1996, Sisters of St. Joseph of La Grange. Audio recording. Used by permission.

17. Kathy Sherman, CSJ, "Dance in the New Day," lyrics and music, *Dance in the Dawn* © 1993, Sisters of St. Joseph of La Grange. Audio recording. Used by permission.

18. "Bless This House" by Helen Taylor, music by Mary Brahe, as sung on *The Mormon Tabernacle's Choir's Greatest Hits* © 1992, Thomas Frost Production. *Verses adapted.

19. Introit, from Common of the Dedication of a Church, in Rev. Hugo H. Hoever, S.O. Cist., Ph.D., ed. *St. Joseph Daily Missal* (New York: Catholic Book Publishing Co., 1959), 1217.

20. Marsie Silvestro, "Walk Through These Doors," *Crossing the Lines* © 1987, Moonsong Productions. Audio recording. Used by permission.

21. Carolyn McDade, "Song of Community," *Rain Upon Dry Land* © 1981, Surtesy Publishing. Audio recording. Used by permission.

22. Carolyn McDade, "We're Coming Home," *This Ancient Love* © 1990, Surtesy Publishing. Audio recording. Used by permission.

23. Miriam Therese Winter, "Sing of a Blessing," *WomanSong* © 1987, Medical Mission Sisters. Audio recording. Used by permission.

24. Gwen Benjamin, written August 1991 for the birth of her granddaughter, Millicent, and sent to WATER on the birth of Cecilia Ann Lapp Stolzfus. Used by permission.

25. Carole Etzler, "Womanchild," from *Womanriver Flowing On* © 1977 Carole Etzler. Audio recording available on tape from Carole Etzler Eagleheart, 1180 VT Route 22A, Bridport VT 05734. Used by permission.

26. Holly Near and Jeff Langley, "Good For the World," words and music, HARP © 1985, 2001, Hereford Music (ASCAP). Audio recording. Used by permission.

27. "The Earth, the Air, the Fire, the Water," source unknown, in *A Circle Is Cast,* by Libana © 1986, Libana. Audio recording. Used by permission.

28. Carolyn McDade, "We're Coming Home," *This Ancient Love* © 1990, Surtesy Publishing. Audio recording. Used by permission.

29. Betty Wendelborn, music, "We Are a Wheel," words by Hildegard of Bingen, *Sing Green: Songs of the Mystics,* 2d ed. (Auckland, New Zealand: Pyramid Press, 1999), 1. Used by permission.

30. Rae E. Whitney, "Make Wide the Circle," stanza 1 adapted, music by Donna Kasbohm, *Bring the Feast* (Cleveland: Pilgrim Press, 1997), 24. Used by permission.

31. Alice Walker, "The Gospel According to Shug," *The Temple of My Familiar* (New York: Simon and Schuster, 1989), 288–89.

32. Joan Prefontaine, "Bring the Feast to Ev'ry Hillside," music "Feast" by Jane Ramseyer Miller, *Bring the Feast* (Cleveland: Pilgrim Press, 1997), 7. Used by permission.

33. Colleen Fulmer, "Blessed Is She," *Cry of Ramah* © 1985, Heartbeats. Audio recording. Used by permission.

34. Marsie Silvestro, "Blessing Song," *Circling Free* © 1983, Moonsong Productions. Audio recording. Used by permission.

35. Ibid.

36. Carolyn McDade, "Sister, Carry On," *Sister, Carry On* © 1992, Surtesy Publishing. Audio recording. Used by permission.

four

HONORING WOMEN'S BLOOD MYSTERIES

When you first realize your blood has come,
smile; an honest smile,
For you are about to have
an intense union with your magic.

Ntozake Shange

Woman am I.
Spirit am I.
I am the infinite within my soul.
I can find no beginning
And I can find no end.
All this I am.

Source unknown

The most creative force in the world is the
menopausal woman with zest.

Margaret Mead

Wisdom is bright, and does not grow dim.
By those who love her she is readily seen,
And found by those who look for her.

Wisdom 6:12

INTRODUCTION

From menarche to menopause, my grandmothers experienced biological-psychosocial-spiritual processes unique to their life cycles yet similar to those of my mother and me, namely, the flow of blood. Women's blood represents our life-giving powers. Each month we feel in our own bodies the meaning of the words of the eucharist, "This is my body; this is my blood."

In recent history in Western cultures, many women learned to talk about monthly menstruation in secret whispers as "the curse," rather than embrace it as "the blessing." Many girl children receive the message, subtly and not so subtly, that menses is associated with pain and limitation rather than creativity and power. Some women who feel physical pain during menses can experience creativity and power during this time. Some women and men are working to change these taboos, social attitudes, and behaviors about women's bleeding so that the next generations of girls and boys can realize the sacred, holy power in women's blood.

In the Native American tradition, a woman is considered to be her most powerful, physically and spiritually, when she is menstruating. In many Native societies, before traditional practices were suppressed, women went to a menstrual hut (a bleeding lodge or a moon lodge), gathered with other such women, and retreated for two to three days to pass their bleeding time.[1] They rested, relaxed, and gathered spiritual wisdom. The Cherokee believe that the menstruating woman is performing a function of cleansing and gathering wisdom that benefits not only herself but the whole tribe.[2]

Biblical and religious traditions have not only not honored women's blood mysteries, they have oppressed women and men by viewing menstruation negatively as a blood taboo. Blood is the source of life and it is dangerous to the patriarchy. In the first chapter of the Book of Lamentations, Jerusalem is portrayed as the wayward "daughter Zion" whose uncleanness of her menstrual flow is but one aspect of her humiliation and shame.[3] In Genesis 29:31–30:25, Rachel escapes with the gods because she is sitting on them when she is menstruating and therefore "untouchable" to the men. In chapter 16 of Ezekiel, menstruation symbolizes dirtiness and shamefulness, a liability that betrayed God.[4] The Pentateuch, particularly Leviticus 12–15 and 17–26, traces the prophets' bewailing of females and menstruation. Tobit 3:7–8, 14–15, 8:1–9 recounts the dangerous young woman who is exorcised and the demon driven away. New Testament writers speak only twice about menstruation: Mark 5:25–34 and Acts 15. Mark records the healing of the hemorrhaging woman and shows that when Jesus interacted with the bleeding woman he went against prevailing customs, disregarded the Torah's admonitions regarding physical contact with a menstruating woman, and ministered to a socially outcast woman.[5] In Acts 15, while menstruation is not the main issue, it is one of the cultic purity concerns mentioned in the passage, which keeps women from being delegates to go from Jerusalem to Antioch to help resolve a dispute.[6]

How do we overcome these negative cultural and biblical images so that all women and the next generations of girl children will have healthy self-concepts and claim their power? How do we reclaim women's bodies as holy? How do we help women and whole cultures see that women image the Divine?

Some women and their communities worldwide are creating rites to honor women's blood mysteries. Two examples follow. The first story from San Bernardo, Argentina, celebrates menstruation. The second account from Manitoba, Canada, describes a croning ceremony.

San Bernardo, Argentina: Celebrating Our Menstruation[7]

The context: Safina Newbery, an anthropologist with Catholic roots, and Zulema Palma, a medical doctor with a Jewish background, are both founders and members of La Urdimbra de

Aquehua, a women's group that comes together for study, celebration, and action. They gathered women, myself among them, at the ocean during the 5th Encuentro of Latin American and Caribbean Women to reclaim our power and celebrate our menstruation. The participants were from most of the Latin American countries.

The rite: They placed a multicolored indigenous cloth on top of the sand to create the space, then put around the cloth four statues of women deities representing the spirits of women from the south, east, north, and west. Around the cloth they put various seeds, rice, and flowers. They gathered the women in a circle and began singing, "Gracias a la Vida (Thanks to Life)."

A young woman gave each participant a flower to symbolize the flower of her sexuality. Safina asked us to imagine our first menstruation: our thoughts, fears, sensations, and beliefs. She invited us to speak out a word that we associate with the negative side of the day—fears, anger, horrors, death, and more. At the end of this litany we shouted, "Be gone, patriarchy!"

Then Zulema invited us to think about our bodies, and where we put our menstruation: in a pad, tampon, cotton, synthetic fiber. She asked us how we could reconnect our bodies, our selves to the earth. She invited us to offer our blood to the Pacha Mama (the Latin American name for Mother Earth), saying, "that our blood renew the earth and fertilize it; that our blood strengthen us and our sisters."

Safina invited women who were menstruating that day to touch women who were not menstruating, and to reach out to those who had not yet had their first menses. She asked the menstruating women to symbolically offer their blood, representing all women's blood, to the Pacha Mama. Everyone said, "I found the Pacha Mama in myself and I love her passionately." We closed embracing one another and singing, "Soy Paz, Soy Pan, Soy Mas (I am Peace, I am Bread, I am More)."

Reflection: This liturgy was a powerful and moving experience for the women. As we sat beside the Atlantic ocean with the waves flowing in and out, we focused on the major taboo in women's lives, our flow of blood. Beginning the rite with "Gracias a la Vida," the political song of Latin America, created a space of gratitude that opened women up to thanksgiving for our menstruation. Most women had never imagined our thoughts, fears, sensations, and beliefs from our first menses. Shouting "Be gone, patriarchy!" to the negative side of the day was cleansing. To think about where we put our blood and how it connects us to the earth was a new concept for most of the gathered. When menstruating women touched women who were not menstruating, a powerful connection happened in the group. Menstruating women were symbolically and actually raised up as imaging Wisdom Sophia.

Manitoba, Canada: Croning[8]

The context: Denise Kuyp, a Roman Catholic Sister, invited twelve women to her home to honor a wise woman in her community on her sixty-fifth birthday. They came together to mark Sheila's passage to the next stage of her life. They wanted to honor her as a crone. The group gathered on the eve of the birthday under a full moon.

The rite: Denise welcomed the twelve and acknowledged Sheila as a very special person among them. Another woman gave Sheila a rock with a wolf painted on it. The wolf is a special animal in the Canadian wilderness and one that feminists use to reclaim power. The wolf symbolizes connection with instinct, energy, and personal power. The group invited her to keep the rock under her pillow that night as a symbol of consciously opening herself to communication from other realities, such as nature, communion of saints, and her Celtic ancestors. The next day the women met in the upper room of the house, prayed, and enacted, with Sheila's consent, a rebirthing experience of her to help her face her fears and demons so that she could be freed from them to enter this next stage of her life. They blindfolded Sheila, carried her down steps as through a birth canal, rocked her, and placed her carefully on the floor of the main level of the house. Each person gave her a symbol to represent the gift of Sheila to each of them, and what she may need for the next stage of her life. Symbols included seeds and a shawl with a wolf painted on it. They sang, danced, and ate festive foods together to honor this Celtic woman of deep faith.

Reflection: Gathering outside in the Canadian wilderness under the full moon and using the wolf as a symbol offered these women an unconscious level of connection to the power of the universe. Giving Sheila the rock with the wolf on it and inviting her to put it under her pillow and sleep on it welcomed her into a liminal state. Meeting in the upper room has a Pentecost feel to it where the women put themselves in the position to receive inspiration from the Holy Spirit, Wisdom Sophia. The rebirthing experience of blindfolding, carrying, rocking, and placing on the floor embodies the life-changing journey for Sheila, at least the part where she is accompanied by her friends. A small group of twelve can personalize a ceremony and add a dimension of intimacy that a larger group cannot because of size. Twelve is a symbolic number in Jewish and Christian history: twelve tribes of Israel, twelve disciples, twelve pillars of the church.

Silver Spring, Maryland, USA: Honoring Women's Blood Mysteries

The context: I was asked to design the liturgies in this section to bless a woman in her blood cycle and to offer faith communities a way to make holy women's life cycles.

The rites: The liturgical texts are given here.

Reflection: "Praise Our Bodies: Women Image the Divine" proclaims that all women's bodies image the Divine and recognizes that all women's bodies are beautiful. "From Developing Girl to Changing Woman: A Celebration of Menses" honors a young girl for her transition from childhood into adolescence and subsequent adulthood. "Honoring Sacred Blood: A Woman's Monthly Blessing" invites a woman to pause during her bleeding time to give thanks for the month that has been, to let unresolved issues and draining worries rest in peace, and to refocus on her wisdom to greet the coming month.

"Change of Life: Journey through Menopause" marks the changes in a woman's life as she enters menopause, a pathway to her empowerment. "Choosing Wisdom: A Croning Ceremony" honors a woman elder as she transitions beyond child bearing, beyond menopause, and sometimes beyond professional life, and comes into the fullness of her wisdom. "Blessed Be: Honoring Women's Cycles" sums up this chapter by celebrating women's life cycles of birth, menstruation, mid-life/menopause, and aging.

PRAISE OUR BODIES:

Women Image the Divine

Women's bodies belong to women. This is a fundamental concept of feminism. We are our bodies and we have only one for a lifetime. We are learning to accept our embodied selves the way we are, not the way the beauty ads want us to be. This is not easy work. It calls us to overcome many myths about womanhood, race, ability, and age.

This liturgy praises our bodies and recognizes that all women's bodies are beautiful. Use it, or parts of it, for personal reflection. Adapt it for a group ritual.

Preparation

Ask six women to read the texts. Place mirrors on a table in the center of a circle. Provide a loaf of bread, two carafes of wine and juice, and cups.

Introductions

Welcome to this liturgy "Praise Our Bodies: Women Image the Divine." We have come together to celebrate our bodies. What do you think and feel when you hear the word "body"? (*Pause*) Let us introduce ourselves by speaking our names and sharing a thought or feeling about our bodies. (*Sharing*)

Call to Gather

Our bodies are ourselves. They reveal, literally and truthfully, the stories of our lives. We present ourselves to the world through our bodies or not at all. We experience the presence of Wisdom Sophia in our bodies or not at all. For we are simply no-bodies without our bodies. Our bodies are sacred, beautiful, and wise.

Let us give thanks for our bodies, ourselves, by singing. Let us walk in a circle as we sing, then stand still for the last line of the chant.

Song: "We Bring Who We Are," by Colleen Fulmer[9]

I am who I bring from yesterday.
I am who I am today.
I am who I am for all the days to come.
I am a Woman, a glorious creation of praise.

We are who we bring from yesterday,
We are who we bring today,
We are who we are for all the days to come.
We are Women—glorious creations of praise.

Readings

Listen to what women say about our bodies. Let us respond to each one with "All women's bodies are beautiful."

Reader One: The body is a sacred garment. (Martha Graham)[10]

Response: All women's bodies are beautiful.

Reader Two: The body has its own way of knowing, a knowing that has little to do with logic, and much to do with truth, little to do with control, and much to do with acceptance, little to do with division and analysis, and much to do with union. (Marilyn Sewell)[11]

Response: All women's bodies are beautiful.

Reader Three: Over the years our bodies become walking autobiographies, telling friends and strangers alike of the minor and major stresses of our lives. (Marilyn Ferguson)[12]

Response: All women's bodies are beautiful.

Reader Four: The rain beats on me, but the rain cannot wash off the beauty of my body. (Yoruba proverb)[13]

Response: All women's bodies are beautiful.

Reader Five:

The bodies of grownups
come with stretchmarks and scars,
faces that have been lived in,
relaxed breasts and bellies,
backs that give trouble,
and well-worn feet:
flesh that is particular,
and obviously mortal.
They also come
with bruises on their heart,
wounds they can't forget,
and each of them
a company of lovers in their soul
who will not return
and cannot be erased.
And yet I think there is a flood of beauty
beyond the smoothness of youth;
and my heart aches for that grace of longing
that flows through bodies
no longer straining to be innocent,
but yearning for redemption. (Janet Morley)[14]

Response: All women's bodies are beautiful.

Reader Six:

Thru animate eyes
I divide the seasons
of time.

I am aware of what they are.
I am aware of their potential.

With my mouth
I kiss my own chosen creation

I uniquely,
lovingly,
embrace every image
I have made
out of the earth's clay.

With a fiery spirit
I transform it
into a body
to serve
all the world. (Hildegard of Bingen)[15]

Response: All women's bodies are beautiful.

Reflection

Take a mirror. (*Pause*) Look at your self. (*Pause*) Look at your body. (*Pause*)

Reading: Song of Songs 4:1–5, translated by Marcia Falk[16]

How fine
you are, my love,
your eyes like doves'
behind your veil

Your hair—
as black as goats
winding down the slopes

Your teeth—
a flock of sheep
rising from the stream
in twos, each with its twin

Your lips—
like woven threads
of crimson silk

A gleam of pomegranate—
your forehead
through your veil

Your neck—
a tower
adorned with shields

Your breasts—
twin fawns
in fields of flowers

Litany of Thanksgiving for Our Bodies[17]

Let us give thanks for our bodies. For this antiphonal blessing, stand and repeat the last line of each verse in the first person.

Speaker One: Praise to you, Wisdom Sophia, for creating us in your image.

Response: Praise to you, Wisdom Sophia, for creating me in your image.

Speaker One: Praise the heart. Feel your pulse. Place your hand on your heart. Pay attention to your heart beat. (*Pause*)

The heart weighs only half a pound. Its rhythmic contraction pumps the circulation of blood. Its millions of cells work together to beat each second for about four billion heartbeats in a lifetime.

Praise to you, Wisdom Sophia, for our hearts.

Response: Praise to you, Wisdom Sophia, for my heart.

Speaker Two: Praise blood. Stretch and move, bend forward and backward. Pay attention to the circulation of blood throughout your body. (*Pause*)

Blood is the fluid that circulates in the heart, arteries, capillaries, and veins. It carries nourishment and oxygen to all parts of the body and takes away waste products from all parts of the body.

Praise to you, Wisdom Sophia, for our blood.

Response: Praise to you, Wisdom Sophia, for my blood.

Speaker Three: Praise lungs. Place your hands on your rib cage, take a deep breath, inhale and exhale, expand and contract your lungs. (*Pause*)

The lungs, our basic respiratory organ, draw in oxygen essential to living cells, and blow out the carbon dioxide cast off by those cells.

Praise to you, Wisdom Sophia, for our lungs.

Response: Praise to you, Wisdom Sophia, for my lungs.

Speaker Four: Praise the brain. Place one hand on the top of your skull and the other over the back of your skull. Gently massage your scalp. (*Pause*)

The brain constitutes the organ of thought and neural coordination; the center of intelligence, memory, and control of muscular movements.

Praise to you, Wisdom Sophia, for our brains.

Response: Praise to you, Wisdom Sophia, for my brain.

Speaker Five: Praise eyes. Open and close your eyes. Look around the room. Look into the eyes of those here. (*Pause*)

The eyes are the organs of sight. They mirror our interior wisdom.

Praise to you, Wisdom Sophia, for our eyes.

Response: Praise to you, Wisdom Sophia, for my eyes.

Speaker One: Praise ears. Place one hand over each ear. Remove your hands. Listen to the sounds around you. (*Pause*)

The ears, organs of hearing and equilibrium, consist of a sound-collecting outer ear separated by a membranous drum from a sound-transmitting middle ear that in turn is separated from a sensory inner ear. Ears translate vibrations into what we hear.

Praise to you, Wisdom Sophia, for our ears.

Response: Praise to you, Wisdom Sophia, for my ears.

Speaker Two: Praise vocal chords. In a whisper, all at the same time, say your name. (*Pause*) Say it louder. (*Pause*) And louder. (*Pause*)

Vocal chords are two pairs of folds of mucous membranes that project into the cavity of the larynx. They give voice to our uniqueness.

Praise to you, Wisdom Sophia, for our vocal chords.

Response: Praise to you, Wisdom Sophia, for my vocal chords.

Speaker Three: Praise bones and muscles. Touch some of your bones and muscles. (*Pause*)

More than two hundred bones covered with muscle give the basic framework to our bodies.

Praise to you, Wisdom Sophia, for our bones and muscles.

Response: Praise to you, Wisdom Sophia, for my bones and muscles.

Speaker Four: Praise breasts, wombs, and ovaries. Touch your breasts and womb, or where they used to be. (*Pause*)

Breasts are the external symbol of our womanhood associated with nurturance. The uterus is the center of reproduction. The ovaries in our reproductive years release an egg each month, and in age continue to produce female sex hormones.

Praise to you, Wisdom Sophia, for our breasts, wombs, and ovaries.

Response: Praise to you, Wisdom Sophia, for my breasts, womb, and ovaries.

Speaker Five: Praise female bodies. Recognize the design of your body. (*Pause*)

Our bodies are ourselves.

Praise to you, Wisdom Sophia, for our beautiful bodies.

Response: Praise to you, Wisdom Sophia, for my beautiful body.

Song: "I Am Enough," by Colleen Fulmer[18]

I am enough, I am enough,
Just as I am, I am enough.
Just as I am, just as I am,
I am enough, just as I am.

I am a woman, I am a woman,
My body's sacred, I am a woman.
My body's sacred, my body's sacred,
I am a woman, my body's sacred.

In God's own image, in God's own image,
I am created, in God's own image.
I am created, I am created,
In God's own image, I am created.

Reflection

Our bodies are ourselves. They image Wisdom Sophia, the Divine Feminine. They are sacred, beautiful, and wise. What have you noticed about your body tonight? (*Pause*) Let us share our feelings and thoughts with one another. (*Sharing*)

Song: "I Am Enough," by Colleen Fulmer[19]

In God's own image, in God's own image,
I am created, in God's own image.
I am created, I am created,
In God's own image, I am created.

Blessing the Bread

(*One woman takes the bread, saying:*)
As it was and is in the beginning, at a woman's breast,
Real milk, nourishing food,
I say, this is your sacrament:

Take. Eat. This is my body
Which I give for the life of the world.
Let us eat, remembering the bread of life.
(*She breaks the bread and passes it for all to eat.*)

Blessing the Wine and Juice

(*One woman takes the fruit of the vine, saying:*)
As it was and is every month in a woman's body,
Real flow of blood, life force shed for many,
I say, this is your sacrament:
Take. Drink. This is my blood
Which I give for the life of the world.
Let us drink, remembering the blood of life.
(*She pours the fruit of the vine and passes the cups for all to drink.*)

Greeting of Beauty

Let us close by acknowledging that we are beautiful. Look around this circle. Notice the women here. Women are beautiful. All shapes, colors, and sizes. Let us affirm our beauty by hugging one another and saying, "You are beautiful."

Song: "We Bring Who We Are," by Colleen Fulmer

I am who I bring from yesterday.
I am who I am today.
I am who I am for all the days to come.
I am a Woman, a glorious creation of praise.

We are who we bring from yesterday,
We are who we bring today,
We are who we are for all the days to come.
We are Women—glorious creations of praise.

FROM DEVELOPING GIRL TO CHANGING WOMAN:

A Celebration of Menses

Transformation can be so ordinary that its very familiarity renders it invisible. This is often true of menstruation. Girl children experience first menses. Women know the full meaning of this passage to womanhood. Every girl who so wishes needs to have a celebration of this special time in her life.

This liturgy invites women to share with the next generations the treasures of womanhood. Use it as a guide to create the celebration that you and the women in your life need. You may wish to create a ceremony for one or for several girls who are passing into womanhood at approximately the same time.

Preparation

Buy a tambourine, red ribbons, a decorative egg, a ring, and herbs that will be given as gifts. Place a red candle, a green one, and a purple one in the center of a circle of chairs. Put a basket of red fruits and pitchers of red drinks along with them.

Call to Gather

Welcome to this celebration for N. (*name of girl passing into womanhood*). We gather today to welcome you, N., to womanhood. You are a symbol of the passage to womanhood that each of us here and women of every culture experience. We gather today to honor menarche. We gather today to proclaim our sacred power as women.

Our flow of blood represents our life-giving powers. As changing women, we celebrate the transmission of our fertility, our creativity, our spirit, and our intuition. As changing women, we dedicate the fertility of our life force to the next generations.

Naming the Circle

Let us begin by naming our circle here. Think of what the time of first menstruation means to you, what it did mean to you, or what it will mean to you. (*Pause*)

Let us create our circle by speaking our names, sharing a word or phrase that comes to mind when thinking of menses, and giving a hand to the person on the right saying, "I am a woman" or "I will be a woman." (*Sharing, for example, "I am Diann. I honor women's sacred powers. I am a woman."*)

Blessing the New Woman

(*The woman who started the naming completes the circle by raising the joined hands and saying:*)

We are women together and our life-giving circle is sacred. May we be blessed beneath the wings of Shechina, Wisdom Sophia. May the Holy Source of Life wrap us in the mantle of her love and protection. May N.'s passing to womanhood be blessed with the power of women's energy. May we each be blessed with the power of N.'s energy as she enters womanhood.

Amen. Blessed be. Let it be so.

(*The namer begins a swaying movement with the hands joined as the singing starts. When the song ends, she lets go of the joined hands.*)

Song: "Womanriver Flowing On," by Carole Etzler[20]

Womanriver flowing on,
Womanriver flowing on and on (*Repeat*)
Womanriver flowing on.

Lighting the Candles

We light three candles today to express our experience as women. The red one is for those who are fertile, those who bleed each month. (*The young woman honored in the celebration lights the red candle.*)

The purple is for the wise women who have passed beyond the biological capacity to give birth and have channeled their energies through their whole selves: mind, spirit, and body. (*A menopausal woman lights the purple candle.*)

The green is for the young girls who will soon pass into womanhood. (*A young girl lights the green candle.*)

Reading

Today as we celebrate menses let us listen to this reading, "Marvelous Menstruating Moments," by Ntozake Shange (As Told by Indigo to Her Dolls as She Made Each and Every One of Them a Personal Menstruation Pad of Velvet)[21]:

When you first realize your blood has come, smile; an honest smile, for you are about to have an intense union with your magic. This is a private time, a special time, for thinking and dreaming. Change your bedsheet to the ones that are your favorite. Sleep with a laurel leaf under your head. Take baths in wild hyssop, white water lilies. Listen for the voices of your visions; they are nearby. Let annoying people, draining worries, fall away as your body lets what she doesn't need go from her. Remember that you are a river; your banks are red honey where the Moon wanders.

Reflection

We women are rivers of life. Today we celebrate life as it is flowing on to another generation. Mother(s), what do you want to pass on to your daughter(s)? (*Pause*)

Let this tambourine represent our voices and let these ribbons represent our blessings for N. (*the girl*). As we pass the tambourine around the circle, shake it, attach a ribbon, and share what you want to pass on to N., who embodies the next generation of women. (*Sharing begins with the mother.*)

Song: "Womanriver Flowing On"

Womanriver flowing on,
Womanriver flowing on and on (*Repeat*)
Womanriver flowing on.

Giftgiving

N., we have gifts for you to remind you of this special day.

(*The mother gives her daughter a ring, saying:*)

N., you traveled the road from nursing (or cuddling, if not the biological mother) in my arms as a baby to maturing into a young woman. I bless you for these and all the seasons of your life. Take this ring as a symbol of the passage well done.

(*The godmother, or significant mentor, gives her godchild an egg, saying:*)

N., womanhood means that you have the power to give birth. Use this awesome power maturely and lovingly. Protect yourself from dangerous pressures to misuse this power. I bless you for using your reproductive years wisely. Take this egg as a symbol of your reproductive powers.

(*Another friend gives her the tambourine, saying:*)

N., this tambourine represents our vision of womanhood. Treasure it and add to it your own wisdom. Keep your body sacred. Use it wisely. Preserve your reproductive power for the time when you are fully prepared to take responsibility for another life. We bless you for becoming the woman you will be.

(*Another friend gives her herbs, saying:*)

N., take these herbs for soothing cramps and calming irritations. Don't be angry with your body. When your body is in pain, listen to it and help it heal. I bless you for caring for your body.

(*Other gifts are shared.*)

Blessing Ourselves

Filled with the fullness of Wisdom Sophia we take time to bless one another and ourselves. To embody our prayer we use an ancient tradition, the laying on of hands.

Touch your eyes and echo these words:
Bless my eyes that I may notice the beauty of women. (*Echo*)
Touch your ears, saying:
Bless my ears that I may hear women's wisdom. (*Echo*)
Touch your heart, saying:
Bless my heart that I may love well. (*Echo*)
Touch your mouth, saying:
Bless my mouth that I may speak my truth. (*Echo*)
Touch your body over your womb, or where your womb used to be, saying:
Bless my womb that I may give birth to my creativity. (*Echo*)
Touch your feet, saying:
Bless my feet that I may walk the path of justice. (*Echo*)
Touch your hands, saying:
Bless my hands that I may touch others and myself tenderly. (*Echo*)
Touch and embrace the women around you and bless them with your own words. (*Embracing*)

Song: "I Am Enough," by Colleen Fulmer[22]

I am enough, I am enough,
Just as I am, I am enough.
Just as I am, just as I am,
I am enough, just as I am.

I am a woman, I am a woman,
My body's sacred, I am a woman.
My body's sacred, my body's sacred,
I am a woman, my body's sacred.

In God's own image, in God's own image,
I am created, in God's own image.
I am created, I am created,
In God's own image, I am created.

I am enough, I am enough,
I walk in beauty, I am enough.
I walk in beauty, I walk in beauty,
I am enough, I walk in beauty.

Blessing the Fruit, Wine, and Drinks

Red is the color of women's life source. Red is the color of women's passion. Red is the color of women's creativity. We eat and drink food that is red today to remind us of women's life-giving energy. (*Women hold up the food and drink.*)

Blessed are you, Life-giving Holy Source, Wisdom Sophia, for ripening fruit on the vine and for weaving women's energies into a generational tapestry. Bless us as we eat and drink, remembering our life passages, and honoring women's sacred blood. (*The blessers pass the food and drink around the circle.*)

Sending Forth

We have welcomed our sister and daughter, N., into womanhood. We have remembered our journeys to womanhood. We have praised women's powers.

Let us open our circle now in song, remembering that we will be there for one another.

Song: "Let the Women Be There," by Marsie Silvestro[23]

If ever I give birth to another person
Or create a work with my mouth, my eyes, my hands

Refrain:
Let the women be there (*Repeat*)
Let the women be there by my side.

If ever I should cry from the pain of injustice
Let the tears I cry run down like a river
And set us free.

(*Refrain*)

And when I am walking,
Spirit breath's last journey,
Let the wisdom I carry be the vision
I'm passing on.

(*Refrain*)

Greeting of Peace

Let us hug one another and promise that we will be there for one another.

HONORING SACRED BLOOD:

A Woman's Monthly Blessing

Each month, when a woman bleeds, she manifests her power. This newness and renewal is a special time for thinking and dreaming, for wishing and visioning, for connecting with sacred powers.

In recent history, many women have grown up cursing monthly menstruation. This is the message girl children receive about their power. It is time women and men, girls and boys, change these attitudes about women's bleeding so that the next generations can realize the power in their blood.

Formerly in some cultures when a woman bled monthly, she went to a menstrual hut or a bleeding lodge, gathered with other such women, and retreated for two to three days. Today, some women make a sacred space in their homes or in any private place where they can be safe and uninterrupted.

This liturgy invites a woman to take a monthly pause, a retreat time, a day of rest by herself, to let go of the previous month and to get ready for the forthcoming one. It is created to be used monthly when a woman begins to bleed. It can be used at the beginning, throughout and/or at the end of menstrual days. Adapt it to your needs.

Preparation

Place a red candle in a favorite place. If you wish, circle twenty-eight shells around the candle to represent the usual twenty-eight-day cycle. Fill an earthenware bowl with salt water. Prepare tea or a drink of choice, gather bath oils or bubbles, choose meditative music, and be ready to draw a bath.

Centering

For the month that has been,
I give thanks.
To unresolved issues, conflictual relationships,
 and draining worries,
I say rest in peace.
For the month that is yet to come,
May I choose wisely.

Candle Lighting

(Light a red candle and gaze at the burning flame.)

Meditation

(Hold an earthenware bowl of salt water for purification. Salt water symbolizes the origins of life and the connection between womb-blood and the water of the sea.)

Praise to you, Wisdom Sophia, for creating me a woman.
Like the moon, I retreat in order to emerge whole.
Like the moon, I rest.

Let my body and its blood teach me:
Let go, let go, let go.
Give up harmful control.

Unshed tears, flow from me.
Pent up tension, flow from me.
Closed emotions, flow from me.
Harmful thoughts, flow from me.
Unforgiven deeds, flow from me.
Unfulfilled expectations, flow from me.
. . . (*Add others*), flow from me.

Wisdom Sophia, breathe into me the breath of life.
Womb of life, bring me home to myself.
Source of Renewal, refresh and restore me again.
Praise to you, Wisdom Sophia, for creating me a woman.

Blessing for the New and for Renewal

(*Touch your hair, saying:*)

Bless to my hair the flow of life that revives and sustains.
(*Touch your eyes, saying:*)
Bless to my eyes the flow of life that revives and sustains.
(*Touch your nose, saying:*)
Bless to my nose the flow of life that revives and sustains.
(*Touch your mouth, saying:*)
Bless to my mouth the flow of life that revives and sustains.
(*Touch your ears, saying:*)
Bless to my ears the flow of life that revives and sustains.
(*Touch your breasts, or where they used to be, saying:*)
Bless to my breasts (*or where they used to be*) the flow of life that revives and sustains.
(*Touch your womb, saying:*)
Bless to my womb (*or womb space*) the flow of life that revives and sustains.
(*Touch your legs, saying:*)
Bless to my legs the flow of life that revives and sustains.
(*Touch your feet, saying:*)
Bless to my feet the flow of life that revives and sustains.
(*Touch your entire body, saying:*)
Bless my entire body with the flow of life that revives and sustains.

Prayer for the New Month

Wisdom Sophia, Womb of Life, Source of Renewal,
Let this new month be filled with blessings:

Of health and joy,
Of goodness and peace,
Of satisfaction and love.
Let truth and justice guide my actions.
Let wisdom and grace blossom within me.
Amen. Blessed be. Let it be so.

Personal Reflection

What do I wish for the new month? (*Take time to reflect on your life and your work, your gifts and your dreams.*)

(*Drink herbal tea or spiced cider to cleanse and calm, take a sauna to purify, get a massage to heal, or take a bath pampering your five senses: light a candle; play music; sip a drink of choice; add aromatic oils or bubbles, and soak in the bath water.*)

Closing

For the month that has been,
I give thanks.
To unresolved issues, conflictual relationships,
and draining worries,
I say rest in peace.
For the month that is yet to come,
May I choose wisely.

CHANGE OF LIFE:
Journey through Menopause

Menopause, a natural and momentous event in the life of a woman, has been neglected historically by society, religion, history, and mythology. Women's communities around the world are reclaiming this aspect of a woman's life and marking it with a rite of passage, a pathway to empowerment. Each woman's experience of menopause is unique. Yet this common passage of adult womanhood deserves attention as a time of psychological integration and growth, spiritual strength, and wisdom.

A woman who experiences menopause may yearn to mark this change in her life. She may desire to invite her friends and family to witness her life-cycle transition by celebrating a rite of passage. This liturgy provides a model. Use it to honor a woman beginning menopause, in the midst of menopause, or at the end of menopause. It is an invitation to create a ceremony for the menopausal women in your community, perhaps for you.

Preparation

Gather four red candles, red sashes (one for each menopausal woman), purple sashes (one for each crone—a wise woman who is post-menopausal), fruit, bread, herbal tea, a bowl of water, and either flowers, a tree, or fans.

Arrange a circle of chairs, one for each participant. Place a table in the center of this circle and put on it the symbols you will use for the ceremony.

Call to Gather

(*A friend begins the ceremony.*)

Welcome, N. (*name of the woman entering menopause*), to your rite of passage, a pathway to empowerment. Today we honor and witness your change of life as you enter menopause. We acknowledge that menopause is a natural and momentous event in the life of every woman even though it has been so neglected by society, mythology, history, and religion. We mark your change and every woman's changes. We are women who live out our cycles of birth, menstruation, menopause, and death.

Let us stand, join hands, and create a circle of celebration by singing.

Chant: "Women Come," traditional round

(*The numbers indicate where parts can begin.*)

1. Women, come; friends, come;
2. Come and join our circle now,
3. Celebrate N.'s change of life,
4. Journey through menopause.

Naming the Circle

(*The friend continues.*)

Who are we here? With whom have we been singing? What comes to your mind when you think of menopause—your own or someone else's? To introduce yourself, speak your name and a word or phrase you associate with menopause. (*Naming*)

The Rite of Passage

(*A menopausal woman explains menopause.*)

Menopause is all of what we have said and more. Translated from the Greek, *menos* means month and *pauein* means to cause to cease. Webster defines menopause as the permanent cessation of menstruation, normally between the ages of forty-five and fifty; female climacteric, or change of life.

This is a time in a woman's life when the blood that was available for giving life to others is now held within as wise blood to nurture oneself and renew the earth. The menopausal woman is freed from birth control, from menstrual periods, from the emotional swings of the reproductive years.

This universal, biological destiny is a critical turning point in a woman's life cycle, equal in significance to the menarche, the first orgasm, or, for some, the birthing of a baby. For many women the time of menopause becomes the beginning of deeper self-discovery, a time to reevaluate and realize values; for others, it marks a major crisis. Shifting into a whole new phase of being can bring up fears and anxieties. Yet women can be energized and transformed during this change of life.

Chant: "Woman Am I," traditional[24]

Woman am I. Spirit am I.
I am the infinite within my soul.
I can find no beginning
And I can find no end.
All this I am.

Candle Lighting

(*The menopausal woman lights the four red candles, saying something appropriate for her, such as:*)

I light four red candles to mark four aspects of my bleeding.

(*Lighting the first candle:*) For the bloods that have ceased flowing from me.

(*Lighting the second candle:*) For the children (*if there are any*), the health, the creativity that the red river of life brought me.

(*Lighting the third candle:*) For the passions of my womanhood.

(*Lighting the fourth candle:*) For the wise blood that stays within me to deepen self-discovery and commitment to social justice.

Purification

(*Another friend takes a bowl of water from the table and says:*)

As we stand with N. at a threshold of womanhood, let us purify our thoughts, our words, and our hearts of all the negativity around menopause. Receive the bowl of water; dip your hands in it; then touch your forehead, your mouth, and your heart and cleanse yourself of negative energy. (*She then passes the bowl of water around.*)

Honoring Menopausal Women

(*A young woman says:*)

We recognize those women among us who are in the midst of menopause and those who have journeyed through menopause to become crones. You are the elders who reveal to us the fullness of womanhood. You do it with grace and beauty.

(*She calls out the name of each crone first, then names each menopausal woman, naming the new menopausal woman last.*)

(*For the crone*)

N., receive this purple sash as an outward sign of your inner wisdom. (*Give her the sash as a stole or tie it around her waist.*)

(*For the menopausal woman*)

N., receive this red sash as an outward sign of the withdrawal of the flowing blood from you. (*Give her the sash as a stole or tie it around her waist.*)

Hymn of Praise

(*The woman entering menopause invites the other menopausal women and crones to join her.*)

Menopausal sisters and wise crones, join me in praying a hymn of praise. The rest of you, please respond after each invocation, "We thank you."

Menopausal women/crones: Praise to you, Source of Life,
for placing within me the ebb and flow of life forever and ever.

Source of Life,

Response: We thank you.

Menopausal women/crones: Praise to you, Wisdom Sophia, for creating me in your image.
Wisdom Sophia,

Response: We thank you.

Menopausal women/crones: Praise to you, Wellspring of Life, for the flowering of my creative gifts.
Wellspring of Life,

Response: We thank you.

Menopausal women/crones: Praise to you, Womb of the Universe, for my connection to all living things.
Womb of the Universe,

Response: We thank you.

Song: "May You Walk," by Marsie Silvestro[25]

May you walk in the ways
Of the women who went before you.
And may you hear their voices rise
Like the wind that gently shakes you.

And know that you are not alone
For we all go with each other.
Yes, know that you are not alone
As you seek with courage your path.

And may you walk in the ways
Of the women who went before you.
And may you feel their laboring hands
Working clear the roads you take.

So know that you are not alone
For we all go with each other.
Yes, know that you are not alone
As your tears push through the pain.

And may you walk in the ways
Of the women who went before you.
And may you see that like the rain
They will send deep healing down.

So know that you are not alone
For we all go with each other.
Yes, know that you are not alone
For your sister's by your side.

As you walk in the ways
Of the women who went before you
With the women who are before you . . .
May you walk.

Readings

(*Women of different generations read.*)

From Christine Downing[26]:

Understanding menopause as primarily a physical experience may block access to its spiritual significance. To understand menopause as a soul-event means attending to it imaginally, regarding its symptoms as symbols, and not being surprised at its close association with underworld experience.

My journey through menopause has brought me to Hestia. She comes bearing none of the usual attributes of the goddess but carrying a book with blank pages, the unwritten volume of the new. I am only beginning to sense what will be written there.

Chant: "We Are A Wheel," by Betty Wendelborn[27]

We are a wheel, a circle of life,
We are a wheel, a circle of power.
We are a wheel, a circle of light,
Circling the world this sacred hour.

From "Grandmother Lodge," by Brook Medicine Eagle[28]:

When you pass beyond menopause, you have the opportunity for a renewed and deeply powerful experience of yourself. As you drop away from the silliness and fear that has been generated by the "over the hill" cultural trance, and open yourself to the truth that lives within you—body and spirit—you will find an incredible challenge—a challenge for which you are better equipped than any other two-legged. You have the opportunity to sit in council, and using the power of the blood held among you, create a harmonious world around you.

From Margaret Mead[29]:

The most creative force in the world is the menopausal woman with zest.

From Maura Kelsea[30]:

At menopause life can turn into one long pre-menstrual experience. Hormones slap you up against the doors of your unfinished business.

From Germaine Greer[31]:

What I want to do is draw middle-aged women out of their purdah, make them really joyous. Menopause is the invisible experience. People don't want to hear about it. But this is the time when everything comes good for you—your humor, your style, your bad temper.

Chant: "We Are A Wheel," by Betty Wendelborn

We are a wheel, a circle of life,
We are a wheel, a circle of power.
We are a wheel, a circle of light,
Circling the world this sacred hour.

Telling Menopause Stories

(*The menopausal woman introduces the storytelling.*)

Sisters, friends, we need to tell one another our stories of menopause. What have you experienced going through menopause? What questions do you have about menopause? Let us take a moment to think about these experiences and questions. (*Pause*) Let us share with one another our wisdom and questions about menopause. (*Sharing*)

Chant: "We Are a Wheel," by Betty Wendelborn

We are a wheel, a circle of life,
We are a wheel, a circle of power.
We are a wheel, a circle of light,
Circling the world this sacred hour.

Presentation of Symbols

(*Choose one of the following symbols that is appropriate for the woman you are honoring, or use another. Place the symbol on a table in the center of the circle.*)

Flowers

(*The woman entering menopause gives a flower to each participant and thanks each for the special gifts and knowledge they have given her while they shared bleeding times.*)

(*Or, as an alternative:*)

(A daughter, son, grandchild, godchild, or child close to the menopausal woman places on the woman's head a garland of flowers or gives her a bouquet of herbs, saying:)

Mother (*or name of the woman*), you give me life. Thank you for your love, your wisdom, and your advice.

A Tree

(The woman entering menopause holds a seedling or other tree ready for planting.)

Trees symbolize connections between roots below, which reach to the depths of the earth where life begins and ends, and the canopy above, which stretches to the expanse of the universe where life is visible. May those of you who come after me find nourishment in this tree's beauty and be comforted under its shade. In my youth I cared for trees my ancestors planted. Now I plant trees for those who will come after me. May my spirit continue growing through the life of this young tree. (*She and her friends plant her chosen tree in a special place.*)

Fans

(One woman picks up a fan and says:)

Fans are appropriate symbols for menopause. The fan can bring a cool breeze to hot flesh. It can provide air to a fire to make the embers glow more strongly.

Take a fan and create a breeze for our menopausal women. (*Fanning*) N., may gentle winds and cool breezes comfort you.

Blessing the Fruit

(Someone takes a bowl of fresh fruit and presents it to the group, saying:) Please repeat after me.

Blessed are you, Source of Life, (*Echo*)

Blessed is the fruit of your womb. (*Echo*)

(She takes a piece of fruit and passes the bowl for each one to select a piece and eat.)

Blessing the Bread

(*Someone takes the loaf of freshly baked bread and presents it to the group, saying:*) Please repeat after me.

Blessed are you, Bread of Life, (*Echo*)
Blessed are those who nourish others. (*Echo*)

(*She breaks a piece of bread and passes the loaf for each one to take a piece and eat.*)

Blessing the Tea

(*Someone takes a cup of herbal tea and presents it to the group, saying:*) Please repeat after me.

Blessed are you, Calming Healer, (*Echo*)
Blessed are the creators and caretakers of life. (*Echo*)

(*She sips the tea and passes the cup for each one to take a sip.*)

Blessing One Another

(*The woman being honored says:*)

A ceremony like this one reminds us that we are connected to all women—those who do not yet bleed, those who do bleed, and those who no longer bleed. Please repeat after me.

Blessed are you, Connector of the Universe, (*Echo*)
Blessed is the community of women. (*Echo*)
Let us share a blessing with one another.

(*She begins the blessing by hugging the women next to her and invites others to do the same.*)

Chant and Spiral Dance: "Woman Am I," traditional

Woman am I. Spirit am I.
I am the infinite within my soul.
I can find no beginning
And I can find no end.
All this I am.

Sending One Another Forth

(*A friend says:*)

Let us go forth from this ceremony filled with the life-giving power of this community of women.

Let us go forth strengthened by witnessing N.'s change of life through menopause.

Let us go forth empowered to journey through our own life cycle transitions.

Amen. Blessed be. Let it be so.

Our circle is now open.

CHOOSING WISDOM:

A Croning Ceremony

Aging, the transition to elderhood, is a phenomenon in world cultures that needs to be celebrated. Groups of women around the world are creating and participating in croning ceremonies, rites of initiation into full-bodied wisdom for women age fifty-six to seventy. Choosing to be an elder and honoring these wise ones recaptures the importance of the passage to later years. It transforms cultural attitudes that are hostile toward older women and old age. Historically, a crone was a woman past menopause who was recognized by others for her wisdom. She was a spiritual elder, a wise mentor, one who had lived long enough to reflect fully and sensitively about the human enterprise.

Croning ceremonies honor a woman for her transition beyond child bearing, beyond menopause, and sometimes beyond active professional life. Each ceremony expresses the idiosyncratic nature of the woman being celebrated. Each is different; each is unique. Use this liturgy as a model to stretch your imagination to plan the one you and your friends and family need to celebrate. It can also be a model for a retirement observance.

Preparation

Invite friends, family, and colleagues to the celebration. Mention that a festive potluck will follow the ceremony and suggest guests be prepared to tell stories about the crone-to-be. Hold the ceremony in a place that is sacred to the crone-to-be: her home or garden, a place by water or in a park, a retreat center or church sanctuary, a women's shelter or community center, a friend's home or a daughter's backyard.

Decorate the space with symbols that are dear to the crone-to-be: quilts or cloths, shells or rocks, nature symbols or herbs, flowers or plants, special clothing or candles, objects for each decade or major period of her life. Bake bread with her, using her favorite recipe, or ask a friend to make the bread. Buy champagne or sparkling cider. Choose an oil that is a favorite of hers, perhaps scent it with her perfume, and pour it into a special bowl. Place these elements on an altar covered with a cherished cloth of the crone-to-be, or with one that will become a treasure. Gather additional gifts that will be given to the crone: crown of flowers, purple stole, declaration, crystal, and bell.

Welcome

(*Spoken by a daughter, sister, or special friend or colleague.*)

Welcome, each of you, to this croning ceremony for N. (*crone-to-be*). We are here to honor you, N., for attaining wisdom in your life. We recognize the beauty of your bodily changes, the wisdom of your life experiences, and the integrity of your intimate relationships. (*Continue to add what reflects the characteristics of the one being honored.*)

Naming the Circle

Wise women are our ancestors, our mentors, and our friends. They have gone before us; they are here with us; they will come after us. Think of the wise women in your life. (*Pause*) Speak your name and the names of these crones as we create our circle and call upon their wisdom to be with us. (*Naming*)

Song: "Standing Before Us," by Carole Etzler[32]

These are the women who throughout the decades
have led us and helped us to know.

Where we have come from and where we are going,
The women who've helped us to grow.
Standing before us, making us strong.
Lending their wisdom to help us along.
Sharing a vision, sharing a dream,
Touching our thoughts, touching our lives
Like a deep flowing stream.

Call to Celebrate the Crone

When Saturn, the teaching planet, spins back for the second time in your natal chart, you are fifty-six years old. This age is recognized as the doorway into the years of wisdom. We are gathered to honor N. and to bless her as she walks through the doorway into the age of wisdom. We are gathered to make history by creating a new ceremony for our wise elders.

A croning ceremony is a rite of initiation into the wisdom years of life. A crone is a woman who is fifty-six years of age or older, who has gone through menopause, and who is recognized by others as a wise woman. She is a spiritual elder and a wise mentor. She is a treasure of power and wisdom. In our historical time, as women live longer than ever before, we need new rituals for this life passage into later life.

Croning ceremonies empower the elder woman by affirming her attainment of wisdom. They acknowledge her beauty, her new status, her contribution to society, and her ongoing transformation. They challenge the oppression by patriarchal societies of elder women as old, unbeautiful has-beens, and useless.

Look around and notice the wisdom, beauty, and power of our elder women. This is what we celebrate tonight by honoring our dear friend N. This is indeed the wisdom of the ages and we are creating and dancing wisdom's circle.

Dancing a Circle: "Wisdom's Circle," adapted from "Jacob's Ladder," an African American spiritual

(*Women join hands in a circle and dance.*)

We are dancing N.'s (*name of crone*) circle,
We are dancing N.'s circle,
We are dancing N.'s circle,
Sisters one and all!

On and on the circle's moving . . .
Wisdom flowing all around us . . .

Readings

(*Friends share a few poems, scripture passages, journals, diaries, or writings that are favorites of the crone-to-be or written for her. Some we have used include:*)

From Julian of Norwich[33]

Thus
I saw God
and sought God.
I had God
and failed to have God.
And this is,
and should be,
what life is all about,
as I see it.

From Wisdom 6:12–16

Wisdom is radiant, and unfading. Easily discerned by those who love her and found by those who seek her, Wisdom hastens to make herself known to those who desire her. The one who rises early to seek wisdom will have no difficulty, and will find wisdom sitting at the gates. To fix one's thought on wisdom is perfect understanding, and the one who is vigilant on account of wisdom will soon be free from care, because wisdom goes about seeking those worthy of her, graciously appears to them in their paths, and meets them in every thought.

Song: (*Play or sing a favorite of the crone-to-be.*)

Choosing the Croning Path

The croning path is available to all women if we so choose it. We need our wise crones to share with us what it means to follow this path. N. (*names of other crones*), tell us what it means to be a crone. (*Sharing by crones.*)

Your stories reaffirm that each crone's journey is unique. N. (*crone-to-be*), share with us what choosing to become a crone means to you. (*Sharing*)

Witnessing to Wisdom

How have you seen N.'s wisdom revealed? Share with us stories about our new crone's wisdom. (*Sharing*)

Chant: "All Knowing Spirit," three-part round, traditional[34]

(*Numbers indicate where parts can begin.*)

1. All knowing wisdom with me,
2. Teach me to see
3. You are my own true self through all eternity.

Blessing the Crone

(*A dancer escorts the crone to the center of the circle, where she is invited to sit. All gather around her. The youngest in the group sits beside the crone holding a bowl of oil.*)

Today we recognize that you, N., have walked through the doors of wisdom. Receive now our blessing in thanksgiving for you and your life. We bless you for all the parts of yourself that you have shared with us. Oil is a symbol of anointing, of strengthening, of soothing, and of healing.

Come, sisters, put oil on your hands, and bless our crone by touching her with the oil and naming an aspect of her that reveals her wisdom. (*Such as:*)

Loving friend,
Compassionate listener,
Creative visionary,
Hard-working colleague,
Tender poet,
Surprise package,
Profound thinker,
Revolutionary patience,
Unexpected laughter,
Committed feminist,
Skillful carpenter,
Eternal well,
Transforming grace,
(*Add others.*)

Come close to our wise woman, and put your hands on her as we pray: (*The participants simultaneously lay hands on the crone.*)

Blessed are you, O Holy Crone, Wisdom Sophia, for bringing N. into our lives. You, N., are a precious treasure throughout every decade of your life. As you journey through your croning years, may you enjoy

Integrity, to make peace with where you have traveled;

Companions, to share your wisdom and your longings;

Laughter, to stay connected with the joys of life;

Challenges, to stretch your imagination and deepen your knowledge;

Solitude, to enter the well of your being and the womb of the universe.

Blessed are you, O Holy Crone, Wisdom Sophia. Surround our beloved sister, N., with grace, energy, and wisdom. Walk beside her all the days of her life. Let your Spirit, Wisdom Sophia, radiate through her. Bless her on her journey through her wisdom years as she comes home. Amen. Blessed be. Let it be so.

Honoring the Crone

N., we honor you with gifts that remind us of you. (*She is honored with gifts that are appropriate for her. The following, together or in combination, have been given to other crones.*)

(*She is given a crown of flowers.*)

N., receive this crown of flowers as a symbol of your beauty. Remember, you are beautiful.

(*She is given a purple stole.*)

N., receive this stole of wisdom as a symbol of your new status. It weaves together the decades of your life.

(*She is given a declaration.*)

N., receive this declaration as the official document that states you are a crone, a wise woman. We, as witnesses, will sign it later.

(*She is given a crystal.*)

N., receive this crystal as a symbol of your ongoing transformation.

(*She is given a bell.*)

N., receive this bell as a symbol of the sounds you have made for ____________ (*saying the years of her age*). We will pass it around the circle to ring it for each year of your life.

Song: "Standing Before Us," by Carole Etzler

(*Sing in the singular, for example, "She is the woman . . ."*)

Blessing the Bread

(*The crone takes the bread, blesses it, breaks it, and shares it with the participants.*)

Blessed are you, Bread of Life, Wisdom Sophia,
For this bread that makes us wise.

Blessing the Champagne or Sparkling Cider

(*Another blesser pops the champagne or sparkling cider, pours it into a glass, blesses it, and shares glasses of the drink with the participants.*)

Blessed are you, Transforming Grace, Wisdom Sophia,
For this fruit of the vine that calls us to festivity and celebration.

Blessing the Food

(*Another blesser invites everyone to gather around the table of food, extend their hands, and pray after her.*)

Blessed are you, Nourishing Friend, Wisdom Sophia, (*Echo*)
For these gifts of women's hands (*Echo*)
Which feed our hunger, (*Echo*)
Strengthen our bodies, (*Echo*)
And comfort our souls. (*Echo*)

Eating the Festive Meal

Let us share this festive meal.

Sending Forth

We have honored our sister N.

We have shared in this festive meal.

We have celebrated a croning ceremony.

Let us go forth remembering that wisdom surrounds us as together we pray:

Closing Prayer

Wisdom Sophia, be with us now.
Wisdom Sophia, be in my mind and in my thinking;
Wisdom Sophia, be in my heart and in my perceiving;
Wisdom Sophia, be in my mouth and in my speaking;

Wisdom Sophia, be in my hands and in my working;
Wisdom Sophia, be in my feet and in my walking;
Wisdom Sophia, be in my body and in my loving.
Wisdom Sophia, be with me all the days of my life,
  and beyond.
Wisdom Sophia, be with me now.

Greeting of Peace

Filled with this Wisdom, let us embrace one another as wise women. (*Hugging*)

Closing Song and Spiral Dance: "O, Freedom," African American spiritual

(*The crone leads the group in a spiral dance.*)

O freedom, O freedom, O freedom over me,
And before I be a slave, I'll be buried in my grave,
And go home to my God and be free.

They'll be dancing . . .
They'll be singing . . .
They'll be laughing . . .

BLESSED BE:

Honoring Women's Cycles

As each woman passes through another cycle of her life, she is indeed blessed among women. Most women need to be reminded of this because the day-to-day grind of working, parenting, surviving can keep us from remembering that we are blessed.

This liturgy honors women by blessing our life passages of birth, menstruation, mid-life/menopause, and aging. Use it during May for a celebration that honors women, as a croning ceremony, a friendship festival, or an annual observance "In Memory of Her." As springtime blossoms with new life, the earth and her sisters are honored for their life-giving powers. The best setting for this springtime celebration is outside.

Preparation

Gather seven candles and place them on a circular symbol table (altar). Bring a bowl of water, carafe of red wine, carafe of tomato juice, two goblets, pieces of chocolate, and nutbread, and give them to the blessers.

Ask people coming to the celebration to bring a fertility symbol, reading, song, or food, and have them include each contribution in the liturgy as they see fit.

Naming the Circle

Let us begin this liturgy by gathering around the symbol table, introducing ourselves, and saying why we have come to bless women's cycles. (*Introductions*)

Call to Celebration

May 1 is a day to celebrate the fertility of the earth. For years before us and hopefully years after us, May Day is a day dedicated to the fertility of our foremothers. May Day, Beltane, or May Eve has been dedicated to Brigid, the Celtic goddess and saint; to Maia, the goddess of increase; to Flora, the flower goddess; to Aphrodite, goddess of love; to Vesta and her Virgins; to the Bona Dea/Damis, goddess of healing; to Rauni, the Nordic goddess; and to Sappho, symbol of our love for each other. The month of May is dedicated to Mary, the Mother of Jesus, the Christ.

Festivals during this season praised the virgin or "flower" aspect of these holy women. They were a time of "wearing of the green" to honor the earth's new green garment of spring, as well as a time to celebrate sexuality, a symbol of nature's fertilization and pleasure.

Tonight we reclaim this symbol of fertility. We gather to give thanks for the bounty of the earth and for the fruitfulness of women's lives.

Chant: "And She Will Rise," by Dakota Butterfield[35]

The earth is a woman and she will rise.
The earth is a woman and she will rise.
We will live in her.
We will live in her.

Candle Lighting

To remember and restore to women the traditions of our sisters who were the keepers of the seven fires, we light seven candles. They represent the seven directions—north, south, east, west, above, below, and center.

(One person lights all the candles or seven different people light one each. As each candle is lit, the candle lighter names the direction and says:)

Sister Spirits of the N. (*name the direction*), may your fires and passionate desires be with us this night.

Litany of Naming[36]

Holy One, Sister Spirit, Wisdom Sophia, you reveal yourself in surprising ways and in daily names. We name you as you have revealed yourself to us:

Source
Wellspring
Quilter
The One Who Gives Birth
Guide

Source of Solace
Gentle Sister
One Who Laughs
Compassionate One
Bright Morning Star

Old Crone
Ever Growing Integrity
Holy Wisdom
Wisdom Sophia
Wholly Holy

Mother
Mirror
Strong Woman
Blessing One
Sower of Seeds

Spark
Counselor
The Ebb and Flow
Bakerwoman
Giant Tear

Goddess of Beauty
Ocean Wave
Bending Branch
Breath of Life
Silence

Safe Haven
Lover
Dancer
The Ultimate Telephone
Open Arms

Big Lap
The One Who Does Not Judge
The Navel of the Universe
The Last Journey
Justice-Seeker

The First Step
Journey's End
Journeyer
The Patient Walk
Companion on the Road

Through every name that gives us a glimpse of your relationship to us, O Holy One, Wisdom Sophia, you call us to be woman and to bless women's cycles.

Song: "Woman Am I," traditional, with gestures[37]

(Gestures for "Woman Am I" follow. Hum the song first while swaying to its melody, then sing the song using the gestures.)

"Woman am I" (*both arms waist high and extended out to side, bring energy into the center of the body with a sweeping motion*),

"Spirit am I" (*both arms, starting from center of the body with hands closed, move outward to left side with fingers bursting open*),

"I am the infinite" (*both arms outstretched, hands open*),

"within my soul" (*sway together, left to right*),

"I can find no beginning" (*left hand, palm open, reaches to person on the left*),

"and I can find no end" (*right hand, palm open, touches the left palm of the person on the right side*).

"All this I am" (*palms drop and make a circle in front of the body*).

CYCLES OF WOMEN'S LIVES

A woman's life is filled with many cycles. Tonight we celebrate four obvious ones: birth, menstruation, menopause, and aging. As we name each one we place a symbol on the altar, read a poem, and sing "Woman Am I."

BLESSED BE THE BIRTH OF A GIRL-CHILD

(*The reader announces the title of this section, "Blessed Be the Birth of a Girl-child," and places a bowl of water on the altar. If others have brought symbols of birth, invite them to speak of the significance of their choices and place each on the altar. Then the reader says:*)

Remembering and Naming

Let us remember and name women who have given life and women to whom we have given life. (*Naming. If there are new mothers among you, recognize them.*)

Reading: "Rise Up, Child of Earth," by Pat Kozak[38]

Rise up, child of earth
Let life rise up in you,
Full-term, new-born.
Time enough in wondrous darkness,
Echoed sounds of voices, stirrings,

Splashings of new life.
Relinquish to memory this one mystery
We yearn to know and will again
In after-death.
So much latent
Still to rise
Until our rising lifts us to a depth
That questions every truth
We've ever known.

Mud-stirred of first-clay.
Plaything of a potter who fell in love
With her hands' work.
Blessed be her handiwork.
Blessed be the work of her hands.
Blessed be.

Blessing the Water

(*The blesser raises the bowl of water, breathes over it, and prays:*)

Blessed are you, One Who Gives Birth, for giving us living water. (*She places the bowl back on the table, gestures the people to come forward, and says:*)

Come to the water, bless yourself, and remember your birth or the birth of another.

(*Women bless themselves with water.*)

Song: "Woman Am I"

BLESSED BE THE CREATIVITY THAT FLOWS WITH WOMEN'S MENSTRUAL CYCLE

(*The reader announces the title of this section, and places carafes of red wine and tomato juice on the altar. If others have symbols of menstruation, invite them to place these on the altar and speak of their significance. Then the reader says:*)

Remembering and Naming

Let us remember and name young girls who are beginning or will be beginning soon their menstrual cycles. (*Naming. If there are any among you, give each a special seashell or nutshell.*)

Reading: "Invocation of the Gifts," traditional Gaelic[39]

We bathe your palms
  In showers of wine,
In the crook of the kindling,
  In the seven elements,
In the sap of the tree,
  In the milk of honey,

We place nine pure, choice gifts
  In your clear beloved face:

The gift of form,
  The gift of voice,
The gift of fortune,
  The gift of goodness,
The gift of eminence,
  The gift of charity,
The gift of integrity,
  The gift of true nobility,
The gift of apt speech.

Blessing the Wine and Juice

(*The blesser pours the wine and juice into the goblets and prays:*)

Blessed are you, Breath of Life, for your life, which flows through girl children coming of age.

Drink this wine and juice in thanksgiving for the blood of life that flows through women.

(*The blesser passes the goblets around for all to drink.*)

Song: "Woman Am I"

BLESSED BE THE POWER AND THE PASSION OF MENOPAUSAL WOMEN

(The reader announces the title of this section and places chocolate on the altar. If others have brought symbols of this cycle, she invites them to place these on the altar and to speak about them. Then she says:)

Remembering and Naming

Let us remember and name menopausal women who are important in our lives. (*Naming. If there are any among you, recognize them.*)

Reading: "The Mystique of Age" (an excerpt), by Betty Friedan[40]

I had menopause myself somewhere back then in the midst of the women's movement, after *The Feminine Mystique,* but I can't remember when. By now the change that I had seen only in a few women was absolutely epidemic in society. By now millions of women, who were supposed to decline and get ready for death after menopause, were back in colleges, universities, going to work, marching, talking back to male chauvinists, revolutionizing home life, revolutionizing concepts of sexuality, demanding to be preachers and rabbis and priests, moving into space as astronauts. No longer were women three percent of the students in medical school and law school; they were 35 percent. And many of these wonderful, vibrant new women were over 45. The whole picture of aging for women was changing.

Blessing the Chocolate

(The blesser raises the chocolate and prays:)

Blessed are you, Companion on the Road, for filling us with passion.

Eat this chocolate and remember your passion. (*She passes the chocolate around the group.*)

Song: "Woman Am I"

BLESSED BE THE WISDOM OF OLDER WOMEN

(A woman walks to the center and invites people to bring forward and speak about symbols for this cycle that they may have brought. Then she says:)

Remembering and Naming

Let us remember and name older women, the wise crones, the ancestors in our lives. *(If there are any among you, recognize them.)*

Reading: "The Great Transparencies," by May Sarton[41]

Lately I have been thinking much of those,
The open ones, the great transparencies,
Through whom life—is it wind or water?—flows
Unstinted, who have learned the sovereign ease.
They are not young; they are not ever young . . .

Youth is too vulnerable to bear the tide,
And let it rise, and never hold it back,
Then let it ebb, not suffreing from pride,
Nor thinking it must ebb from private lack.
The elders yield because they are so strong—

Seized by the great wind like a ripening field,
All rippled over in a sensuous sweep,
Wave after wave, lifted and glad to yield,
But whether wind or water, never keep
The tide from flowing or hold it back for long.

Lately I have been thinking much of these,
The unafraid although still vulnerable,
Through whom life flows, the great transparencies,
The old and open, brave and beautiful . . .
They are not young; they are not ever young.

Blessing the Bread

(*The blesser takes bread in her hands and prays:*)

Blessed are you, Wisdom Sophia, for filling us with the beauty and wisdom of our ancestors. Let us eat this bread in memory of our foremothers.

(*The blesser breaks the bread and passes it around for all to eat.*)

Song: "Woman Am I"

Reflection and Sharing the Food

Our dancing comes to a close so that our feasting can begin. Let us feast on the fruits of our labors. As we eat, let us talk about our lives, let us share stories about a holy part of us, our fertility.

How have I celebrated each of my life cycles?
How have I used my sexuality?
What choices have I made? (*Sharing*)

Sending Forth

(*When the eating and feasting come to a natural close, the hostess begins to chant "Woman Am I" and gestures for everyone to gather in a circle.*)

Our celebration has come to a close. As we open our circle to move on from this place, we remember that we are intertwined with the cycles of all life. May we be attentive to our cycles. May we be sensitive to the cycles of others. And may we be respectful of the cycles of Mother Earth. Amen. Blessed be. Let it be so.

NOTES

1. Anne Cameron, *Daughters of Copper Woman* (Vancouver: Press Gang, 1981), 103. See also Anita Diamant, *The Red Tent* (New York: St. Martin's Press, 1997); Nancy Jay, *Throughout Your Generations Forever: Sacrifice, Religion, and Patriarchy* (Chicago: University of Chicago Press, 1992).

2. Laura Owen, *Her Blood is Gold* (New York: HarperCollins, 1993), 46.

3. Kathleen M. O'Connor, "Lamentations," in *The Women's Bible Commentary*, ed. C.A. Newsom and S.H. Ringe (Louisville: Westminster John Knox, 1992), 179–80.

4. Kathryn Pfisterer Darr, "Ezekiel," in Newsome and Ringe, *The Women's Bible Commentary*, 183–88.

5. Mary Ann Tolbert, "Mark," in Newsome and Ringe, *The Women's Bible Commentary*, 267–68.

6. Luke Timothy Johnson, *The Writings of the New Testament: An Interpretation*, rev. ed. (Minneapolis: Fortress Press, 1999), 244–45.

7. Safina Newbery, e-mail to Diann L. Neu, Buenos Aires, Argentina, 3 May 2002.

8. Denise Kuyp, interview by Diann L. Neu, Accra, Ghana, 16 January 2002.

9. Colleen Fulmer, "We Bring Who We Are," *Dancing Sophia's Circle* © 1994, Heartbeats. Audio recording. Used by permission.

10. Martha Graham, from *Blood Memory* © 1991, in Rosalie Maggio, "Body," *The New Beacon Book of Quotations by Women* (Boston: Beacon Press, 1996), 74.

11. Marilyn Sewell, from *Cries of the Spirit* © 1991, in Rosalie Maggio, "Body," *The New Beacon Book of Quotations by Women* (Boston: Beacon Press, 1996), 74.

12. Marilyn Ferguson, from *The Aquarian Conspiracy* © 1980, in Rosalie Maggio, "Body," *The New Beacon Book of Quotations by Women* (Boston: Beacon Press, 1996), 74.

13. Yoruba Proverb, in Terri L. Jewell, ed., *The Black Woman's Gumbo Ya-Ya: Quotations by Black Women* (Freedom, CA: Crossing Press, 1993), 8.

14. Janet Morley, "The bodies of grownups," in Hannah Ward, Jennifer Wild, and Janet Morley, eds., *Celebrating Women* (London: SPCK, 1995), 130–31. Used by permission.

15. Gabriele Uhlein, ed., *Meditations with Hildegard of Bingen* (Sante Fe, NM: Bear & Co, 1982), 35. Used by permission.

16. Copyright © by Marcia Lee Falk. Excerpted from *The Song of Songs: A New Translation and Interpretation by Marcia Falk* (San Francisco: HarperCollins, 1990), 15. Used by permission. Available at www.marciafalk.com.

17. Another version of this appears in *Creation Spirituality*, May/June, 1991.

18. Colleen Fulmer, "I Am Enough," *Dancing Sophia's Circle*, © 1994, Heartbeats. Audio recording. Used by permission.

19. Ibid.

20. © 1977 Carole Etzler, from *Womanriver Flowing On*, available on tape from Carole Etzler Eagleheart, 1180 VT Route 22A, Bridport, VT 05734. Used by permission.

21. Ntozake Shange, "Marvelous Menstruating Moments," *Sassafrass, Cypress & Indigo* (New York: St. Martin's Press, 1982), 19–20.

22. Colleen Fulmer, "I Am Enough," *Dancing Sophia's Circle* © 1994, Heartbeats. Audio recording. Used by permission.

23. Marsie Silvestro, "Let the Women Be There," *Crossing the Lines* © 1991, Moonsong Productions. Audio recording. Used by permission.

24. Author unknown, "Woman Am I," in Anna Kealoha, ed., *Songs of the Earth* (Berkeley, CA: Celestial Arts, 1989), 181.

25. Marsie Silvestro, "May You Walk," *On the Other Side* © 1993, Moonsong Productions. Audio recording. Used by permission.

26. Christine Downing, *Women of the 14th Moon: Writings on Menopause,* ed. Dena Taylor and Amber Coverdale Sumrall (Freedom, CA: Crossing Press, 1991), 319.

27. Betty Wendelborn, "We Are a Wheel," *Sing Green: Songs of the Mystics,* 2d ed. (Auckland, New Zealand: Pyramid Press, 1999), 1. Used by permission.

28. Brook Medicine Eagle, "Grandmother Lodge," in Taylor and Sumrall, *Women of the 14th Moon,* 260.

29. Margaret Mead, from Taylor and Sumrall, *Women of the 14th Moon,* 203.

30. Maura Kelsea, from Taylor and Sumrall, *Women of the 14th Moon,* 151.

31. Germaine Greer, from Taylor and Sumrall, *Women of the 14th Moon,* 1.

32. © 1983 Carole Etzler, from *Thirteen Ships,* available on tape from Carole Etzler Eagleheart, 1180 VT Route 22A, Bridport, VT 05734. Used by permission.

33. In Brendan Doyle, ed., *Meditations with Julian of Norwich,* (Sante Fe, NM: Bear & Co., 1983), 34. Used by permission.

34. Author unknown, "All Knowing Spirit," in Anna Kealoha, ed., *Songs of the Earth* (Berkeley, CA: Celestial Arts, 1989), 108.

35. Dakota Butterfield, "And She Will Rise," on *Fire Within* by Libana © 1990, Dakota Butterfield. Audio recording. Used by permission.

36. These are among the many names of God revealed to members of a WATER feminist liturgy class. The women imaged the Holy One and spoke aloud the names they heard in a stream of consciousness process.

37. Author unknown, "Woman Am I," in Kealoha, *Songs of the Earth,* 181.

38. Pat Kozak, "Rise Up, Child of Earth," in Janet Shaffron and Pat Kozak, *More than Words: Prayer and Ritual for Inclusive Commu-*

nities (Oak Park, IL: Meyer-Stone Books, 1986), 135. Used by permission.

39. Traditional Gaelic, "Invocation of the Gifts," in Caitlin and John Matthews, eds., *Ladies of the Lake* (London: Thorsons, 1992), vi–vii. Used by permission.

40. Betty Friedan, an excerpt from "The Mystique of Age," from Taylor and Sumrall, *Women of the 14th Moon*, 312–13.

41. May Sarton, "The Great Transparencies," *Collected Poems 1930–1993* (New York: W.W. Norton, 1974), 334. Used by permission.

MAKING REPRODUCTIVE CHOICES

Praise our choices, sisters, for each doorway
open to us was taken by squads of fighting
women who paid years of trouble and struggle,
who paid their wombs, their sleep, their lives
that we might walk through these gates upright.

Marge Piercy

Let the women be there, let the women be there,
Let the women be there by my side,
And I in turn will be for them.

Marsie Silvestro

As often as I have witnessed the miracle,
held the perfect creature with its tiny hands and feet,
each time I have felt as though I were entering a cathedral
with prayer in my heart.

Margaret Sanger

I uniquely, lovingly, embrace every image
I have made out of the earth's clay.
With a fiery spirit I transform it into a body
To serve all the world.

Hildegard of Bingen

INTRODUCTION

Each woman, from grandmothers to mothers, from daughters to the next generations, from every race, class, and culture, makes reproductive choices for her life or has reproductive choices made for her. Healthy reproductive choice includes the best medical, psychological, and social support available. It also includes spiritual support that we sometimes forget in making all-important decisions and undergoing momentous life events. We—friends, family, ministers, and counselors—need to develop and celebrate liturgies that affirm women's reproductive choices. Many women may need encouragement to consider such a liturgy because traditional churches and societies do not provide them.

The political, economic, cultural, and intellectual environments surrounding reproductive choices have changed over the last thirty years. In the 1960s and '70s, the women's movement in the United States opened doors for all women—heterosexual, bisexual, and lesbian—regarding a variety of choices including birth control, abortion, self-insemination, and adoption. Reproductive freedom is a tenet of most forms of feminism. Control over fertility and reproduction is a precondition to self-determination. The struggle for reproductive choice (including the right to abortion) is a call for a new social order in which women define rather than are defined by their reproductive contribution.[1]

Religious traditions are often a source of oppression to women concerning reproductive choices. Many religious authorities refuse to acknowledge women's rights to control reproductive choices. In the past and still today for some, the expectation was that girls married, had intercourse for the purpose of procreation, and became mothers and homemakers. The choices open to them were motherhood if they were married, or celibacy if they chose to enter a religious order or to remain single.

Today a growing number of women have the option of birth control, pregnancy, self-insemination, abortion, birthing, and adoption. Yet most women in many countries still need to bear children so that they will have someone to care for them and help them survive old age. As we prepare a young girl for her first menses, we need to share with her the reproductive choices available to her and to encourage her to respect and use her body wisely and choose carefully.

Rather than name the myriad ways in which patriarchal, kyriarchal traditions try to control women, I will focus instead on the female body, the object of patriarchal control. The body has caused many problems for theologians over the centuries. Is it merely flesh? Does it carry within it a soul? Do women's bodies image the Divine? The Christian scriptures have embodiment at their heart. From the moments Sarah, Elizabeth, and Mary each agree to conceive and birth a special child, their bodies become sites of revelation and redemptive action.

Some women worldwide are creating feminist liturgies that support women in making reproductive choices for their life journeys. Two examples follow. The first story from Tonga describes a blessing for conception. The second account from Montevideo, Uruguay, describes a liturgy that affirms a woman's choice not to be a mother.

Tonga: Blessing For Conception[2]

The context: 'Asinate Samate of the Methodist Church of Tonga joined her father, a Methodist minister, in offering a blessing for conception for a Tongan couple living in Australia who could not become pregnant. The couple had seen doctors and had taken Tongan fertility medicine (a special mixture from Tongan healers). They made an appointment with 'Asinate Samate's father when they heard he was coming to Australia.

The rite: When the couple arrived, 'Asinate, her father, her sister, the couple, another minister, and his wife (all seven Tongans) sat in a circle on the floor in the sitting room. They prayed silently for a while, then her father knelt in front of the couple, laid hands on the woman's head, and prayed while the others affirmed loudly with "yes," "amen," "let it be" as is the Tongan tradition. The prayer included "if it is God's will for you to have children, let it be. If you have faith and trust that you need children, and it is God's will, then let it be." As the couple were leaving, the husband said he "felt relieved and hopeful, and would let them know if anything happened." Within the year word came that the wife was pregnant.

Reflection: This liturgy brought women's life cycle needs directly into the church, where a caring pastor and a loving community received the woman and her husband, surrounded them with love, and prayed for their fertility. The blessing reveals much about the island culture, for example, the importance of sitting on the floor, trust in Tongan fertility medicines, comfort with a Tongan minister. It reminds us that at intimate times like fertility some women and men need to be with healers from their own culture. It encourages women and couples to ask for such a blessing, and it invites pastors to do the same. I am left with the question, what would the minister say to women who do not become pregnant?

Montevideo, Uruguay: Deciding Not to Be Mother[3]

The context: Dorys Zeballos of Catolicas por el derecho a decidir (Catholics for a Right to Decide) wrote this liturgy for Latin American women who have decided not to be mothers. This is a political action since the social pressures on Latin American women to be mothers are very strong.

The rite: Participants formed a circle around a table with a cloth, napkins, vases, knives, candles, a pitcher of milk, and a bowl of honey. They spoke about the social pressures in their countries to be mothers. They affirmed that each woman is a total person herself and can be holy whether she chooses to have children or not. They named women who decided not be mothers: Sor Juana

Ines de la Cruz, Gabriella Mistral, Simone de Beauvoir, and anonymous others. They named women who could not have children, such as Frida Kahlo.

They took milk and honey, symbols in the bible of freedom, and the elements that are perfect for humans from birth to old age. They all extended their hands, palms up, and blessed the milk and honey, uniting with women of Latin America and the world who live and work that the life of each and the humanity of all will be fertile lands flowing with milk and honey. They then ate the honey, drank the milk, sang, and feasted.

Reflection: These women, who have lived much of their lives under dictatorships, broke silence, talked about the social pressures to be mothers, and supported those among them who choose not to be mothers. They affirmed that single women, women who choose not to have children, and women who cannot bear children are holy and complete. This, of course, challenges the Catholic church position that women should be mothers. Naming women of faith and well-known Latin American women who did not have children supports their position. By blessing and sharing milk and honey, perfect food and symbols of freedom, similar to women's breast milk, they showed that they did not need motherhood to offer milk and honey.

Silver Spring, Maryland, USA: Making Reproductive Choices

The context: I was asked to create the liturgies in this section to offer models to individuals and communities to support a woman as she honors her body and makes the reproductive choices necessary for her, her partner (if there is one), and her family.

The rites: The liturgical texts are given here.

Reflection: "Standing with Women: Making Reproductive Choices" celebrates women's spirituality by affirming the integrity and holiness of women's choices regarding a variety of reproductive options: birth control, pregnancy, self-insemination, abortion, birthing, adoption. "That Waters May Run: A Prayer for Conception" supports women who want to conceive, especially those who find it a struggle to get and stay pregnant.

"You Are Not Alone: Seeking Wisdom to Decide" guides a woman to discover her own wisdom to make a choice about her unexpected pregnancy. "A Difficult Decision: Affirming a Choice for Abortion" provides a woman with strength and healing after making a difficult choice. "Blessing a Mother-to-Be: A Shower Awaiting Birth or Adoption" marks the transition into motherhood for a woman, her family, and her community.

STANDING WITH WOMEN:
Making Reproductive Choices

Women throughout history have made many different choices about reproduction. Some have been made against our wills; others we have chosen ourselves. Unfortunately for many women, choice is a luxury and coercion is more the norm. It is important for all women to be aware of our reproductive options, of those choices made by our family and friends, as well as others in our community and around the world. Politically and personally, women need to stand together to insure that each of us can make the reproductive choices that are best for us.

This liturgy affirms the variety of reproductive choices available to women. It is an effort to stand with women regardless of their reproductive choices. A version of it was celebrated with the Women-Church Convergence at the time of the "Women's Equality, Women's Lives" march in Washington, D.C., in which six hundred thousand women, men, and children participated to affirm women's right to reproductive choice. Variations have been celebrated around the world. Many stories and litany petitions are given here. Use the ones that are appropriate for your situation and time frame.

Preparation

Gather daffodils or flowers in season, place them in a vase, and give them to the woman who will read the first story in the script. Place a candle, a loaf of seven-grain bread, a carafe of wine, a carafe of juice, and two cups on a central table. Invite seven people to be blessers.

Call to Gather

(*The celebrant lights a candle.*)

We come to this liturgy with our questions, our concerns, and our stories about making reproductive choices. We come remembering the women who have made choices about reproduction—our mothers, our sisters, our friends, our relatives, unnamed women, women from every race and culture, ourselves. We come remembering women who have had reproductive decisions made for us against our wills.

Today we place this loaf of seven-grain bread and these carafes of wine and juice in the center of our circle to represent for us women's lives, women's choices. (*Two women place the bread and drink on the table.*)

Let us begin this liturgy in solidarity with those who make reproductive choices. Let us stand together as women who choose.

Song: "Stand Together My Sisters," by Marsie Silvestro[4]

Come to me now, women spirit. Come to me now, sister of life.
Come to me now, mother of my being,
and sing in me a melody of love.

Stand together, my sisters, stand together again.
Stand together in a circle. Stand together as friends.

Let the spirit come on down. Let her touch you all around.
Let the spirit come on down. Let her touch you all around.

Prayer

Praise to you, Wisdom Sophia, for giving your people the power for reproduction. Open our hearts to listen compassionately to one another's stories. Fill us with insight that we may choose wisely. Strengthen us to make such options available to all women. Amen. Blessed be. Let it be so.

Introduction to Stories

The following stories celebrate women's spirituality by affirming the integrity and holiness of their decisions. Listen to each woman's story as if she were someone very close to you. She is your sister. These daffodils, beautiful and plentiful at this time of year, symbolize these women who are everywhere.

(The first reader places a vase of daffodils on the table.)

Song: "Listen, Listen, Listen," by Paramahansa Yogananda[5]

Listen, listen, listen to my heart song, *(Repeat)*
I will never forsake you; I will always be with you. *(Repeat)*

A Story from Margaret Sanger[6]

Pregnancy was a chronic condition . . . Then one stifling mid-July day of 1912, I was summoned to a Grand Street tenement . . . Jake Sachs, a truck driver scarcely older than his wife, had come home to find the three children crying and her unconscious from the effects of a self-induced abortion . . . At the end of three weeks, as I was preparing to leave the fragile patient to take up her difficult life once more, she finally voiced her fears, "Another baby will finish me, I suppose?"

"It's too early to talk about that," I temporized. But when the doctor came to make his last call, I drew him aside. "Mrs. Sachs is terribly worried about having another baby."

"She well may be," replied the doctor, and then he stood before her and said, "Any more such capers, young woman, and there'll be no need to send for me."

"I know, doctor," she replied timidly, "but," and she hesitated as though it took all her courage to say it, "what can I do to prevent it?" . . . Picking up his hat and bag to depart, the doctor said, "Tell Jake to sleep on the roof."

. . . Even through my sudden tears I could see stamped on her face an expression of absolute despair. We simply looked at each other, saying no word until the door had closed behind the doctor. Then she lifted her thin, blue-veined hands and clasped them beseechingly. "He can't understand. He's only a man. But you do, don't you? Please tell me the secret, and I'll never breathe it to a soul. Please!" . . . I really did not know what to say to her or how to convince her of my own ignorance; I was helpless . . .

The telephone rang one evening three months later, and John Sachs' agitated voice begged me to come at once; his wife was sick again and from the same cause . . . Mrs. Sachs was in a coma and died within ten minutes. I folded her still hands across her breast, remembering how they had pleaded with me, begging so humbly for the knowledge that was her right. . . . I resolved to seek out the root of evil, to do something to change the destiny of mothers whose miseries were vast as the sky.

Response: "Sabbath of Mutual Respect," by Marge Piercy[7]

Praise our choices, sisters, for each doorway
open to us was taken by squads of fighting
women who paid years of trouble and struggle,
who paid their wombs, their sleep, their lives
that we might walk through these gates upright.
Doorways are sacred to women for we
are the doorways of life and we must choose
what comes in and what goes out. Freedom
is our real abundance.

Song: "Listen, Listen, Listen," by Paramahansa Yogananda

Listen, listen, listen to my heart song, (*Repeat*)
I will never forsake you; I will always be with you. (*Repeat*)

A story from Ellen and Julie (a.k.a. Beth and Merle)[8]

I'm beginning to believe in miracles. We are pregnant. Yep, it's true. After just one cycle of inseminations, Merle is "with child" and I am filled with joy. At times I feel that I should be cautious, perhaps withhold some of my excitement given that miscarriage is a possibility, but my heart takes over. In fact, Merle and I had agreed that until the end of the first trimester we would tell only close friends and family. But we can't seem to shut up about it. Thirty-eight days into our pregnancy, it seems that our entire world has been made aware of our forthcoming bundle.

Several days after the insemination, Merle was convinced that she was pregnant ("oy vay, I'm nauseous and I have a headache") but over the course of about ten days she began to feel "normal" and expected to get her period. Then her period didn't arrive on schedule, nor the next day, and then another day passed. Once Merle was three full days late—keeping in mind that she is very regular—I went to the local pharmacy and picked up an E.P.T., ready to know the truth. As a butch dyke, one thing I was sure I'd never purchase was a pregnancy test! Oh, have times changed.

Response: Praise our choices, sisters . . .

Song: Listen, listen, listen to my heart song, (*Repeat*)
I will never forsake you; I will always be with you. (*Repeat*)

A Story from Gloria Steinem[9]

My own had taken place in a time of such isolation, illegality, and fear that afterward, I did my best to just forget. Only a decade later when a new wave of feminism was encouraging women to share "secrets"—allowing us to learn, for example, that as many as one in three or four adult American women probably had risked abortion even when it was criminal and dangerous—did I begin to think about my own experience as a microcosm of what millions of women had gone through. Belatedly, I questioned how the female half of the human race, whose bodies bear all the consequences of reproduction, were allowed so few of its decisions: on the legality of abortion, contraception, or sterilization; on the workplace or medical treatment of pregnancy and childbirth; on even what was considered "normal" in female sexuality.

Gradually, I figured it out . . .

Response: Praise our choices, sisters . . .

Song: Listen, listen, listen to my heart song, (*Repeat*)
I will never forsake you; I will always be with you. (*Repeat*)

A Story from Nancy[10]

Unexpectedly, the phone call came the night before we were to board the plane. We had planned a weekend of celebrations: my husband's birthday, our second wedding anniversary, our friends' new home. A renewing of our friendship. With their call, the mood changed.

"You're our friends," she began. "You've also been our ministers. I know we've planned a weekend of celebration. But we also wanted to ask you to help us with some grief work. Would you help us to do a memorial service for Isaac—the child we will never have?"

How will this change your life? we asked. What dreams do you let go? What new dreams are free to form? They spoke of renewed joy in each other, friendships, work. But mostly they spoke of the relief at letting go of their continuous roller coaster of emotions, of an end to counting the sad waiting for signs that never came, nurturing hopes that were never fulfilled.

Response: Praise our choices, sisters . . .

Song: Listen, listen, listen to my heart song, (*Repeat*)
I will never forsake you; I will always be with you. (*Repeat*)

Reflection

We have just heard stories of some of the reproductive choices that women make or have had made for them. And there are many others. Most women have many choices regarding reproduction.

What choices have you made or not made concerning reproduction? How do you enable other women to claim their power in their choices? (*Pause. Repeat the questions.*)

Let us form groups of three or four and share as much or as little as we wish. (*Sharing*)

Song: Listen, listen, listen to my heart song, (*Repeat*)
I will never forsake you; I will always be with you. (*Repeat*)

Litany of Solidarity

(*Two readers alternate the reading of each section.*)

Let us remember all women who are making reproductive choices. Our response to this litany is: We remember and we stand with you.

Reader One: We remember all women, young and old, educated and illiterate, rich and poor, who were denied access to contraception and who were forced into decisions they could have avoided if contraception were available to them.

We remember married women who were told by religious leaders that limiting the number of their children was a denial of God's will.

We remember women with chronic illnesses or hereditary conditions who did not want to leave a legacy of pain and limitation to any children they might have conceived, but who were unable to obtain reliable and safe means of preventing conception, and so in solidarity we say,

Response: We remember and we stand with you!

Reader Two: We remember lesbian women and single women who want to have children, who find it difficult to obtain information about self-insemination and who are devalued by the medical profession for their desire to bear and raise a child.

We remember women who want to have children with their life partners and who are exploited by fertility clinics, made to undergo repeated and needless tests, to pay large sums of money for procedures, and who are not given a realistic assessment of their chances of conception.

We remember women who induced their own abortions, who sought out back-alley abortionists, who were rendered infertile, who were made gravely ill, and who died from illegal abortions that were unsafe and inhuman, and so in solidarity we say,

Response: We remember and we stand with you!

Reader One: We remember women who have been harassed and assaulted going to legal abortion clinics by people who value the fetus more than a woman's own conscience.

We remember women who have grappled with their own beliefs and the traditions they have been taught as they sought to make choices about pregnancies resulting from rape or incest.

We remember unmarried teenage women, professional women in an era when single motherhood was unacceptable, women caught in the cycle of poverty, and others who would have kept their babies but chose to give their children up for adoption because of lack of family and societal support, and so in solidarity we say,

Response: We remember and we stand with you!

Reader Two: We remember women forced to carry pregnancies to term because bearing and relinquishing their children was the only option presented to them.

We remember struggles of women who were abandoned by their partners and who worked long and hard to keep their children, often having to leave their children in unloving and unsafe conditions.

We remember women who experienced unplanned pregnancies and who had to make decisions that involved remaking their plans for their lives no matter which decision they made, and so in solidarity we say,

Response: We remember and we stand with you!

Reader One: We remember all those who have worked to make contraceptive education available to women of all classes, statuses, and economic backgrounds.

We remember those who proposed legislation, educated lawmakers, lobbied, those who brought cases to trial and argued against those who denied a woman's right to choose, in order to bring the requirement for safe, legal abortion for all women to the consciousness of their nations.

We remember those health care professionals who train women to use contraception safely and responsibly, who educate teenagers about heterosexual intercourse and its consequences, who counsel women contemplating abortion, who counsel women at risk who conceive children with genetic and hereditary defects, who support women through abortion procedures, who refer women to responsible adoption agencies, and who recognize the rights of women to make reproductive choices, and so in solidarity we say,

Response: We remember and we stand with you!

Song: "Weaving a New Creation," by Ruth Duck[11]

Refrain:
We have labored, and we have baked the bread.
We have woven cloth, we have nurtured life.

Now we're weaving a new creation, too.
Praise, O God, all praise to you!

God of simple, common things,
God of cloth and bread,
Help us, mend our tattered lives.
Spirit be the thread.

(Refrain)

As we change our daily lives,
Justice is our call:
Safer homes and city streets,
Bread and drink for all.

(Refrain)

Weave our frayed and varied strands,
Shaping one design.
May our colors richly blend,
As our lives entwine.

(Refrain)

Clothed in wisdom, may we live
Robed in love and praise,
May our labor turn to joy,
As we learn your ways.

(Refrain)

Knead us, make us but one loaf,
Mixed from varied grain.
May our flavors richly blend,
Foretaste of your reign.

Blessing the Bread

This seven-grain bread symbolizes all our sisters around the world who decide for themselves when and how and how many children to have. Let us bless it in their names:

(Seven women bless the bread. Each one uses her own gesture for the blessing.)

Blesser One: In the name of the women of the Middle East, who make their choices in the context of ethnic and religious struggles, in refugee camps, and in ongoing struggle for justice for peoples deeply connected to their lands.

Response: We bless this bread.

Blesser Two: In the name of the women of sub-Saharan Africa, who make their choices in the context of HIV-AIDS, of drought and famine, of wars that produce huge migrations of refugees, of struggles against apartheid and continuing effects of colonialism.

Response: We bless this bread.

Blesser Three: In the name of the women of Asia, who make their choices in the context of growing populations, one-child policies, limited land and resources, and economic exploitation from transnational corporations.

Response: We bless this bread.

Blesser Four: In the name of the women of the Pacific rim, who make their choices in the context of the exploitation of natural resources and the trafficking in prostitution and pornography.

Response: We bless this bread.

Blesser Five: In the name of the women of North America, who make their choices in the context of racism, sexism, heterosexism, ableism, and ageism; of the growing gap between rich and poor, and of the threat of criminalization of women who choose abortion.

Response: We bless this bread.

Blesser Six: In the name of the women of Latin America and the Caribbean who make their choices in the context of class struggle and intervention by foreign powers in their quest for liberation, economic security, and peace.

Response: We bless this bread.

Blesser Seven: In the name of the women of Europe, who make their choices in the context of ongoing ethnic and religious struggles and ecological threats.

Response: We bless this bread.

Let us extend our hands, palms out, and touch the palms of the persons on either side of us. Let us bless this bread as the bread of solidarity and friendship, in praise of women's bodies, in praise of women's choices.

Song: "Weaving a New Creation," by Ruth Duck

Refrain: We have labored, and we have baked the bread.
We have woven cloth, we have nurtured life.
Now we're weaving a new creation, too.
Praise, O God, all praise to you!

Blessing the Wine and Juice

We will pass around several carafes and cups. When you receive them, speak a word of solidarity with our sisters and pour from the carafe into the cup, then pass both on to the next person.

(If the group is large, pass several carafes around at the same time. The people who end up with the last cups for each choice of drink offer the blessing.)

We bless this drink in the name of all women whose blood has been shed in their quest to remain true to themselves through their reproductive choices.

Let us extend our hands, palms out, and touch the palms of those on either side. Let us bless this fruit of the vine as the drink of solidarity and friendship, in praise of women's bodies, in praise of women's choices.

Song: "Weaving a New Creation," by Ruth Duck

Refrain: We have labored, and we have baked the bread.
We have woven cloth, we have nurtured life.
Now we're weaving a new creation, too.
Praise, O God, all praise to you!

Sharing the Bread and Drinks

This bread, wine, and juice represent women's lives. Let us pass the baskets and cups around our circle and partake of the bread and drink. (*Eating and drinking*)

Blessing the Women

Blessed are you, Wisdom Sophia, for giving women the power of choice. We sing women's praises. Please echo after me.

Praise women for our wisdom. (*Echo*)
Praise women for our power. (*Echo*)
Praise women for our mighty acts. (*Echo*)
Praise women with timbrels and dance. (*Echo*)
Praise women for our courage and insight. (*Echo*)
Praise women for our faithfulness. (*Echo*)
Praise women for . . . (*Add others, echo*)
Let all that has breath praise women for our choices. (*Echo*)

Sending Forth

Leader: When I raise my hand, please say "Let us go forth."

All: Let us go forth.

Leader: To stand, sit, cry, and pray with women making reproductive choices.

All: Let us go forth.

Leader: To speak to family members, friends, and legislators of our support for women's decisions.

All: Let us go forth.

Leader: To challenge our synagogues, churches, and holy congregations to affirm women as moral agents.

All: Let us go forth.

Leader: To encourage rabbis, ministers, priests, and counselors to counsel women about free choice.

All: Let us go forth.

Leader: To the city centers and country corners to tell women that all of their choices, including their choice for abortion, are holy and healthy.

All: Let us go forth.

Leader: In the name of the Holy One, Wisdom Sophia, to bring about justice for all women.

All: Let us go forth.

Song: "Stand Together My Sisters," by Marsie Silvestro[12]

Come to me now, women spirit. Come to me now, sister of life.
Come to me now, mother of my being,
and sing in me a melody of love.

Stand together, my sisters, stand together again.
Stand together in a circle. Stand together as friends.

THAT WATERS MAY RUN:

A Prayer for Conception

Some women desire to conceive a child. For many, conception comes easily. For others, it is a struggle. They cry out to God, their friends and family, the medical system. They feel alone. Some women conceive after a long struggle and they give birth to a child. Still others wait endlessly and never conceive.

This liturgy is a prayer for conception. It uses water, the symbol of life's beginnings. Use it as a model for the prayer you or your friends and community need.

Preparation

Take a special bowl and fill it with water. Invite a friend or several to join you, if you wish. Gather in silence, sing, or play music.

Centering

This is the season to cherish life.

Wisdom Sophia, Source of Life (*whatever name you call the Divine*), embrace me.

Thank you for what has been, what is, and what will be.

Hold the Bowl of Water

Prayer

Praise to you, Source of Life, for you choose the good time. Fill me with new life, Wisdom Sophia, that I may conceive and bear a child. How many and wonderful are your works, O Loving Creator. I honor and praise you now and forever. Amen. Blessed be. Let it be so.

Calling on the Spirits of the Earth

(Pray, and if comfortable and convenient, face each direction.)

Spirit of the East, Winds of the Air Cycle,
You breathe in oxygen to awaken new life;
You breathe out carbon dioxide to the flowers.
Fill me with your life that I may conceive.

Spirit of the South, Metabolism of the Fire Cycle,
You touch seeds with sun that fuels all life;
You embrace the world with fertility.
Fill me with your life that I may conceive.

Spirit of the West, Flow of the Water Cycle,
Blood, lymph, mucus, sweat, tears;
You make powerful waters run.
Fill me with your life that I may conceive.

Spirit of the North, Creation of the Earth Cycle,
You replace each cell in the human body every seven years;
You contain all nourishment, all verdancy, all germinating power.
Fill me with your life that I may conceive.

Breathe into the Water

Reflection

(Ask yourself: Why do I want to conceive a child now? What actions will I take to conceive? Sit and watch the water. Breathe into the water again.

Write down or draw your thoughts in a journal, dance your feelings, and/or share your insights with another. Reflect for as long as you like . . . Bless yourself with the water when you are finished.)

Blessing

May new life be before me. (*Stretch hands in front*)
May new life be behind me. (*Stretch hands behind*)
May new life be below me. (*Stretch hands down to feet*)
May new life be above me. (*Raise hands toward sky*)
May new life be all around me. (*Turn around, with outstretched arms*)
May new life be within me. (*Hug yourself*)

Closing

This is the season to cherish life.

Wisdom Sophia, Source of Life (*whatever name you call the Divine*), embrace me.

Thank you for what has been, what is, and what will be.

Afterwards

(*Do something comforting now. Drink a cup of tea, take a warm shower, listen to soothing music, take a walk in the garden. Then make love with your partner or inseminate.*)

YOU ARE NOT ALONE:

Seeking Wisdom to Decide

When a woman discovers she is unintentionally pregnant, she experiences a variety of emotions and may feel that no one shares or understands her situation. She needs to seek her own wisdom to make a choice about her pregnancy.

This liturgy will help her focus on whether to bring her pregnancy to term or to have an abortion. I have used it with women in counseling, including long-distance telephone conversations. It can be used in the quiet of one's own room or with a trusted friend. I have written it to be used with a friend so women will know they are not alone.

Preparation

Gather a candle, paper and pencil, favorite instrumental music. Choose a comfortable place in a favorite location. First play soothing instrumental music quietly in the background. Then light a candle, absorb its power, and pray.

Prayer

Gracious and loving Wisdom Sophia, fill N. (*name of the woman*) with wisdom that she may know clearly the choice that she needs to make. Bless her and comfort her with your Spirit.

Guided Meditation

(*Guide the woman through this visualization.*)

N., close your eyes, take a deep breath, and feel your body begin to relax. Imagine yourself walking on a path through the woods. You are walking into the future, your future. At the end of this path imagine yourself in ten years if you decide to bring this pregnancy to term. (*Pause for three minutes and let mind and body realize this prospect.*)

Now begin again. (*Pause fifteen seconds.*) Imagine another path through the woods. Walk along this path. At the end of this path experience yourself in ten years if you do not bring this pregnancy to term. (*Pause for three minutes and experience what this is like.*)

After you have visualized these two pathways, think of a favorite place, the place where you feel most comfortable, and imagine yourself there. Take a deep breath, let your body relax, and think about what you have experienced. (*Pause for as long as you like.*)

Reflection

Sit and watch the candle burn. Write down or draw your thoughts in a journal, dance your feelings, and/or share your insights with another. Reflect for as long as you like . . . Blow out the candle when you are finished.

Closing

(*When closure is appropriate*)

Wisdom comes when we reflect on our life and make choices based on honesty and truth. Wisdom lives within us. Listen to her. Trust her. Talk with her whenever you need to. She is your friend. She is the Holy One who is with you always. Seek to find wisdom and love her fiercely.

Song: "Blessing Song," by Miriam Therese Winter[13]

May the blessing of God go before you.
May Her grace and peace abound.
May Her Spirit live within you.
May Her love wrap you 'round.
May Her blessing remain with you always.
May you walk on holy ground.

Afterwards

N., do something comforting now. Drink a cup of tea, take a warm shower, listen to soothing music, take a walk in the garden.

A DIFFICULT DECISION:

Affirming a Choice for Abortion

When a woman decides to have an abortion, she usually makes a difficult decision. She needs support from her family, friends, and religious community. She needs counseling and affirmation.

This liturgy affirms that a woman has made a good and holy decision to have an abortion. It provides strength and healing after making a difficult choice. It brings closure to an often intense and emotional process. It is intended to be celebrated with friends.

Preparation

Place on a cloth in the center of the circle: oil, symbols such as flower petals or dried flowers, and a bowl that will be given to the woman as a gift. Invite her to choose a favorite song, poem, reading, or scripture verse for the ritual.

Invite the woman who has made the decision, if appropriate her partner, and supportive friends to gather for affirmation.

Call to Gather

Welcome. Today we gather with our friend, N. (*name of the woman*), to affirm her and her choice to have an abortion. She needs our support.

Song

(*Play or sing a favorite, comforting song, one that the woman likes.*)

Prayer

Let us pray. Blessed are you, Wisdom Sophia, for your presence with N. Praised be you, Mother Goddess and Father God, that you have given your people the power of choice. We are saddened that the life circumstances of N. (*woman's name and, if appropriate, her partner's name*), are such that she has had to choose to terminate her pregnancy. Such a choice is never simple. It is filled with pain and hurt, with anger and questions, but also with integrity and strength. Our beloved sister has made a very hard choice. We affirm her and support her in her decision. We promise to stand with her in her ongoing life.

Blessed are you, Wisdom Sophia, for your presence with N.

Reading

(Choose a poem, reading, or scripture verse that captures the message of the liturgy.)

Reflection

(The celebrant invites the woman [and her partner] to speak about her [their] decision to have an abortion. If there is a symbolic gesture that expresses her [their] feelings, such as sprinkling flower petals or sharing dried flowers, invite her [them] to incorporate it into the sharing.)

Blessing

N., we love you very deeply. As a sign of our affirmation of you and of your choice, we give you this oil and this bowl. Oil soothes bones that are weary from making a difficult decision. Oil strengthens and heals. Oil . . . (*Add sentences that reflect what the woman spoke in her story. Pour the oil into the bowl.*)

N., we would like to bless you with this oil. May we? (*If yes, continue with oil. If no, invite her to put oil on her hands or just offer words of support.*) Come, friends, take oil from the bowl, massage N.'s hands, face, feet, neck, shoulders, or head. Offer her words of support and embrace her.

N., the bowl is a tangible symbol of this day. When times are difficult—and such days come to each of us—look at this bowl and remember our love for you. We bless you, N., and promise to be with you on your journey.

Closing Song: "Blessing Song," by Marsie Silvestro[14] (or another blessing song that is comforting to the woman)

Bless you, my sister, bless you on your way
You have roads to roam before you're home
And winds to speak your name.

So go gently, my sister, let courage be your song
You have words to say in your own way
And stars to light your night.

And if ever you grow weary,
And your heart song has no refrain
Just remember we'll be waiting
To raise you up again.

And we'll bless you, our sister, bless you in our way
And we'll welcome home all the life you've known
And softly speak your name. (*Repeat*)
Bless you, our sister, bless you on your way.

BLESSING A MOTHER-TO-BE:
A Shower Awaiting Birth or Adoption

The transition into motherhood is an important life stage that needs to be marked. In Western cultures, many friends plan a baby shower and offer the woman gifts for the child. While this is important economic support, the woman herself also needs to be blessed by friends before she gives birth or adopts so that she will have the support of the community with her during labor or during the adoption process. A woman benefits from a blessing ceremony and the woman's community needs to be with her before the birth or adoption to offer their support to her.

This liturgy celebrates preparation for giving birth or adopting. It was created and celebrated for a WATER staff member. Use it for a woman you know who needs a blessing as she awaits the birth or adoption of her child. If two women are adopting, adjust the script accordingly. This liturgy could replace the traditional baby shower. The best time for the celebration is as close to the woman's due date or adoption time as seems appropriate. Don't wait too long!

Preparation

Ask the mother-to-be for her guest list, then invite these friends to a liturgy and a meal to honor her. (You may want to include the prospective father and other men, too). Ask each to bring a candle and a piece of fruit that will be given to the woman during a blessing of her. In the center of a circle, place several special objects on a cloth or small table: an egg-shaped candle, a basket, an egg-shaped loaf of bread, a pitcher of milk, a glass, and the woman's favorite flower floating in a bowl of water. Choose vessels for the milk and bread that will be given to the woman as reminders of this occasion. Give each person one of the quotes from the Readings section.

Candle Lighting

(The mother-to-be lights the egg-shaped candle.)

Call to Gather

(Either the mother-to-be or a friend welcomes people. The friend continues:)

Welcome to this blessing of N. (*name of the woman*). N., your life will be filled with new life very soon. We have gathered to be with you to mark your transition into motherhood. You and we are awaiting the arrival of your child.

This special time invites us to recall our own birthing lines. Think for a minute about your matrilineage. (*Pause*) Let us create our circle by speaking our names, reciting our matrilineage, lighting our candle, and each passing the flame on to the next person on the left. (*Example: I am Diann Lynn, mother of Catherine Fei Min, aunt of Angie, Christie, Jenifer, Tabatha, Tiffany, Julie, Maria, Michelle, Chrissie, Lisa, Katie, Sarah, Debbie, and Jessica; daughter of Mary Catherine; granddaughter of Catherine Anna; granddaughter of Emma Marie; great-granddaughter of Catherine; great-granddaughter of Anna. I share their lives with you.*) N., come light the candle and begin. (*Sharing*)

Song: "Sisters' Spiral," by Colleen Fulmer[15]

Spiraling, spiraling circle of Wisdom
Sisters together a body of praise.
Born of earth her rhythms, cycles
Love that's flowing from ancient of days . . .

Prayer

Our circle is filled with the power of women. Let us extend our hands with our candles in them. Pray with me by repeating:

Blessed are you, Mother Creator, for bringing us to this joyous moment. (*Echo*)

Blessed are you, Sister Wisdom, for your presence with N. (*Echo*)

Blessed are you, Source of Life, for blessing us with life. (*Echo*)

Let us surround this home with candlelight. Place your candle where you wish.

Readings: from *The New Beacon Book of Quotations by Women*, compiled by Rosalie Maggio[16]

(Each participant reads the quote she was given when she feels moved to do so. Many of these quotes focus on birthing. If the occasion is adoption, choose accordingly.)

One pain like this should be enough to save the world forever.

—Toi Derricotte, title poem, *Natural Birth* (1983)

Envy the kangaroo. That pouch setup is extraordinary; the baby crawls out of the womb when it is about two inches long, gets into the pouch, and proceeds to mature. I'd have a baby if it would develop in my handbag.

—Rita Rudner, *Naked Beneath My Clothes* (1992)

Every pregnant woman should be surrounded with every possible comfort.

—Dr. Flora L. S. Aldrich, *The Boudoir Companion* (1901)

If men had to have babies they would only ever have one each.

—Diana, Princess of Wales, in *The Observer* (1984)

All night I have suffered; all night my flesh has trembled to bring forth its gift. The sweat of death is on my forehead; but it is not death, it is life!

—Gabriela Mistral, "Dawn," *Desolation* (1922)

If God were a woman, She would have installed one of those turkey thermometers in our belly buttons. When we were done, the thermometer pops up, the doctor reaches for the zipper conveniently located beneath our bikini lines and out comes a smiling, fully diapered baby.

—Candice Bergen, in *Woman's Day* (1992)

Little fish, / you kick and dart and glide / beneath my ribs / as if they were your private reef.

—Ethna McKiernan, "For Naoise Unborn," *Caravan* (1989)

In the dark / Defiant even now, it tugs and moans / To be untangled from these mother's bones.

—Genevieve Taggard, "With Child" (1921), *Collected Poems* (1938)

As often as I have witnessed the miracle, held the perfect creature with its tiny hands and feet, each time I have felt as though I were entering a cathedral with prayer in my heart.

—Margaret Sanger, *Margaret Sanger* (1938)

The burning embers within me burst into flame / My body becomes a fire-lit torch. / Ho someone! Send for the mid-wife.

—Amrita Pritam, "The Annunciation," in Joanna Bankier and Deirdre Lashgari, eds. *Women Poets of the World* (1983)

Having a baby is definitely a labor of love.

—Joan Rivers, *Having a Baby Can Be a Scream* (1974)

Reflection from the Mother-to-Be

(The woman speaks about her fears and hopes about becoming a mother of this child. Others in the group share what they choose of their experiences of motherhood and caring for children.)

Sharing the Fruit

Let us share with N. our wishes for her and her baby. We have each brought fruit to symbolize a blessing. Let us speak our wishes and then give N. the fruit. (*Give N. a basket. Sharing*)

May our wishes empower you, N., as your day of giving birth [*or* of adoption] draws near.

Song: "Blessing the Divine Womb," by Colleen Fulmer[17]

Refrain:
O Sacred Womb of love and grace.
We can feel you all around us.
We lift our hearts to touch and bless you
For we are held and carried in this holy place.

Blessed be this womb where we can move and dance
and dream.
Blessed be this womb that holds us safe and warm within.

(*Refrain*)

Blessed be this womb where Mama's heart is beating
strong.
Blessed be this womb she rocks us gently to her songs.

(*Refrain*)

Blessed be this womb where we're accepted as we are.
Blessed be this womb where we can rest and feel secure.

(*Refrain*)

Blessing the Mother-to-Be

(If the woman is comfortable, invite participants to lay hands upon her. She can sit or stand in the center of the circle and each person can put her hands somewhere on the woman's body.)

Let us close this time together by blessing our beloved pregnant sister and blessing the fruit of her womb. [*For adoption:* . . . by blessing our beloved sister.] N., come and sit in the center of the circle so we can lay our hands on you in blessing. Let us each offer a word of blessing. (*Each participant offers her own blessing, or the following is prayed.*)

Blessed are you, Womb of the Universe, Wisdom Sophia, for filling N. with new life. Bless her womb that she may give birth quickly. [*For adoption:* Bless her womb that she may feel connected to her child.] Bless her eyes that she may see her child and herself as they grow and change. Bless her mouth that she may tell the story of birthing [of adoption]. Bless her hands that she may hold her child and all life tenderly. Bless her breasts that she may nourish her child. Bless her ears that she may hear the sounds of her child. Bless her feet that she may walk with her child throughout all the journeys that lie ahead. Bless her heart that she may deepen her connection with you, O Womb of the Universe, Wisdom Sophia. Amen. Blessed be. Let it be so.

Let us gather around the table.

Blessing the Milk

(N.'s mother pours milk into the glass, and prays:)

Mother's milk of union,
Earliest communion.

Let us together touch and bless this life-force.
Blessed are you, Source of Life, Wisdom Sophia,
For you desire health, safety, and well-being for your
offspring.

Blessing the Bread

(Another woman takes the bread and prays:)

Bread of life,
Nurturing, sustaining, Grandma's life.

Touch and bless this common thread.
Blessed you are, Bakerwoman God, Wisdom Sophia,
For you give your loved ones food for the journey.

Bless the Fruit

(Another takes the fruit and prays:)

Fruit of blessing,
Patience, strength, and love abounding.

Touch and bless this sweet food.
Blessed are you, Sweet Friend, Wisdom Sophia,
For you empower birthing [adopting] sisters with blessings.

Let us eat, drink, and celebrate together.

Giftgiving

N., take these vessels used for the milk, bread, and fruit as a reminder of this occasion. (*Give N. the basket, pitcher, and glass.*)

Song: "Blessing the Divine Womb," by Colleen Fulmer

Refrain:
O Sacred Womb of love and grace.
We can feel you all around us.
We lift our hearts to touch and bless you
For we are held and carried in this holy place.

Closing Prayer

Compassionate Creator Mother, Wisdom Sophia, protect N. that she may be healthy of mind and body. May she give birth to her child safely and in good health. [*Adoption*: May her trip to receive her child be safe.] May our foremothers sustain her through her time of danger. May her waters and birth canal open so that her child is born safely and with little pain. [*Adoption*: May she and her child bond lovingly.] May her recovery be quick, easy, and comfortable. May her child be a blessing.

Blessed are you, Mother Creator, for bringing us to this joyous moment. (*Echo*)
Blessed are you, Sister Wisdom, for your presence with N. (*Echo*)
Blessed are you, Source of Life, for blessing us with life. (*Echo*)

NOTES

1. Maura A. Ryan, in *Dictionary of Feminist Theologies*, ed. Letty Russell and J. Shannon Clarkson (Louisville: Westminster John Knox Press, 1996), 2.

2. 'Asinate Samate, interview by Diann L. Neu, Accra, Ghana, 16 January 2002.

3. Dorys Zeballos, ed., "Decidiendo no ser Madre," *No Estas Sola: Reflexiones y Liturgias sobre Procreasion Responsible* (Montevideo, Uruguay: Catolicas por el derecho a decidir, 1991), 11–12.

4. Marsie Silvestro, "Stand Together My Sisters," *Circling Free* © 1983, Moonsong Productions. Audio recording. Used by permission.

5. Paramahansa Yogananda, "Listen, Listen, Listen," *Cosmic Chants* © 1974, Self-Realization Fellowship, Los Angeles, in Julie Forest Middleton, ed., *Songs of Earthlings* (Philadelphia: Emerald Earth Publishing, 1998), 276. Used by permission.

6. Tillie Olsen, ed., *Mother To Daughter, Daughter To Mother: A Daybook and Reader* (New York: Feminist Press, 1984), 107–8.

7. Marge Piercy, "Sabbath of Mutual Respect," *The Moon Is Always Female* (New York: Alfred A. Knopf, 1980), 107. Used by permission.

8. Ellen Kahn and Julie Drizen, "Baby Talk," *Woman's Monthly* (February 1999), 20. Used by permission.

9. Gloria Steinem, "A Basic Human Right," *Ms.* (July/August 1989), 39. Used by permission.

10. Nancy Gieseler Devor, "A Service for Isaac," copyright 1988 Christian Century Foundation. Reprinted by permission from the April 20, 1988, issue of the *Christian Century*. Subscriptions: $49/yr. from P.O. Box 378, Mt. Morris, IL 61054. 1-800-208-4097.

11. Ruth Duck, "Weaving a New Creation," music by Donna Kasbohm, *Bring the Feast* (Cleveland: Pilgrim Press, 1997), 43. Used by permission.

12. Marsie Silvestro, "Stand Together My Sisters," *Circling Free* © 1983, Moonsong Productions. Audio recording. Used by permission.

13. Miriam Therese Winter, "Blessing Song," *WomanSong* © 1987, Medical Mission Sisters. Audio recording. Used by permission.

14. Marsie Silvestro, "Blessing Song," *Circling Free* © 1982, Moonsong Productions. Audio recording. Used by permission.

15. Colleen Fulmer, "Sisters' Spiral," *Dancing Sophia's Circle* © 1994, Heartbeats. Audio recording. Used by permission.

16. Rosalie Maggio, comp., *The New Beacon Book of Quotations by Women* (Boston: Beacon Press, 1996), 74, 102–3, 545.

17. Colleen Fulmer, "Blessing the Divine Womb," *Dancing Sophia's Circle* © 1994, Heartbeats. Audio recording. Used by permission.

MOURNING LOVED ONES

Those who have died have never, never left.
The dead are not under the earth.
They are in the rustling leaves,
They are in the growing woods,
They are in the crying babes,
They are in the morning light.
The dead are not under the earth.
Listen more often to things than to beings (Repeat)
'Tis the ancestors' prayer when the fire's voice is heard.
'Tis the ancestors' prayer in the voice of the waters.

Sweet Honey in the Rock

I'm not going to die, honey;
I'm going home like a shooting star.

Sojourner Truth

O God, I cry to you day and night!
Will you listen to my prayer?

Psalm 88:1–2

In one of the stars I shall be living.
In one of them I shall be laughing.
And so it will be as if all the stars were laughing,
When you look at the sky at night.

Antoine de Saint Exupery

INTRODUCTION

A colleague has a miscarriage and grieves that the hoped-for birth is no longer. Two close friends who have been partners for twelve years choose to end their relationship as lovers. A child born with HIV-AIDS takes his last breath before his fifth birthday. A beloved friend who has been active in the international ecumenical movement dies when she is almost ninety. My grandmother becomes a young widow with a child after the sudden death of my grandfather.

The examples of women mourning loved ones are endless. All living creation eventually completes its earthly cycle by dying. Life and death are interconnected. The question before us is how do we mourn well those we have loved?

Most societies and religions honor the dead of every age with a wake and/or burial rite. In the village of San Pedro Zacatepeques near Antigua, Guatemala, family and friends gather to honor the dead with a last meal the day before the burial. They reminisce and mourn, pause for a blessing at the village church, and bury the deceased loved one on the slopes of El Agua volcano. In the Chinese traditions of Taoism, Buddhism, and Confucianism, death is the gateway to rebirth, and therefore a joyous occasion. Mourners wear white, the color of death, and throw a handful of dirt on the grave as a positive act of closure. Every year on August 6, the people of Hiroshima create a pathway of candles to mark the anniversary of the day an American B-29 dropped the first atomic bomb.[1]

A few societies and religions mourn with a woman over infertility, a lost pregnancy, or a stillbirth. In Judaism, there are no mourning or burial rites for a fetus less than five months old, and a fetus up to forty days old is considered, by law, merely water. (BT Yevamot 69b).[2] Most Christian churches do not have mourning or burial ceremonies for infertility and early losses. Many more ceremonies are needed to support a woman and a couple during this difficult time.

Since divorce has become an acceptable option in many cultures and religions for ending a relationship, some are beginning to create divorce rites, yet a divorce liturgy is still rare for others. Widowhood ceremonies are not as common and are needed so the community can be with a woman as she grieves the loss of her lifelong partner.

The following two examples show how some women worldwide are creating feminist liturgies that mourn loved ones. The first story from Mendoza, Argentina, describes a woman's funeral. The second account from Ghana, Africa, relates a ceremony to bless a woman who is coming out of widowhood.

Mendoza, Argentina: Funeral of a Woman[3]

The context: Alieda Verhoeven, a Methodist pastor who is known for her work with the human rights community, receives a call that a woman has died. She goes immediately to the woman's home to be with the family who has lost their loved one. She talks with them about the woman's life: artistic works, hobbies, and expressions of her spirit and work. She suggests that the family and friends bring symbols of the woman to the cemetery.

The rite: The family and friends sit on the woman's grave. They recall creative things that the woman has done. They share their symbols and put them on the grave. They tell how they feel and how the deceased has enriched them. As they talk, they take a ball of yarn, hold it, throw it, and weave a web over the beloved's grave.

Reflection: Graves are very important to Argentines because during the dictatorship and dirty wars many were disappeared, tortured, killed, and buried in no-name graves. Groups such as the Mothers and Grandmothers of the Plaza de Mayo still march in the Plaza de Mayo every Thursday at 3:30 P.M. to demand the reappearance or accounting of their loved ones. To know where the graves of their loved ones are would give them great consolation. Sitting on the grave offers a very tactile way to connect with the loved one. Weaving the web symbolizes the way each person is connected to the deceased and shows how this loved one wove together each person present.

Ghana, Africa: Coming Out of Widowhood[4]

The context: Laurene Nyarko was asked by a widow in her congregation to create a coming out of widowhood liturgy and celebrate it in church on Sunday. The church serves a large congregation that is diverse in terms of age, class, and gender. I was honored to attend a Sunday worship service when I was in Ghana.

The rite: At the end of a liturgy one Sunday, Laurene invited the widow to come forward into the center of the sanctuary. She said a prayer as an older widow replaced the widow's black dress with a white one to represent her new life. Then Laurene asked the whole congregation to pray silently with the widow. She summed up these prayers by asking God to give the widow the peace of mind she needs and a way to take care of herself and her children. To close, Laurene asked the whole congregation to shake hands with the widow and offer her blessings and words of encouragement.

Reflection: This simple blessing is so profound. This widowhood liturgy challenges women and congregations worldwide to create liturgies to honor widows, not oppress them. Having the blessing within the Sunday worship is political. In the African context, the fate of a widow is an unhappy one. A widow does not stand to inherit her husband's property. If she is childless there is no one to care for her. Asking a blessing for the widow to take care of herself and her children is what the woman needs in this context. Taking off the black dress and replacing it with a white one symbolizes bringing closure to intense mourning and transitioning to a new life. Inviting the congregation to shake the women's hand offers her support and can encourage the congregation to help care for the widows among them.

Silver Spring, Maryland, USA: Mourning Loved Ones

The context: I designed the liturgies in this final section to support those who are grieving because they have lost significant ones in their lives.

The rites: The liturgical texts are given here.

Reflection: "Tears from the Womb: Mourning a Lost Pregnancy" supports a woman (and partner) grieving a miscarriage, stillbirth, abortion, or lost pregnancy. "Ending a Relationship: Divorcing a Partner" honors a couple's choice to divorce, offers each of them family and community support during this difficult time, and helps them bring closure to their life together.

"A Child's Wake: Going Home" mourns the painful death of a beloved child. "A Feminist Funeral: In Memory of Her" gathers the community of family and friends to bid farewell to a loved one and honor her spirit and beliefs. "Honoring Widowhood: Grieving a Partner" gives encouragement and support to a widow during her bereavement and blesses her for her journey of grief.

TEARS FROM THE WOMB:

Mourning a Lost Pregnancy

The journey toward peace and acceptance after a miscarriage, stillbirth, or abortion is usually long and painful. A woman and her family need comfort, support, and sympathy after a lost pregnancy. Grief needs to be acknowledged. The grieving person needs a support system. It is impossible to calculate the emotional, psychological, and spiritual cost of losing a pregnancy or an infant.

Behind the statistics of lost pregnancies are women who suffer. These women are devastated both by the loss of the potential child and by the fear that they may not bear another. If the woman has experienced sexual abuse, she probably will experience additional issues and emotions. Friends, family, religious leaders, and health care workers often greet those who have lost a pregnancy with insensitive, awkward platitudes. Embracing such feelings of loss is uncommon in our culture. Grieving mothers and fathers need people to accept their right and their need to mourn.

This rite of mourning is meant to help cope with the loss of a pregnancy. It acknowledges pregnancies that have ended in sorrow. It makes the loss real. I have used variations of this liturgy with women who were rushed past grief when they experienced a stillbirth twenty years before, with women who mourn a miscarriage, with women who have chosen abortion, and with women who have lost pregnancies for a variety of other reasons. It is never too late to remember a milestone that went unmarked. Anniversaries can be a time publicly to affirm the loss. Use this service in the hospital or in a small private gathering. Adapt it as you find appropriate.

Preparation

Ask the would-have-been parents what symbol expresses their grief. (For example, a bird cage with an open door, a balloon that has burst, a picture of the sonogram, the death certificate, a rose.) Place this symbol on an altar table. Put a candle beside the symbol. Gather hard chairs for the participants to sit on, reflecting the hard place in which they find themselves.

Call to Mourn

Compassionate family and friends, we gather with N. (*name the one who experienced the loss*) to mourn the death of a dream, the end of a life. N. was anticipating the birth of a child, but her hope ended too soon. We gather to grieve with her this loss of the child she and we will never have, and to express what this potential child meant. We bring this presence into this room. Let our rite of mourning heal wounds all of us bear as the result of our losses. Let it invite us to comfort one another. Let it give us the chance to say farewell to one we will never know.

Introduction of Friends

We are here because we know N. Some of us know one another. Others are just meeting. Let us speak aloud our names, say how we know N., and end with "N., I support you in your grief." (*Naming*)

Candle Lighting

(The would-have-been parent[s] light a candle and say:)

I (we) light this candle in memory of the little one we will never know.

(Another woman lights a second candle, saying:)

I light this candle to remember all women who have lost an anticipated baby.

Opening Prayer

O Compassionate One, Wisdom Sophia, God of Our Ancestors, we weep and mourn today. Our beloved N. was anticipating the birth of a child into her life. She had imagined their future together. (*Share any specifics here.*) Yet the seed of life could not grow in her. Now, her womb is empty and her heart is aching. She is angry and confused. Her yearnings to cradle new life, to sing hushed lullabies, and to welcome a little one into her home will not be fulfilled at this time.

O Compassionate One, Wisdom Sophia, God of Our Ancestors, we weep and mourn with N. today.

Song: "Balm in Gilead," African American spiritual

There is a balm in Gilead, to make the wounded whole
There is a balm in Gilead, to heal the mourning soul.

Sometimes I feel discouraged and think my work's in vain
But then the Holy Spirit revives my soul again.

Readings

(These are some of the ones I have used. Choose ones that express the sentiments of those involved.)

"Sharon's Legacy" by Dottie Ward-Wimmer[5]
(Written on the twentieth anniversary of the birth of her stillborn daughter)

somewhere between a heartbeat and tomorrow
she lived.
snuggled within, she waited patiently
for me to want her.

then she listened
quietly, softly
to the giggles of her big sisters
and the off key crooning of her mom . . .

and the voice i couldn't hear.
a voice that said,
    "little one, like all children, you bring
    lessons for your mother,
    lessons she may not fully know
    for some time.
    you cannot wait that long my child,
    come home."
so she left the lessons behind
    and went.

and now i know . . .
that she taught me to be gentle with words,
to care about the hearts that must hear them.
she taught me that dreams, like
unborn babies, are to be loved
and remembered.
she taught me that the sweetness of truth
is worth the search.
she taught me that it's never too late to
say hello
or to forgive.
and finally,
with that absolute certainty
known only to children,
she taught me that when it's over,
you say "good bye."

Response

Let us sit for a minute with open hands as a sign of letting go.

"This Is My Broken Body," by Cynthia Lapp[6]

On World Communion Sunday I had a miscarriage. I lay in bed for a week, finally forced to stop and grieve.

In the recesses of my mind I began to hear the words of Jesus, "This is my body, broken . . ." I began to feel it in my body. "This is my body, broken . . ." My body had been broken, my blood poured out . . . I had tried to continue my life as if not much had changed. But I had changed. My ability to trust and love was greatly diminished, while my capacity for anger, doubt, and self-reliance had increased exponentially.

But then that little body—that had gestated only twelve weeks, that sent me to the hospital, that took me away from my two children—spoke the words. "This is my body broken, for you." It was not only my body that had been broken, my blood poured out, it was the lifeblood of that little being. That broken body became bread for my soul, as I lay in bed, weak from my own loss of blood.

I saw that I could not go it alone. I did need God, in the community and in myself. The bread of the community, women who shared their stories of miscarriage and loss, fed me. Friends bearing cinnamon rolls, foot lotion, and candles ministered to me. My children were cared for, meals made, the laundry washed, the house cleaned. After months of death, loss, anger, and grief I began to learn to trust and love again. Through the brokenness of that little creature I was given a new life, a new calling, a new understanding of the Christian story.

Response

Let us take one another's hands and, for a time, hold them tight.

Psalm of Lamentation: Psalm 88:1–12, by Marchiene Vroon Rienstra[7]

O God, I cry to You day and night!
Will You listen to my prayer?
My soul cries out, full of pain.
I feel that my life has come to an end.
I might as well be dead.
There is no strength or joy left within me.
I am forgotten as if I were long dead.
Do You remember those who lie in the grave?
Am I, with them, cut off from Your help?

You have thrust me into a pit of deep darkness.
Sorrow overwhelms me, sweeping over me in monstrous waves.
You have taken my loved ones away from me;
They shun me like a pariah.
I am walled up in my grief, without escapes.
My eyes are blurred with tears.

Every day I call upon You, O God.
I stretch out my arms to You, pleading for help.
Do You work wonders for the dead?
Will they rise and give You thanks?
Do those in the grave proclaim Your mercy?
Do those without breath declare Your faithfulness?
Are Your wonders known in the darkness?
Is Your generosity known in the land of the dead?

Sharing the Loss

N., this loss has been difficult for you and for us. Let us talk together about our memories. (*Sharing*)

(*The loss could be shared in any of the following ways: 1) Write thoughts about the lost child and give them to the woman; 2) Share a wished-for name; 3) Write a memory on a silver star and hang it on a paper sky; 4) Engrave the name on a gold bracelet; 5) Stitch the name into a cloth and hang it with pictures of the other children; 6) Light a candle, a symbol of hope and healing, every morning and evening to commemorate the lost one; 7) Tear a cloth (baby blanket); 8) Wash hands as a symbol of letting go of the life that would have been (use a bowl of water with rose petals in it, which later can be sprinkled on a garden as a symbol of returning a loved one to the Earth); 9) Weep together as a group (those who are uncomfortable remain silent, or sit outside the circle) to offer a way to express grief in a safe environment; 10) Plant a tree or flower to honor the lost one.)*

Choosing Life Again

To bless this moment of transition to the next phase of life, we invite you to wash your hands as a symbol of letting go of what may have been or of wanting to let go. (*Handwashing*)

Final Blessing: A reading from *The Little Prince*, by Saint Exupery[8]

In one of the stars I shall be living.
In one of them I shall be laughing.
And so it will be as if all the stars were laughing,
When you look at the sky at night.

And when your sorrow is comforted (time
soothes all sorrows), you will be content
That you have known me.

You will always be my mother
You will always be my friend
You will want to laugh with me . . .

Candle Snuffing

(The would-have-been parent blows out the candle and says:)

Goodbye, my little one, until we meet again.

Greeting of Peace

N. (*name of the lost one*) leaves us the gift of peace. Tonight look up at the stars, hear the laughter and remember. (*If the loss was in the past, add something like: We are mindful of the nineteen years that it has taken for this peace to reveal itself.*) Let us greet one another with this peace.

ENDING A RELATIONSHIP:

Divorcing a Partner

Divorce, the death of a once significant intimate relationship, is a rite of passage that causes each person in the family to reevaluate self. Many divorcing people feel rejected, betrayed, vulnerable, and fearful. Some feel relieved and experience a deep sense of health and wholeness. Some experience growing alienation, more hurt than healing, and more offense than forgiveness. Others know an increasing inability to communicate that results from the radically different life paths each has taken. Others struggle with the pain and the need to let go. Still others separate amicably making their paths parallel but not joined, moving from lovers to friends. While each divorce is unique, most couples need community support. And most communities need to change their understandings about marriage and divorce.

This liturgy honors a couple's choice to divorce and offers each of them family and community support during this difficult time. It presupposes the willingness of both people to meet for a liturgy of reconciliation. It is designed to help a couple and their family and friends bring closure to their life together. Use it for married women and men who divorce, partnered lesbians who separate, friends who are parting ways, or any relationship that is ending. Adapt it to your needs. If both people cannot come together, one of the partners may need a liturgy of healing after divorce.

Preparation

Place a copy of the marriage certificate and a rose for each child, if there are children, on a table that is in the center of a circle of chairs.

Call to Gather

Today we gather together in this place because we love you, N. and N. (*names of those divorcing*). We wish to support you in this time of transition in your lives. We ask Wisdom Sophia to bless each of you as you face the challenge of walking a new journey. May the gracious and loving Holy One, Wisdom Sophia, fill you each with peace now and in the days to come.

N. and N. were married in (*city, state, country*) on (*month, day, year*) and are now seeking a new form of relationship. They announce the closure of their marriage on this day (*month, day, year*) in (*city, state, country*).

Telling the Story

N. and N., what have you called us together to witness today?

(*N. and N. say together*): Today we mark the closure of our marriage.

(Each speaks a paragraph about the journey. Examples from a ceremony: Marie said, "My inner guide and my deeper self called me beyond the limits and endurance of our life together. She called me to places where you, N., did not wish to and could not join me, though you first helped me glimpse the mountains to which I might fly. For this I thank you deeply. I also thank you deeply for the children we share. I will respect you always."

John said, "I seek patterns and pathways of my own; I sense my God's call in directions other than yours. Although our ways part and I will take care of our children, N. and N., I will do all I am able to help them know you as their mother, take them to you, and invite you often to be with us. I will respect you always.")

Reaffirming the Parental Covenant

(Use this section if there are children or perhaps animals that need to be cared for jointly.)

N. and N., you are blessed with wonderful children. They embody your love and they need to know that you will continue to love them and provide for them. What do you promise to your children?

(*N. and N. respond separately to each child*): N., I will love you and care for you as long as I live. This rose is a symbol of your beauty and of my love for you. (*Each gives each child a rose or some other symbolic gift*).

Response of the Child(ren)

Mom, I will love you and care for you forever and always. Dad, I will love you and care for you forever and always.

Call to Reconciliation

Pain and sorrow, hurt and anger have been part of your relationship. It is right and just that you ask forgiveness of one another. Using the words "Forgive me for . . . ," what do you ask that you may forgive and be forgiven?

(N. and N. speak a spontaneous litany to one another, something like:
Forgive me for taking a path that is different from yours.
Forgive me for not listening to you.
Forgive me for not trusting that you love me.
Forgive me for being attracted to someone else.
Forgive me for not being there for you.
Forgive me for getting angry with you inappropriately.
Forgive me for not understanding.)

Promise of Respect

(Each speaks of the meaning of their divorce and their feelings toward one another, and/or the following:)

N., I affirm my part in ending our marriage, and tear our marriage certificate to symbolize this. From this day our paths separate and our love changes. Now I enter into a new relationship with you. I shall treasure the vision and good times that we shared. I shall honor the new and joyful in your life ahead. I promise to respect you as an individual. This is my pledge.

Undoing the Vows

This man and this woman have decided after much effort, pain, and anger that they will no longer be husband and wife. They wish to be friends and to respect and care about each other. They will continue to be parents of their children, and will each be responsible for each of them. (*Use words that are appropriate for the situation.*)

(Each gives the minister or a friend her/his wedding ring.)

Let the return of these rings free you from a vow that you once took and have now outlived. You are now free to enter into a new life, a new love, and a new partnership. Let go of all hurts and pains and go forth with hope in your future.

(The minister or friend returns the rings to each former partner.)

N. and N., you have stated to one another your desire to live independently. You have declared your common commitment to the health and well-being of one another and to others in your lives. You have pledged to respect yourself and each other. And so, I now pronounce your marriage to be dissolved.

Response of the Gathered

Family and friends, please say after me:

In this difficult time, we join with you as your friends. (*Echo*)

We have been with you in your joys and struggles. (*Echo*)

We honor you each and support you in your decision to divorce. (*Echo*)

We love you each. (*Echo*)

Blessing

N. and N., may we lay our hands on you and bless you? *(If yes, then proceed.)*

May you, N., and you, N., find peace and good health in your lives.

May you enjoy satisfying work, tender friendships, and the love of your children.

May you dream new dreams and share them with someone who is beloved.

May you know the presence of Wisdom Sophia, who loves you deeply.

Amen. Blessed be. Let it be so.

Hug of Support

Let us remove our hands and give N. and N. a hug of support. *(Each guest greets each of the couple.)*

Sending Forth

Let us go forth promising to support N. and N. during this time of transition.

Let us go forth committed to reconciling our differences with the divorced and their children.

Let us go forth promising to love the children all the days of our lives.

A CHILD'S WAKE:

Going Home

The death of a child brings overwhelming heartache. Burying the body of a young one is a painful task. It is vitally important for family and friends to be together during this time to support one another and say farewell to their loved one. Death marks a "going home" that is a mystery for all.

This wake service[9] was held in the family home. Those gathered, especially the nurses and doctors, grieved for N. (*the child*) and for all the children they have known who have died. Use it as a model for the one your community needs to celebrate. Include readings and music that are meaningful to the child and the parents.

Preparation

If the wake is at home, place the child's body where it is most visible. For this service, the casket was moved to the doorway between the dining room and the living room. Gather candles, one for each year of the child's life, and give one to an equal number of candlelighters. Have a special candle for the parents to light, perhaps the baptismal candle, if there is one. Have a smaller candle for each participant. Put a pitcher of water and a large bowl near the casket.

Call to Gather

Today we come together with N. and N. (*names of the parents*) to mourn the death of N. (*the child's name*), and to celebrate N.'s life. This is a very difficult time for all of us because N.'s days with us were so few. "Why?" we ask. "Why the death of a child?" And we have no answers that satisfy us. Now, we give thanks that (*age of the child*) years were given to N., and we mourn because life, as we knew it, is no longer. Burying this child is a painful task that reminds us that love that sparks and ignites our hearts is what matters finally.

Candlelighting

(The parent[s] light the child's baptismal candle, and put the candle by the casket.)

Parent One: As we light N.'s baptismal candle we remember the energy that sparked her (his) breath;

Parent Two: The flame that danced into our lives.

Parent One: And the fire that singes our hearts this night as we remember her (him):

Parent Two: Her (his) beginning;

Parent One: Her (his) full little life;

Parent Two: Her (his) fun;

Parent One: Her (his) suffering;

Parent Two: Her (his) death;

Parent One: Her (his) absence;

Parent Two: Her (his) spirit, which may live on and spark each of us if we allow it to do so.

Prayer

Let us pray. Loving and Caring God of our Mothers and Fathers, Wisdom Sophia, give N. a hug for all of us and share with her (him) your gifts of heaven. Invite the angels and saints to dance with her (him) now. Bless her (him) with many surprises. We love her (him) and are so sad that she (he) is no longer here to laugh and cry with us. Be with her (him) now and always. Amen. Blessed be. Let it be so.

Song: "The More We Get Together," traditional

(N. loved this song. Let us sing it remembering the happiness she [he] gave us.)

The more we get together, together, together,
The more we get together, the happier we'll be.
For N.'s friends are my friends and my friends are your friends,
The more we get together, the happier we'll be.

Lighting the First-Year Candle

(A close friend lights a candle from N.'s baptismal candle and tells a story of the child's first year of life. When she finishes, she puts the candle by the casket, and invites those who knew N. during the first year to light a candle from the one she lit and tell a first-year story.)

Storytelling

Song: "Angels Watchin' Over Me," traditional

All night, all day; angels watchin' over me, my God.
All night, all day; angels watchin' over me.

Day is dying in the west; angels watchin' over me, my God.
Sleep my child and take your rest; angels watchin' over me.

Now I lay me down to sleep; angels watchin' over me, my God.
Pray to God my soul to keep; angels watchin' over me.

If I die before I wake; angels watchin' over me, my God.
Pray to God my soul to keep; angels watchin' over me.

Lighting a Second-Year Candle

(Another friend lights a candle from N.'s baptismal candle and tells a second-year story. When she finishes she puts her candle by the casket and invites those who knew N. during the second year to light a candle from the one she had lit and tell a second-year story.)

Storytelling

Song: "This Little Light of Mine," traditional

This little light of mine, I'm gonna let it shine, (*Sing three times*)
Let it shine, let it shine, let it shine.

Everywhere I go, I'm gonna let it shine, (*Sing three times*)
Let it shine, let it shine, let it shine.

Lighting a Third-Year Candle

(Another lights a candle from the baptismal candle and tells a third-year story. When he finishes, he puts the candle by the casket, and invites those who knew N. during this third year to light a candle from the one he had lit and tell a third-year story.)

Storytelling

Song: "Over the Rainbow," by E. Y. Harburg and Harold Arlen[10]

Somewhere over the rainbow way up high
There's a land that I heard of once in a lullaby
Somewhere over the rainbow skies are blue
And the dreams that you dare to dream really do come true

Someday I'll wish upon a star
And wake up where the clouds are far behind me
Where troubles melt like lemon drops
Away above the chimney tops, that's where you'll find me

Somewhere over the rainbow bluebirds fly
Birds fly over the rainbow, why then, O why can't I?
If happy little bluebirds fly beyond the rainbow
Why, O why can't I?

Lighting a Fourth-Year Candle

(Another lights a candle from the baptismal candle and tells a fourth-year story. When she finishes, she puts the candle by the casket, and invites those who knew N. during this fourth year to light a candle from the one she had lit and tell a fourth-year story.)

Storytelling

Song: "Twinkle, Twinkle, Little Star," traditional

Twinkle, twinkle, little star,
How I wonder where you are.
Up above the world so high,
Like a diamond in the sky.
Twinkle, twinkle, little star,
How I wonder where you are.

Lighting the Fifth-Year Candle

(The parents light the fifth-year candle, tell a fifth-year story, put the candle by the casket, and pour water into the bowl.)

Storytelling

Song: "We All Come from the Mother," traditional[11]

We all come from the Mother, and to her we shall return.
Like a drop of rain, flowing to the ocean.

We all come from *blessing, and to *it we shall return.
Like a drop of rain, flowing to the ocean

(**words adapted*)

Storytelling

(A celebrant invites people to think of a story about the child that was precious to them, then turn to two or three people around them and share stories.)

Song: "The More We Get Together," traditional

The more we get together, together, together,
The more we get together, the happier we'll be.
For N.'s friends are my friends and my friends are your friends,
The more we get together, the happier we'll be.

Sending Forth

Leader: Filled with the spirit of N., let us go forth.
May her (his) strength continue through us.
Let us say: Amen. Blessed be. Let it be so.

Response: Amen. Blessed be. Let it be so.

Leader: May (*names of parents, siblings, guardians*) be comforted by the presence of friends and family, and the knowledge that they loved N. well.

Response: Amen. Blessed be. Let it be so.

Leader: May we each live our lives with honesty, integrity, and faithfulness as we prepare for our own death.

Response: Amen. Blessed be. Let it be so.

Hug of Peace

Today we need all the hugs we can give and receive. Let us greet one another with love and peace, the gifts that N. leaves with us. (*Greeting*)

A FEMINIST FUNERAL:

In Memory of Her

Death will befriend each of us one day. This reality urges us to pay attention to the lasting memory we wish for ourselves and for our friends. When a beloved friend dies, we need to take care how we say good-bye. We must think carefully about how we will carry on her legacy and tell her story. When a friend or colleague dies, the community wants to gather to bid farewell.

For centuries, religion and its accompanying rituals offered space, time, and place in which the bereaved could express grief. These days, with changing belief patterns, many feminists find church rituals inadequate. They need more meaningful wake and funeral liturgies to say good-bye and to honor the loved one's spirit and beliefs.

This liturgy is a feminist farewell. I have used variations of it for the funerals of several friends and colleagues. Some of them had planned their service before they died. Their faces are before me now as I write this liturgical text to capture these sacred memorials. Use this text as a guide for your own feminist farewell or for the one you will plan with another. Use prayers, music, and readings that respect the beliefs of the bereaved and the deceased. Observe significant dates, such as holidays and anniversaries, after a loved one's death.

Preparation

Prepare a memorial card that has a photo of the person and a favorite quote. Provide one for each participant. Celebrate this liturgy at the home of the loved one who has died, in the backyard of a friend, at a funeral home, or in an appropriate place such as by the sea. If there is a casket, place it in a central location and cover it with a quilt, shawl, or scarf of the beloved. If the person was cremated, place the urn of ashes on a central table and form a circle of chairs around it. Place pictures and symbols of the loved one around the room. Invite family and friends to sit in a circle around the casket, urn, or photos. Have one candle to represent the loved one and a candle for each participant.

Prelude Music: *(Play music that the loved one enjoyed.)*

Call to Gather

(Sound a bell, triangle, or tambourine to call people to gather around the casket, urn, or pictures. A family member, close friend, or community representative says:)

Welcome to this "Feminist Farewell: In Memory of Our Beloved N." (*name of person*). We gather to bid her a final farewell and to support her loved ones and one another in our sorrow. It is so hard to believe that N. is not here with us. Let us celebrate her power in life and in death and give thanks that we knew her.

Candle Lighting

(A family member, loved one, or colleague offers a biographical sketch of the loved one and then lights a candle, saying:)

I light this candle to remember N., especially her smile. You each have a candle. Light yours from this one and share a memory you have of N. *(She passes the candle around the circle. Sharing)*

Reading: "Song: 'Now let us honor with violin and flute'" by May Sarton[12]

Now let us honor with violin and flute
A woman set so deeply in devotion
That three times blasted to the root
Still she grew green and poured strength out.

Still she stood fair, providing the cool shade,
Compassion, the thousand leaves of mercy,
The cherishing green hope. Still like a tree she stood,
Clear comfort in the town and all the neighborhood.

Pure as the tree is pure, young
As the tree forever young, magnanimous
And natural, sweetly serving: for her the song,
For her the flute sound and the violin be strung.
For her all love, all praise,
All honor, as for trees
In the hot summer days.

Song: "This Tough Spun Web," by Carolyn McDade[13] **(or a favorite of the beloved or of the community)**

We are the forest of ten thousand seeds
in shades of green that hold the sun.
With mingled roots our limbs together lean,
we are the many and the one.
We are the waters, each small drop of rain,
life-spawning ponds and stream-filled sea.
We run the blood that flows in living veins
to live and die that all be free.

Chorus: This circle opening moves with deepened faith,
our lives to birth a living dawn.
As love renewed turns in our common way,
creating hope we carry on.

We are the wind-filled song that sounds of joy
and cries from dungeons cast away.
The deep sung dreams of those who labor on
to shape a just and caring way.
We are the sun-fired passionate love of life,
the burning heart within the soul.
We are the love that grows resisting chains
to free the bound and make us whole.

(Chorus)

We are the hands proud ache to knead the bread
from golden seed we raise as corn.
We harvest thoughts to feed the hungering mind,
translating life into a poem.
We are the faith beyond all mystery,
beneath the deep yon skies above.
We are the hope in solidarity
profoundly shaped by human love.

(Chorus)

Our healing love, our hands reach out and touch
the cherished body, the quiv'ring mind.
Our lives like grass, like bread, like falling rain,
the ordinary our sublime.
Hold true this tough spun web as hard times come
and much be lost or taken away.
We struggle not for things that best be gone,
integrity rewebs our way.

(Chorus)

Readings: Excerpts from Wisdom

(Read alternately by two readers)

Proverbs 9:1, 5
Wisdom has built herself a house; she has prepared her food, mixed her wine, and set her table . . . she calls to all in the city and in the towns . . . come and eat my food and drink the wine I have made . . .

Proverbs 1:20; 2:1, 6
Wisdom calls aloud in the streets . . . I will pour out my heart to you . . . tune your ear to wisdom and your heart to truth . . . then you will understand who Wisdom Sophia is and discover love of life . . . you will understand justice and the ways of happiness.

Proverbs 31:25, 28, 29
Wisdom is clothed with strength and dignity, and she laughs at the days to come . . . Her children rise up and praise her; her husband, too, extols her. Many are the women of proven worth, but you have excelled them all.

Proverbs 31:31
Give her of the fruit of her hands, and let her works praise her in the gates.

Storytelling

N.'s works tell her praises. She was a wise and amazing woman. When you think of her, what memories do you want to share? Let us tell stories about her now. After each three we will sing. (*Sharing*)

Song: "You Can't Kill the Spirit," traditional

> You can't kill the Spirit, she's like a mountain
> Old and strong she lives on and on and on (*Sing three times*)

Litany of Remembrance[14]

Leader: We will remember N., whom death has taken from our midst. In the rising of the sun and in its going down,

Response: We will remember her.

Leader: In the blowing of the wind and in the chill of winter,

Response: We will remember her.

Leader: In the opening buds and in the rebirth of spring,

Response: We will remember her.

Leader: In the blueness of the sky and in the warmth of summer,

Response: We will remember her.

Leader: In the rustling of leaves and in the beauty of autumn,

Response: We will remember her.

Leader: In the beginning of the year and when it ends,

Response: We will remember her.

Leader: When we are weary and in need of strength,

Response: We will remember her.

Leader: When we are lost and sick at heart,

Response: We will remember her.

Leader: When we have joys we yearn to share,

Response: We will remember her.

Leader: When we look in the mirror and see her smile in our eyes,

Response: We will remember her.

Leader: When we hear her voice in the sea,

Response: We will remember her.

Leader: When we feel her spirit in the mountains,

Response: We will remember her.

Leader: When we gather as women-church,

Response: We will remember her.

Leader: When we celebrate our gifts as women,

Response: We will remember her.

Leader: So long as we shall live, she too shall live, for she is now a part of us, as we remember her.

Song: "Blessing Song," by Marsie Silvestro[15]

Bless you my sister, bless you on your way
You have roads to roam before you're home
And winds to speak your name.

So go gently, my sister, let courage be your song
You have words to say in your own way
And stars to light your night.
And if ever you grow weary
And your heart song has no refrain
Just remember we'll be waiting to raise you up again

And we'll bless you, our sister, bless you in our way
And we'll welcome home all the life you've known
And softly speak your name. (*Repeat*)
Bless you, my sister, bless you on your way.

Closing Blessing: "She Whom We Love," by St. John Chrysostom[16]

She whom we love
And lose
Is no longer

Where she was before.
She is now
Wherever we are.

Sending Forth

Let us go forth remembering N. as we look up at the stars.
Let us love as she loved.
Let us carry on her legacy of hospitality and social justice.
Let us remember that "she is now wherever we are."
Amen. Blessed be. Let it be so.

HONORING WIDOWHOOD:

Grieving a Partner

Jesus spoke and the common people heard him gladly. Why?
Beware of the hypocrisy that exploits,
That pretends to be decent and religious.
Beware of the privileged that seek attention,
Who parade among you in order to court recognition.
Beware of those who have marked seats in the place of worship,
Who are seated at high tables in order to eat of the best.

See! These are those who acquire the houses of widows,
Who receive from them gifts of money and precious goods,
Compensation for the long prayers they say for the widows.
They enrich themselves and the widows get poorer,
The poorer the widows get the more prayers they need.
So those who do the praying get richer.

Just look over there, see that widow?
She has given until she has nothing left.

She has put in the last coins in exchange for the services
of the religious.
Tell me, what will she and the children eat today?
And do not tell me there are social services,
For if they functioned well, she would not be left with
two mites in hand.
Do not tell me the extended family will help her cope,
For if she had received more than enough,
She would not be left with two mites in hand.

Why did she not put in one?
Is this her last protest?
"Here take all I have
I am ready to depart in peace!"

So Jesus spoke, and the common people heard him gladly.
As for the houses built on hypocrisy and greed
Not one stone will be left standing.
So Jesus spoke the mind of the people.
And the common people heard him gladly.
(Mark 12:38-44)

—Mercy Amba Oduyoye[17]

The death of a spouse marks another stage in the life of a woman. Separated from her husband or partner, the widow may be lonely, filled with sorrow and pain, and grieving. She may be left with the responsibility of looking after children. Yet, she must usually do everything on her own. She needs encouragement and support during her bereavement. In many cultures, such as some in Africa, widows are treated unjustly and left with two mites in hand. How can we respond to the cries and protests of widows?

This liturgy is one way. Adapt it to the needs of the widow and her particular community, including those who are lesbian. It could also be used to bless many widows. Use it for a liturgy that occurs within the first month after the death of the spouse or a one-year anniversary.

Preparation

Invite a few friends to bring gifts for N. such as a black scarf, a white scarf, a handkerchief, and herbs. Choose one (or several) symbol(s) meaningful to the widow, such as flowers, rocks, shells, candles, herbs. Have one for each participant or invite participants to bring a symbol. Encourage the widow beforehand to share some of her thoughts about the deceased. Let her know that she may change her mind and ask some family member to speak for her.

Welcome

(Spoken by a daughter, sister, pastor, special friend, or colleague.)

Welcome, each of you, to this liturgy for N. (*name of widow*). We are here to be with you, N., in your loss. We know that the death of N. (*husband or partner*) has brought a major change to your life. We are with you and (*Name the children if there are any and/or others who are appropriate. Continue to add what reflects the characteristics of the widow.*).

Naming the Circle

N. needs our support during her transition to widowhood. Speak your name and say, "N., I am here to support you." (*Naming*)

Song: "We Are A Wheel," by Betty Wendelborn[18]

We are a wheel, a circle of life.
We are a wheel, a circle of power.
We are a wheel, a circle of love,
Circling the world this sacred hour.

Readings

(Use a reading that is meaningful to the widow. Some we have used follow.)

A reading from the book of Ruth 1:16–21 (*or Luke 7:11–17 or Acts 6:1–7, 9 or Mark 12:38–44*)

"Do not urge me to go back and desert you," Ruth answered. "Where you will go, I will go, and where you stay, I will stay. Your people will be my people, and your God, my God. Where you die, I will die and there I will be buried. I swear a solemn oath before God, nothing but death shall divide us." When Naomi saw that Ruth was determined to go with her, she said no more, and the two of them went on until they came to Bethlehem. When they arrived in Bethlehem the whole town was in great excitement about them, and the women said, "Can this be Naomi?" "Do not call me Naomi," she said, "call me Mara [Bitter], for it is a bitter lot that the Almighty has sent me. I went away full and God has brought me back empty. Why should you call me Naomi? God has pronounced against me; the Almighty has brought disaster to me."

Widow's Psalm, by Miriam Therese Winter[19]

All who keep at a distance
come near and see my sorrow,
come close and feel my pain.
The love of my life has been taken away,
I shall never be whole again.

As I stand alone in the shadow of death
I see no green in my Valley.
No flower beside my path,
no bird song breaks the silent void
around my broken heart.

The light has been extinguished.
How can I carry on?
It is hard to hold on to the vision
Hard to find any meaning,

Hard to keep on going
When the point of it is all gone.

(Use the following two verses if appropriate)

O God of the resurrection
Allow me to take my comfort
In the flesh our flesh created.
Let our spirit live forever
In the offspring of our love.

May the child of my girlhood passion
Lift me again into laughter
And be there with me
When the trumpets sound for me
From my heavenly home.

May the one I mourn
Be waiting for me forever.
Hear me, heed me, Shaddai.

Words from the Widow

(If she wants to speak or if she wants another to speak for her.)

Words from the Gathered

Let us share our words of support with N., then take a symbol and give it to her as a sign of this support. (*Sharing*)

Gift Giving

(The widows in the group and/or close friends offer N. gifts that are significant to her.)

Black scarf: N., black is a sign of mourning. Wear this black scarf as a symbol of your mourning. In some cultures women wear black for a year as they mourn. Wear this scarf as long as you wish.

White scarf (*for a one-year anniversary, replace black scarf with a white one*): N., to honor this one-year anniversary of your widowhood, we replace your black scarf with this white one as a sign of your new life.

Handkerchief: N., this handkerchief will catch your tears. May your tears flow. They will cleanse your soul.

Taking off the ring (*some may not want to do this*): N., taking off your wedding ring is a sign that you are beginning to separate from your past life with N. (*spouse or partner*). Take it off gently, remembering.

Blessing the Widow(s)

(If the group is small, ask the widow if the gathered can lay hands on her. If yes, ask her to sit or stand in the center of the circle or invite people to extend their hands toward the woman. Each person can offer their own prayer of blessing or one person can bless for all similar to the following:)

Blessed are you, Gracious and Loving God, Wisdom Sophia, Compassionate Holy One, for you have given us our sister, N. Bless her as she enters this journey of widowhood in her life. Fill her with family and friends to help her through her changes. Give her tears to cleanse her soul. Strengthen her to care for her children. Give her peace of mind and body, and hold her always in the palm of your hand. Amen. Blessed be. Let it be so.

Song: "Blessing Song," by Miriam Therese Winter[20]

May the blessing of God go before you.
May Her grace and peace abound.
May Her Spirit live within you.
May Her love wrap you 'round.
May Her blessing remain with you always.
May you walk on holy ground.

Sending Forth

Let us go forth filled with love and care for N.

Let us go forth in solidarity with all widows worldwide.

Let us go forth committed to work to overcome unjust practices toward widows.

Greeting of Peace

Let us greet N. and one another with a sign of peace, love, and care. (*Hugging*)

NOTES

1. David Cohen, ed. *The Circle of Life: Rituals from the Human Family Album* (San Francisco: HarperSanFrancisco, 1991), 197, 194, 225.
2. Rabbi Debra Orenstein, *Lifecycles* (Woodstock, VT: Jewish Lights Publishing, 1994), 37.
3. Alieda Verhoeven, interview by Diann L. Neu, Accra, Ghana, 13 January 2002.
4. Laurene Nyarko, interview by Diann L. Neu, Geneva, Switzerland, 14 January 2001.
5. Dottie Ward-Wimmer, "Sharon's Legacy," written for this liturgy, unpublished. Used by permission.
6. Cynthia Lapp, "This Is My Body Broken," Mt. Rainier, MD. Previously unpublished. Used by permission.
7. Marchiene Vroon Rienstra, "Psalm 88: 1–12," *Swallow's Nest: A Feminine Reading of the Psalms* © 1992 Wm. Erdmans Publishing Company, Grand Rapids, MI, 101. Used by permission.
8. Antoine de Saint Exupery, *The Little Prince* (New York: Harcourt, Brace & World, 1943, 1971), 104.
9. A version was written with Jackie Lynch and Sally King for the funeral of their child Shawn Sheffield.

10. E. Y. Harburg and Harold Arlen, "Over the Rainbow" ©1938 (Renewed) Metro-Goldwyn-Mayer Inc. ©1939 (Renewed) EMI Feist Catalog, Inc. All rights reserved. Used by permission of Warner Bros. Publications U.S. Inc., Miami, FL 33014.

11. "We All Come from the Mother," in Anna Kealoha, ed. *Songs of the Earth* (Berkeley, CA: Celestial Arts, 1989), 169. *Indicates words adapted.

12. May Sarton, "Song: 'Now let us honor with violin and flute,'" *Collected Poems 1930–1993* (New York: W.W. Norton, 1993, 1988, 1984, 1980, 1974), 76. Used by permission.

13. Carolyn McDade, "This Tough Spun Web," *This Tough Spun Web* © 1985, Surtesy Publishing. Audio recording. Used by permission.

14. "We Remember Them," adapted, *Rabbi's Manual* (New York: Central Conference of American Rabbis, 1988), 130–31. Used by permission.

15. Marsie Silvestro, "Blessing Song," *Circling Free* © 1983, Moonsong Productions. Audio recording. Used by permission.

16. St. John Chrysostom, "She Whom We Love," in Elizabeth Roberts and Elias Amidon, *Life Prayers* (San Francisco: Harper-SanFrancisco, 1996), 341.

17. Mercy Amba Oduyoye, "The Lament Over the Mites," *Heart, Mind and Tongue: A Heritage of Woven Words* (Accra, Ghana: The Circle of Concerned African Women Theologians, 2001), 40–41. Used by permission.

18. Betty Wendelborn, "We Are A Wheel," *Sing Green: Songs of the Mystics* (Auckland, New Zealand: Pyramid Press, 1999), 1. Used by permission.

19. Miriam Therese Winter, "Widow's Psalm," *WomanSong* © 1987, Medical Mission Sisters. Audio recording. Used by permission.

20. Miriam Therese Winter, "Blessing Song," *WomanSong* © 1987, Medical Mission Sisters. Audio recording. Used by permission.

seven

WOMEN'S LIFE CYCLE LITURGIES WORLDWIDE

The liturgies presented here document that some women around the world are creating and celebrating feminist life cycle liturgies that many women need. These rites, which are designed out of diverse contexts, honor women's worth and mark positively women's life transitions from womb to grave. Such a ceremony can be a moment of dramatic teaching and socialization that makes its members more fully and deeply its own.

Life is a journey that requires individuals to differentiate particular moments. Some of these experiences are rooted in biology; some are social constructs; all have a spiritual and religious component. Some women around the globe are beginning to name these moments out of women's experiences in particular contexts. Types of rites for life's journey that women need and are creating include:

1. Beginnings: monthly menstruation, fertility, pregnancy, childbirth, afterbirth, adoption
2. Infertility and early losses: difficulty conceiving, miscarriage, abortion, stillbirth, death of a young child
3. Welcoming a child into community, naming, baptism
4. Adolescence: first menstruation, coming of age
5. Lifestyle choices: being single, coming out, courtship, marriage, entering a religious community, commitment
6. Parenting: breastfeeding or not, weaning, role modeling, teaching, holding on or letting go
7. Transition: divorce, separation, breaking a relationship, empty nest, new job, moving
8. Healing from sexual abuse: rape, incest, domestic violence, marital rape, date rape
9. Health: hysterectomy, medical requirements, recovery from an operation, mastectomy, breast reduction surgery, surgery
10. Midlife: menopause, retirement
11. Aging: croning, widowhood
12. Death, suicide, euthanasia, and mourning

Women and their communities need women's rites for life's journey to nourish women at these life-changing times. As reflected in the liturgies I have presented here, these rites can assist women in transitions, and thereby benefit the community at large. They can lead to individual and communal valuing for women. They can provide spiritual support that reduces anxiety about change. They can make change manageable, allowing the gathered to experience it and celebrate it with others as part of the pattern of living rather than as a threat to it.

Women's rites for life's journey can encourage a sense of self, a sense of family, and a sense of group membership. They can promote emotional, physical, and spiritual well-being during times of intense relationship change. They can assist in the resolution of conflict. They function at many levels, marking individual change (from single woman to coupled woman), relationship change (from dating couple to committed partners), family system change (through addition or loss of members), and family-community change (change in relationship to the outside world). They can create safe places where women can be honored for life transitions.

WOMEN CLAIMING RITUAL AUTHORITY

Christian and Jewish women who are creating and celebrating women's rites for life passages and personal milestones are claiming ritual authority. We are transforming the way we understand the Scriptures and Torah; the way we image the Divine; the way we practice liturgy and ritual; the way we tell and pass on stories; the way we organize our communities; and the way we make sense of sacred mysteries.

Christian women who celebrate feminist liturgies for life's journey are called by Wisdom Sophia to be church. And what is church, we must ask? Theologians still answer that it is the place of assembly for worship, while others affirm that it exists more as an event than a structure. Still others say it is the community that makes the church.

Elisabeth Schüssler Fiorenza speaks of the *ekklesia* of women:

> The diverse women's movements in the churches must come together as the public forum and alliance of the *ekklesia* of women. As a "rainbow" discipleship of equals we can voice and celebrate our differences because we have as a "common ground" our commitment to the liberation

> struggle and vision of God's *basileia,* God's intended world and community of well-being for all. We are not the first to engage in this struggle for ending societal and ecclesiastical patriarchy. Nor are we alone in it. A "great cloud of witnesses" surrounds us and has preceded us throughout the centuries in the *ekklesia* of women. We derive hope and courage from the memory of our foremothers and their struggles for survival and dignity, from the remembrance of our foresisters who have resisted patriarchal dehumanization and violence in the power of the Spirit.[1]

Women-church is gathering worldwide. Mary E. Hunt defines women-church as "a global, ecumenical movement made up of local feminist base communities of justice-seeking friends who engage in sacrament and solidarity."[2] Some ask how will we know that these groups are church? One knew the church historically through its marks: one, holy, catholic (universal), and apostolic. Isabelle Graessle suggests a contemporary reformulation of these marks of the church to be "plurality, solidarity, contextuality and witness."[3]

Women's rites for life's journey reveal these four marks of church. They honor women's reality that is varied in the way we name the Divine and pray. They join in struggle with people of all classes and cultures who are all marginalized by patriarchy and kyriarchy. They are designed out of a particular setting and invite women to create liturgies for their own context, region, culture, and religion. They give testimony to the lives of many holy women from the past. They reveal a pluralistic, caring, contextual, and witnessing church.

Letty Russell offers four more clues to spark the churches into becoming safe and welcoming communities: "the Spirit is poured out on women; good news is preached by women; hospitality is offered to women; and justice is shared by women."[4] Women's rites for life's journey challenge the churches to acknowledge that the Holy Spirit, Wisdom Sophia, Shekinah, is inspiring women to preach the good news of women's rites. These rites invite the churches to offer church space (the space the ancestors of women built) to women's liturgical communities. They remind the churches that justice must be shared within the church with its female members as well as with others who are marginalized.

Jewish women who create feminist rituals are called by Shekinah, She Who Dwells Within, the female presence of God in Jewish tradition, to end the exile that keeps women from shaping the Jewish tradition. Lynn Gottlieb speaks in her book *She Who Dwells Within:*

> Just as Shekinah has been in exile, so Jewish women have been in exile. Our exile, however, has been in the midst of our own culture. Denied access to avenues of public expression, we were denied the ability to shape Jewish culture explicitly. This is the exile *She Who Dwells Within* seeks to end.[5]

Shekinah spoke through her daughter Judith Kaplan, a young girl of twelve and a half, when eighty years ago, she became the first young woman to stand in front of her congregation and recite the Torah blessings and read Torah as a Bat Mitzvah. Sandy Eisenberg Sasso says of this action: "What began that day with the determination of a young girl and the wisdom of her father, Rabbi Mordecai Kaplan, became a revolution in religious creativity. We are still unwrapping that gift."[6]

Jewish women unwrap that gift as they create and celebrate life cycle rituals. Sue Levi Elwell notes "the development of Jewish women's rituals in the last quarter of the twentieth century reflects the unrolling of the 'unwritten scrolls' of Jewish women's lives through the ages, and our first attempts to read those scrolls, piecing together the oral traditions much as our ancestors compiled what we now call the Torah."[7] The early rituals were attempts to establish women as equal to men, such as baby naming for girls, bat mitzvah, egalitarian *ketubot* (marriage contracts), and divorce decrees that fully acknowledge both spouses. Later rites acknowledge rites of passage connected with women's biological experiences, such as weaning, menses, pregnancy loss and abortion, hysterectomy, and mastectomy.

Judith Plaskow reflects on how Jewish women are changing Judaism.

> As Jewish women recognize ourselves as heirs to and shapers of Judaism, as we explore our own experiences and integrate them into the tradition, we necessarily transform the tradition and shape it into something new. How, then, might the central Jewish categories of Torah, Israel, and God change as women appropriate them through the lens of our experience?[8]

For Jewish and Christian women, women's life cycle liturgies help build a community of justice-seeking friends that is changing the religious landscape. These liturgies show that the very creation of women's life cycle liturgies offers resistance to the kyriarchy and patriarchy that coopts women's life journey into the sacramental life of the churches[9] and the synagogues. They are clues to the transformation that women are bringing and returning to liturgies, within and alongside of the churches and synagogues.

Wisdom Sophia, Shekinah, is calling her sisters to recover women's rites as memory and heritage for her people. Memory and imagination, faithfulness and hope are her gifts. Wisdom Sophia, Shekinah, She Who Dwells Within, and the community of women resisters in the scriptures are the source of women's liturgical strength and authority.

Feminist liturgies for life's journey challenge women to be religious and to make the world safe for all children.

Closing: "Inspired by Wisdom Sophia, Shekinah, She Who Dwells Within," by Diann Neu

Let us take the transforming aspects of *Women's Rites: Feminist Liturgies for Life's Journey*
to the city streets and country roads of the world.
Let us go forth in all directions of the universe
to bless and to embrace,
to forgive and to heal,
to welcome and to sanctify.
Let us go forth to be with the homeless and the hospitable,
the hungry and the full,
the thirsty and the justice-seekers.
Let us go forth to be with the elderly and those who seek wisdom,
the exiled and those who understand freedom,
the hopeless and those who see visions.
Let us go forth to church leaders who turn their backs on the needs of their people,
to government officials who are immune to the suffering of the poor,
to world leaders who are numb to the movements for peace.
Let us go forth to the women and to the men of every race and place,
to the young and to the old of every neighborhood,
to the next generations and to their children of every nation.
Let us go forth in the name of Wisdom Sophia, Shekinah
to celebrate feminist liturgies for life's journey,
to bless women at life-changing times,
to make the world safe for all children!

NOTES

1. Elisabeth Schüssler Fiorenza, *Discipleship of Equals: A Critical Ekklesialogy of Liberation* (New York: Crossroad, 1993), 331.

2. Mary E. Hunt, "Women-Church: An Introductory Overview," in Diann L. Neu and Mary E. Hunt, eds., *Women-Church Sourcebook* (Silver Spring, MD: WATERworks Press, 1993), 2.

3. Isabelle Graessle, "From Impasse to Passage: Reflections on the Church," *The Ecumencial Review*, vol. 53, no. 1 (January 2001): "On Being Church: Women's Voices and Visions" (Geneva: World Council of Churches), 27–28.

4. Letty Russell, "Hot-House Ecclesiology: A Feminist Interpretation of the Church," *The Ecumencial Review*, vol. 53, no. 1 (January 2001): "On Being Church: Women's Voices and Visions," (Geneva: World Council of Churches), 52–53.

5. See Lynn Gottlieb, *She Who Dwells Within: A Feminist Vision of a Renewed Judaism* (San Francisco: HarperSanFrancisco, 1995), 6.

6. Sandy Eisenberg Sasso, "Introduction: Unwrapping the Gift," in *Women and Religious Ritual*, ed. Lesley A. Northup (Washington, DC: Pastoral Press, 1993), ix.

7. Sue Levi Elwell, "Reclaiming Jewish Women's Oral Tradition: Rosh Hodesh," in *Women at Worship: Interpretations of North American Diversity*, ed. Marjorie Procter-Smith and Janet R. Walton (Louisville: Westminster John Knox Press, 1993), 123.

8. Judith Plaskow, *Standing Again at Sinai: Judaism from a Feminist Perspective* (San Francisco: Harper & Row, 1990), vii.

9. See Christine E. Gudorf, "The Power to Create: Sacraments and Men's Need to Birth," *Horizons* 14/2 (1987), 296–309. Susan A. Ross explores this in depth in *Extravagant Affections: A Feminist Sacramental Theology* (New York: Continuum, 1998).

SELECTED BIBLIOGRAPHY

Feminist Prayer, Liturgy, and Ritual

Abbott, Margie, RSM. *Sparks of the Cosmos: Rituals for Seasonal Use.* Unley, South Australia: MediaCom Education, 2001.

Adelman, Penina V. *Miriam's Well: Rituals for Jewish Women Around the Year.* Fresh Meadows, NY: Biblio Press, 1986.

Aldredge-Clanton, Jann. *Praying with Christ-Sophia.* Mystic, CT: Twenty-Third Publications, 1996.

Anderson, Virginia Cobb. *Prayers of Our Hearts in Word and Action.* New York: Crossroad, 1991.

Beben, Mary, and Bridget Mary Meehan. *Walking the Prophetic Journey: Eucharistic Liturgies for 21st Century Small Faith Communities.* Boulder: WovenWord Press, 1998.

Bell, Catherine. *Ritual: Perspectives and Dimensions.* New York: Oxford University Press, 1997.

Berger, Teresa, ed. *Women's Ways of Worship: Gender Analysis and Liturgical History.* Collegeville, MN: Liturgical Press, 1999.

________. *Dissident Daughters: Feminist Liturgies in Global Context.* Louisville: Westminster John Knox Press, 2001.

Bowe, Barbara, Kathleen Hughes, Sharon Karam, and Carolyn Osiek, eds. *Silent Voices, Sacred Lives: Women's Readings for the Liturgical Year.* New York: Paulist Press, 1992.

Bradshaw, Paul F., and Lawrence A. Hoffman, eds. *Life Cycles in Jewish and Christian Worship.* Notre Dame, IN: University of Notre Dame Press, 1996.

Breger, Jennifer, and Lisa Schlaff. *The Orthodox Jewish Woman and Ritual: Options and Opportunities—Birth.* New York: Jewish Orthodox Feminist Alliance, 2001.

________. *Bat Mitzvah.* New York: Jewish Orthodox Feminist Alliance, 2001.

Broner, E. M. *A Weave of Women*. New York: Bantam Books, 1978. Reprint, Indiana University Press, 1985.

________. *The Telling*. New York: HarperCollins, 1993.

________. *Bringing Home the Light: A Jewish Woman's Handbook of Rituals*. San Francisco: Council Oak Books, 1999.

Brooten, Bernadette J. *Women Leaders in the Ancient Synagogue: Inscriptional Evidence and Background Issues*. Brown Judaic Studies 36. Chico, CA: Scholars Press, 1982.

Butler, Becky, ed. *Ceremonies of the Heart: Celebrating Lesbian Unions*. Seattle: Seal Press, 1990.

Cady, Susan, Hal Taussig, and Marian Ronan. *Wisdom's Feast: Sophia in Study and Celebration*. San Francisco: Harper & Row, 1989.

Cardin, Rabbi Nina Beth. *Tears of Sorrow, Seeds of Hope: A Jewish Spiritual Companion for Infertility and Pregnancy Loss*. Woodstock, VT: Jewish Lights Publishing, 1999.

Carnes, Robin Deen, and Sally Craig. *Sacred Circles*. San Francisco: HarperCollins, 1998.

Caron, Charlotte. *To Make and Make Again: Feminist Ritual Thealogy*. New York: Crossroad, 1993.

Cherry, Kittredge, and Zalmon Sherwood, eds. *Equal Rites: Lesbian and Gay Worship, Ceremonies, and Celebrations*. Louisville: Westminister John Knox Press, 1995.

Clark, Linda, Marian Ronan, and Eleanor Walker. *Image-breaking/Image-building: A Handbook for Creative Worship with Women of Christian Tradition*. New York: Pilgrim Press, 1981.

Cohen, David, ed. *The Circle of Life: Rituals from the Human Family Album*. New York: HarperCollins, 1991.

Collins, Mary, and David Power, eds. *Can We Always Celebrate the Eucharist?* New York: Seabury Press, 1982.

________. *Blessing and Power*. Edinburgh, Scotland: T. and T. Clark, 1985.

Con-spirando. *Cuaderno de Ritos*. Santiago, Chile: Colectivo Conspirando, 1995.

Dierks, Shelia Durkin. *WomenEucharist*. Boulder: WovenWord Press, 1997.

Driver, Tom F. *Liberating Rites: Understanding the Transformative Power of Ritual*. Boulder: Westview Press, 1998.

Duck, Ruth. *Finding Words for Worship: A Guide for Leaders.* Louisville: Westminster John Knox Press, 1995.

Edelman, Marian Wright. *Guide My Feet: Prayers and Meditations on Loving and Working for Children.* Boston: Beacon Press, 1995.

Eiker, Diane, and Sapphire Eiker, eds. *Keep Simple Ceremonies.* Portland, ME: Astarte Shell Press, 1993.

Elkins, Heather Murray. *Worshiping Women: Re-forming God's People for Praise.* Nashville: Abingdon Press, 1994.

Falk, Marcia. *The Book of Blessings: New Jewish Prayers for Daily Life, the Sabbath, and the New Moon Festival.* San Francisco: HarperCollins, 1996.

Falk, Nancy, and Rita M. Gross, eds. *Unspoken Worlds: Women's Religious Lives in Non-Western Cultures.* San Francisco: Harper & Row, 1980.

Fine, Irene, and Bonnie Feinman. *Midlife and Its Rite of Passage Ceremony with a Midlife Celebration.* San Diego: Woman's Institute for Continuing Jewish Education, 1983.

Fine, Irene. *Midlife, A Rite of Passage: The Wise Woman, a Celebration.* San Diego: Woman's Institute for Continuing Jewish Education, 1988.

Froehle, Virginia Ann. *Called into Her Presence: Praying with Feminine Images of God.* Norte Dame, IN: Ave Maria Press, 1992.

Gjerding, Iben, and Katherine Kinnamon, eds. *No Longer Strangers: A Resource for Women and Worship.* Geneva, Switzerland: World Council of Churches, 1984.

Gottlieb, Lynn. *She Who Dwells Within: A Feminist Vision of a Renewed Judaism.* New York: HarperSanFrancisco, 1995.

Grinnan, Jeanne Frinkman, Mary Rose McCarthy, Barbara S. Mitrano, and Rosalie Muschal-Reinhardt. *Sisters of the Thirteen Moons: Rituals Celebrating Women's Lives.* Webster, NY: Prism Collective, 1997.

———. *Rituals for Women Coping with Breast Cancer.* Webster, NY: Prism Collective, 2000.

Haydock, snjm, Kathy McFaul, and the Women of Weavers. *We Are Sisters: Prayer and Ritual for Women's Spirituality and Empowerment.* Seattle: Intercommunity Peace & Justice Center, 1996.

Henderson, J. Frank, ed. *Remembering the Women: Women's Stories from Scripture for Sundays and Festivals.* Chicago: Liturgy Training Publications, 1999.

Henry, Kathleen M. *The Book of Ours: Liturgies for Feminist People.* Jamaica Plain, MA: Alabaster Jar Liturgical Arts, 1993.

Hoffman, Lawrence A. *Introduction to Life Cycles in Jewish and Christian Worship.* Notre Dame, IN: University of Notre Dame Press, 1996.

Howard, Julie. *We Are the Circle: Celebrating the Feminine in Song and Ritual.* Collegeville, MN: Liturgical Press, 1993.

Imber-Black, Evan, and Janine Roberts. *Rituals for Our Times.* New York: HarperCollins, 1992.

Inclusive-Language Lectionary Committee, ed. *An Inclusive-Language Lectionary: Readings for Years A–C.* Atlanta: John Knox Press and others for the Cooperative Publication Association, 1985–1987.

Katsuno-Ishii, Lynda, and Edna J. Orteza, eds. *Of Rolling Waters and Roaring Wind: A Celebration of the Woman Song.* Geneva, Switzerland: WCC Publications, 2000.

Kirk, Martha Ann. *Celebrations of Biblical Women's Stories: Tears, Milk and Honey.* Kansas City, MO: Sheed and Ward, 1987.

Klug, Lyn, ed. *Soul Weavings: A Gathering of Women's Prayers.* Minneapolis: Augsburg Fortress, 1996.

Knie, Ute, and Herta Leistner. *Lass horen deine Stimme: Werkstattbuch Feministische Liturgie.* Gütersloh: Gütersloher Verlagshaus, 1999.

Leistner, Herta. *Lass spüren deine Kraft: Feministische Liturgie.* Gütersloh: Gütersloher Verlagshaus, 1997.

Leviton, Richard. *Weddings by Design: A Guide to the Non-Traditional Ceremony.* San Francisco: Harper, 1993.

Ling, Coralie. "Creative Rituals: Celebrating Women's Experiences in an Australian Feminist Context," D.Min. diss., San Francisco Theological Seminary, 1998.

Littell, Marcia Sachs, and Sharon Weissman Gutman, eds. *Liturgies on the Holocaust.* Valley Forge, PA: Trinity Press International, 1996.

Luebering, Carol. *Planning the Funeral Liturgy: A Step-by-Step Guide for Families.* Cincinnati: St. Anthony Messenger Press, 1986.

Mahdi et al., eds. *Betwixt and Between: Patterns of Masculine and Feminine Initiation.* LaSalle: Open Court, 1987.

Mananzan, Mary John, ed. *Women and Religion: A Collection of Essays, Personal Histories, and Contextualized Liturgies.* 2d ed. Manila: Institute of Women's Studies, St. Scholastica College, 1992.

Martensen, Jean, ed. *Sing Out New Visions.* Minneapolis: Augsburg Fortress, 1998.

Matthews, Caitlin. *The Little Book of Celtic Blessings.* Elements Books, 1994.

McEwan, Dorothea, Pat Pinsent, Ianthe Pratt, and Veronica Seddon, eds. *Making Liturgy: Creating Rituals for Worship and Life.* Norwich, Norfolk, England: Canterbury Press, 2001.

Mitchell, Rosemary Catalano, and Gail Anderson Ricciuti. *Birthings and Blessings: Liberating Services for the Inclusive Church.* New York: Crossroad, 1991.

———. *Birthings and Blessings II: More Liberating Worship Services for the Inclusive Church.* New York: Crossroad, 1993.

Moore, Sally Falk, and Barbara G. Meyerhoff, eds. *Secular Ritual.* Assen, the Netherlands: Van Gorcum, 1977.

Morley, Janet. *All Desires Known: Inclusive Prayers for Worship and Meditation.* Harrisburg, PA: Morehouse Publishing, 1988, 1992.

Neu, Diann L. "Feminist Liturgies: Claiming Ourselves Church" (M.Div. and STM thesis, the Jesuit School of Theology, Berkeley, CA, 1982).

———. *Women-Church Celebrations: Feminist Liturgies for the Lenten Season.* Silver Spring, MD: WATERworks Press, 1985.

———. *Women and the Gospel Traditions: Feminist Celebrations.* Silver Spring, MD: WATERworks Press, 1989.

———. *Liturgia: Un Jardin Compartido.* Silver Spring, MD: WATERworks Press, 1995.

———. *Peace Liturgies.* Silver Spring, MD: WATERworks Press, 2001.

———. *Gathered at Sophia's Table.* Silver Spring, MD: WATERworks Press, 2001.

———. *Return Blessings: Ecofeminist Liturgies Renewing the Earth.* Cleveland: Pilgrim Press, 2002.

Neu, Diann L., and Mary E. Hunt. *Women of Fire: A Pentecost Event.* Silver Spring, MD: WATERworks Press, 1990.

———. *Women-Church Sourcebook.* Silver Spring, MD: WATERworks Press, 1993.

Neu, Diann L., and Ronnie Levin. *A Seder of the Sisters of Sarah: A Holy Thursday and Passover Seder.* Silver Spring, MD: WATERworks Press, 1986.

Neu, Diann L., Tobie Hofman, Barbara Cullom, and Mindy Shapiro. *Miriam's Sisters Rejoice.* Silver Spring, MD: WATERworks Press, 1988.

Neu, Diann L., Jessica Weissman, and Barbara Cullom. *Together at Freedom's Table.* Silver Spring, MD: WATERworks Press, 1991.

Niethammer, Carolyn. *Daughters of the Earth: The Lives and Legends of American Indian Women.* New York: Collier Books, 1977.

Northrup, Leslie A., ed. *Women and Religious Ritual.* Washington, DC: Pastoral Press, 1993.

________. *Ritualizing Women: Patterns of Spirituality.* Cleveland: Pilgrim Press, 1997.

Orenstein, Rabbi Debra, ed. *Lifecycles: Jewish Women on Life Passages & Personal Milestones.* Woodstock, VT: Jewish Lights Publishing, 1994.

Procter-Smith, Marjorie. *In Her Own Rite: Constructing Feminist Liturgical Tradition.* Nashville: Abingdon Press, 1990.

________. *Praying with Our Eyes Open: Engendering Feminist Liturgical Prayer.* Nashville: Abingdon Press, 1995.

Procter-Smith, Marjorie, and Janet R. Walton, eds. *Women at Worship: Interpretations of North American Diversity.* Louisville: Westminster John Knox Press, 1993.

Richardson, Jan L. *Sacred Journeys: A Woman's Book of Daily Prayer.* Nashville: Upper Room Books, 1995.

Rienstra, Marchiene Vroon. *Swallow's Nest: A Feminist Reading of the Psalms.* Grand Rapids: William B. Eerdmans, 1992.

Roberts, Elizabeth, and Elias Amidon, eds. *Earth Prayers.* San Francisco: HarperSanFrancisco, 1991.

________. *Life Prayers.* San Francisco: HarperSanFrancisco, 1996.

________. *Prayers for a Thousand Years.* San Francisco: HarperSanFrancisco, 1999.

Roberts, Wendy. *Celebrating Her: Feminist Ritualizing Comes of Age.* Cleveland: Pilgrim Press, 1998.

Ross, Susan A. *Extravagant Affections: A Feminist Sacramental Theology.* New York: Continuum, 1998.

Ruether, Rosemary Radford. *Women-Church: Theology and Practice.* San Francisco: Harper & Row, 1985.

Schaffran, Janet, and Pat Kozak. *More Than Words: Prayer and Ritual for Inclusive Communities.* Oak Park, IL: Meyer Stone Books, 1986.

Schmitt, Mary Kathleen Speegle. *Seasons of the Feminine Divine: Christian Feminist Prayers for the Liturgical Cycle.* New York: Crossroad, 1993.

________. *Seasons of the Feminine Divine: Cycle C, Christian Feminist Prayers for the Liturgical Cycle.* New York: Crossroad, 1994.

________. *Seasons of the Feminine Divine: Cycle A, Christian Feminist Prayers for the Liturgical Cycle.* New York: Crossroad, 1995.

Sears, Marge. *Life-Cycle Celebrations for Women.* Mystic, CT: Twenty-Third Publications, 1989.

Sewell, Marilyn, ed. *Cries of the Spirit.* Boston: Beacon Press, 1991.

________. *Claiming the Spirit Within.* Boston: Beacon Press, 1996.

Spiegel, Marcia Shon, and Deborah Lipton Kremsdorf. *Women Speak to God: The Prayers and Poems of Jewish Women.* San Diego: Women's Institute for Continuing Jewish Education, 1987.

St. Hilda's Community. *Women Included: A Book of Services and Prayers.* London: SPCK, 1991.

________. *The New Women Included.* London: SPCK, 1996.

Starhawk. *The Spiral Dance: A Rebirth of the Ancient Religion of the Great Goddess.* 2d ed. San Francisco: Harper & Row, 1989.

Stuart, Elizabeth, ed. *Daring to Speak Love's Name: A Gay and Lesbian Prayer Book.* London: Hamish Hamilton, 1992.

Swidler, Arlene, ed. *Sistercelebrations: Nine Worship Experiences.* Philadelphia: Fortress Press, 1974.

Turner, Victor. *Forest of Symbols.* Ithaca, NY: Cornell University Press, 1967.

________. *The Ritual Process: Structure and Anti-Structure.* Chicago: Aldine Publishing, 1969.

Van Gennep, Arnold. *The Rites of Passage.* Trans. Monika B. Vizedom and Gabrielle L. Caffee. Chicago: University of Chicago Press, 1960.

Walker, Barbara G. *Women's Rituals: A Sourcebook.* San Francisco: Harper & Row, 1990.

Walton, Janet R. *Feminist Liturgy: A Matter of Justice.* Collegeville, MN: Liturgical Press, 2000.

Ward, Hannah, and Jennifer Wild, eds. *Human Rites: Worship Resources for an Age of Change.* London: Mowbray, 1995.

Ward, Hannah, Jennifer Wild, and Janet Morley, eds. *Celebrating Women.* London: SPCK, 1995.

WATERwheel, 17-volume collection including feminist litugies. Silver Spring, MD: WATERworks Press, 1985–present.

Webster, Linda. *Womancircle Rituals: Celebrating Life, Sparking Connections.* Austin, TX: Women's Spirituality Group, First Unitarian Church, 1988.

Winter, Miriam Therese. *WomanPrayer, WomanSong: Resources for Ritual.* Oak Park, IL: Meyer Stone Books, 1987.

________. *WomanWord: A Feminist Lectionary and Psalter. Women of the New Testament.* New York: Crossroad, 1990.

________. *WomanWisdom: A Feminist Lectionary and Psalter. Women of the Hebrew Scriptures: Part One.* New York: Crossroad, 1991.

________. *WomanWitness: A Feminist Lectionary and Psalter. Women of the Hebrew Scriptures: Part Two.* New York: Crossroad, 1992.

Winter, Miriam Therese, Adair Lumis, and Alison Stokes, *Defecting in Place.* New York: Crossroad, 1995.

Women's Ordination Conference. *Liberating Liturgies.* Fairfax, VA: Women's Ordination Conference, 1989.

World Council of Churches. *Prayer & Poems, Songs & Stories: Ecumenical Decade 1988–1998.* Geneva, Switzerland: WCC Publications, 1998.

Zeballos, Dorys, ed. *No Estas Sola: Reflexionnes y Liturgias sobre Procreasion Responsible.* Montevideo, Uruguay: Catolicas por el derecho a decidir, 1991.

Women Musicians and Their Music

Boyce-Tillman, June. *In Praise of All Encircling Love,* Vols. 1 and 2. London: Association for Inclusive Language/Hildegard Press, 1992, 1995. Book and audio recording.

Boyce-Tillman, June, and Janet Wooton, eds. *Reflecting Praise.* London: Stainer & Bell/WIT, 1993.

Duck, Ruth, and Michael G. Bausch, eds. *Everflowing Streams: Songs for Worship.* Pilgrim Press, 700 Prospect Avenue, Cleveland OH 44115-1100. 1981. Book.

Eagleheart, Carole Etzler. *Womanriver Flowing On.* Carole Etzler Eagleheart, 1180 VT Route 22A, Bridport, VT 05734, ceagle @aol.com, www.homestead.com/eagleheart1, 1977. Audio recording.

________. *She Calls to Us.* Eagleheart. 2002. Book, audiocassette, compact disk.

Friedman, Debbie. *And You Shall Be a Blessing.* Sounds Write Productions, 6685 Norman Lane, San Diego, CA 92120, 619-697-6120, www.soundswrite.com. 1988. Audiocassette.

Fulmer, Colleen. *Cry of Ramah.* Heartbeats, 20015 Detroit Road, Cleveland, OH 04416. 800-808-1991. 1985. Book, audiocassette.

________. *Her Wings Unfurled.* Heartbeats. 1989. Book, audiocassette.

________. *Dancing Sophia's Circle.* Heartbeats. 1994. Book, audiocassette, compact disk.

Kealoha, Anna. *Songs of the Earth, Music of the World.* Celestial Arts, P.O. Box 7327, Berkeley, CA 94707. 1989. Book.

Libana. *A Circle is Cast.* Libana, Inc., P.O. Box 400530, Cambridge, MA 02140, 800-997-7757, www.libana.com, libana@aol.com. 1986. Book, audiocassette.

________. *Fire Within.* Libana. 1990. Book, audiocassette.

________. *Night Passage.* Libana. 2000. Book, audiocassette, compact disk.

McDade, Carolyn. *Songs by Carolyn McDade.* Surtesy Publishing, 25 Woodridge Road, Orleans, MA 02653-4806. 1982. Book.

________. *Rain Upon Dry Land.* Surtesy Publishing. 1984. Book, audiocassette.

________. *This Tough Spun Web.* Surtesy Publishing. 1985. Book, audiocassette, compact disk.

________. *The Best of Struggles.* Surtesy Publishing. 1989. Book, audiocassette, compact disk.

________. *This Ancient Love.* Surtesy Publishing. 1990. Book, audiocassette, compact disk.

________. *Songs for Congregational Singing.* Surtesy Publishing. 1991. Book.

________. *Sister, Carry On.* Surtesy Publishing. 1992. Book, audiocassette, compact disk.

Middleton, Julie Forest, ed. *Songs for Earthlings.* Emerald Earth Publishing, P.O. Box 1946, Sebastopol, CA 95473. 707-829-0868, emeraldearth@aol.com. 1998. Book.

Near, Holly. *HARP.* Hereford Music, c/o Alison de Grassi, alison@greatspeakers.com. 1985 and 2001. Audiocassette, compact disk.

Re-Imagining Community. *Bring the Feast Songs.* Pilgrim Press, 700 Prospect Avenue, Cleveland, OH 44115-1100, www.pilgrimpress.com. 1998. Book.

Sherman, Kathy, CSJ. *Touch the Earth.* Sisters of St. Joseph of La Grange, La Grange, IL 60525. 800-354-3504, www.ministryofhearts.org. 1987. Book, audiocassette, compact disk.

________. *Gather the Dreamers.* Sisters of St. Joseph of La Grange. 1991. Book, audiocassette, compact disk.

________. *Upon a Universe.* Sisters of St. Joseph of La Grange. 1992. Book, audiocassette, compact disk.

________. *Dance in the Dawn.* Sisters of St. Joseph of La Grange. 1993. Book, audiocassette, compact disk.

________. *Coming Home.* Sisters of St. Joseph of La Grange, 1994. Book, audiocassette, compact disk.

Silvestro, Marsie. *Circling Free.* Moonsong Productions, 79 Mt. Pleasant Avenue, Glouchester, MA 01930. 978-282-1655. 1983. Book, audiocassette, compact disk.

________. *Crossing the Lines.* Moonsong Productions. 1987. Book, audiocassette, compact disk.

________. *On the Other Side.* Moonsong Productions. 1993. Book, audiocassette, compact disk.

Sweet Honey in the Rock. *Good News.* Flying Fish Records, Inc. 1304 W. Schubert, Chicago, IL 60614. 1981. Book, audiocassette, compact disk.

Ware, SL, Ann Patrick. *New Words for Old Hymns and Songs*. Women's Liturgy Group of New York City, c/o Claire S. Derway, 1120 Fifth Avenue, New York, NY 10128, 212-860-0980. 2000. Book.

Wendelborn, Betty. *Sing Green: Songs of the Mystic*. Pyramid Press, 29 King Edward Street, Mount Eden, Auckland 3, New Zealand. 1988. betty.wendelborn@clear.net.nz. Book, audiocassette.

Winter, Miriam Therese. *Woman Prayer, Woman Song*. Crossroad Publishing, 370 Lexington Avenue, New York, NY 10017. 1990. Book.

________. *Songlines: Hymns, Songs, Rounds and Refrains for Prayer and Praise*. Crossroad Publishing. 1996. Book.

Other Works of Interest

Adams, Carol, ed. *Ecofeminism and the Sacred*. New York: Continuum, 1993.

Allen, Paula Gunn. *The Sacred Hoop: Recovering the Feminine in American Indian Traditions*. Boston: Beacon Press, 1986.

________. *Grandmothers of the Light: A Medicine Woman's Sourcebook*. Boston: Beacon Press, 1991.

Amoah, Elizabeth, ed. *Where God Reigns*. Accra, Ghana: Circle of Concerned African Women Theologians, 1997.

Aquino, Maria Pilar. *Our Cry for Life: Feminist Theology from Latin America*. Maryknoll, NY: Orbis Books, 1993.

Baker-Fletcher, Karen. *Sisters of Dust, Sisters of Spirit: Womanist Wordings on God and Creation*. Minneapolis: Fortress Press, 1998.

Belenky, Mary, Blyhe Clinchy, Nancy Goldbeger, and Jill Tarule, *Women's Ways of Knowing*. New York: Basic Books, 1986.

Berneking, Nancy J., and Pamela Carter Joern, eds. *Re-Membering and Re-Imagining*. Cleveland: Pilgrim Press, 1995.

Brenneman, Walter L., and Mary G. Brenneman. *Crossing the Circle at the Holy Wells of Ireland*. Charlottesville, VA: University Press of Virginia, 1995.

Brown, Judith K., and Virginia Kerns. *In Her Prime,* 2d ed. Chicago: University of Illinois Press, 1992.

Budapest, Zsuzsanna E. *The Grandmother of Time.* San Francisco: Harper & Row, 1979.

Cameron, Anne. *Daughters of Copper Woman.* Vancouver: Press Gang, 1981.

Canon, Katie. *Katie's Cannon: Womanism and the Soul of the Black Community.* New York: Continuum, 1995.

Chodorow, Nancy. *The Reproduction of Mothering: Psychoanalysis and the Sociology of Gender.* Berkeley: University of California Press, 1978.

Christ, Carol. *The Rebirth of the Goddess: Finding Meaning in Feminist Spirituality.* Reading, MA: Addison-Wesley, 1997.

Chung Hyun-Kyung. *Struggle to Be the Sun Again: Introducing Asian Women's Theology.* Maryknoll, NY: Orbis Books, 1990.

Diamant, Anita. *The Red Tent.* New York: St. Martin's Press, 1997.

Doyle, Brendan. *Meditations with Julian of Norwich.* Sante Fe: Bear & Co., 1983.

Eagle, Brook Medicine. *Red Flower: Rethinking Menstruation.* Freedom, CA: Crossing Press, 1988.

Eiesland, Nancy. *The Disabled God.* Nashville: Abingdon Press, 1994.

Fabella, Virginia, M. M., and Mercy Amba Oduyoye. *With Passion and Compassion: Third World Women Doing Theology.* Maryknoll, NY: Orbis Books, 1988.

Fabella, Virginia, M. M., and Sun Ai Lee Park. *We Dare to Dream: Doing Theology as Asian Women.* Seoul, Korea: Asian Women's Resource Center, 1989.

Falk, Marcia. *Song of Songs: A New Translation and Interpretation by Marcia Falk.* San Francisco: Harper, 1990.

Gebara, Ivone. *Levanta-te e anda: Aguns aspectos da caminhada da mulher na America Latina.* Sao Paulo: Edicoes Paulinas, 1989.

________. *Longing for Running Water: Ecofeminism and Liberation.* Minneapolis: Fortress Press, 1999.

Gilligan, Carol. *In a Different Voice: Psychological Theory and Women's Development.* Cambridge, MA: Harvard University Press, 1982.

Gimbutas, Marija. *The Language of the Goddess.* San Francisco: Harper & Row, 1989.

Gudorf, Christine. *Sex and Pleasure*. Cleveland: Pilgrim Press, 1994.

Hayes, Diana L. *Hagar's Daughters: Womanist Ways of Being in the World*. New York/Mahwah: Paulist Press, 1996.

Heyward, Carter. *Our Passion for Justice: Images of Power, Sexuality and Liberation*. Cleveland: Pilgrim Press, 1984.

Hunt, Mary E. *Fierce Tenderness: A Feminist Theology of Friendship*. New York: Crossroad, 1991.

Isasi-Diaz, Ada Maria. *Mujerista Theology*. Maryknoll, NY: Orbis Books, 1996.

Isherwood, Lisa, and Elizabeth Stuart. *Introducing Body Theology*. Sheffield, England: Sheffield Academic Press, 1998.

Jay, Nancy. *Throughout Your Generations Forever: Sacrifice, Religion, and Patriarchy*. Chicago: University of Chicago Press, 1992.

Jensen, Anne. God's *Self-confident Daughters: Early Christianity and the Liberation of Women*. Trans. O. C. Dean, Jr. Louisville: Westminster John Knox Press, 1996.

Jewell, Terri L. *The Black Women's Gumbo Ya-Ya: Quotations by Black Women*. Freedom, CA: Crossing Press, 1993.

Johnson, Elisabeth. *Women, Earth, and Creator Spirit*. New York: Paulist Press, 1993.

Johnson, Luke Timothy. *The Writings of the New Testament: An Interpretation*. Rev. ed. Minneapolis: Fortress Press, 1999.

Jordan, Judith V., Alexandra G. Kaplan, Jean Baker Miller, Irene P. Stiver, and Janet L. Surrey. *Women's Growth in Connection: Writings from the Stone Center*. New York: Guilford Press, 1991.

Jung, Patricia Beattie, Mary E. Hunt, and Radhika Balakrishnan, eds. *Good Sex: Feminist Perspectives from the World's Religions*. New Brunswick, NJ, and London: Rutgers University Press, 2001.

Kanyoro, Musimbi R. A., and Nyambura J. Njoroge, eds. *Groaning in Faith: African Women in the Household of God*. Nairobi, Kenya: Acton Publishers, 1996.

King, Ursula, ed. *Feminist Theology from the Third World: A Reader*. Maryknoll, NY: Orbis Books, 1994.

Kraemer, Ross S., ed. *Maenads, Martyrs, Matrons, Monastics: A Sourcebook on Women's Religions in the Greco-Roman World*. Philadelphia: Fortress Press, 1988.

________. *Her Share of the Blessings: Women's Religions among Pagans, Jews, and Christians in the Greco-Roman World.* New York: Oxford University Press, 1992.

Kwok, Pui-lan. *Discovering the Bible in the Non-Biblical World.* Maryknoll, NY: Orbis Books, 1994.

________. *Introducing Asian Feminist Theology.* Cleveland: Pilgrim Press, 2000.

MacDonald, Margaret Y. *Early Christian Women and Pagan Opinion: The Power of the Hysterical Woman.* Cambridge, England: Cambridge University Press, 1984.

Maggio, Rosalie, comp., *The New Beacon Book of Quotations by Women.* Boston: Beacon Press, 1996.

Mananzan, Mary John, Mercy Amba Oduyoye, Elsa Tamez, J. Shannon Clarkson, Mary C. Grey, and Letty M. Russell, eds. *Women Resisting Violence.* Maryknoll, NY: Orbis Books, 1996.

McCoy, Edain. *Celtic Women's Spirituality.* St Paul, MN: Llewellyn Publications, 1998.

McFague, Sallie. *The Body of God: An Ecological Theology.* Minneapolis: Fortress Press, 1993.

________. *Super, Natural Christians: How We Should Love Nature.* Minneapolis: Fortress Press, 1997.

________. *Life Abundant: Rethinking Theology and Economy for a Planet in Peril.* Minneapolis: Fortress Press, 2001.

Moltmann-Wendel, Elisabeth. *I Am My Body: A Theology of Embodiment.* New York: Continuum, 1995.

Neuger, Christie Cozad. *Counseling Women.* Minneapolis: Fortress Press, 2001.

Newsom, Carol A., and Sharon H. Ringe, eds. *Women's Bible Commentary.* Louisville: Westminster John Knox Press, 1998.

Oduyoye, Mercy Amba. *Daughters of Anowa: African Women and Patriarchy.* Maryknoll, NY: Orbis Books, 1995.

Oduyoye, Mercy Amba, and Musimbi Kanyoro. *The Will to Rise: Women, Tradition and the Church in Africa.* Maryknoll, NY: Orbis Books, 1992.

Olsen, Tillie, ed. *Mother to Daughter, Daughter to Mother: A Daybook and Reader.* New York: Feminist Press, 1984.

Owen, Laura. *Her Blood is Gold.* New York: HarperCollins, 1993.

Piercy, Marge. *The Moon Is Always Female*. New York: Alfred A. Knopf, 1980.

Qoyawayma, Polingaysi. *No Turning Back*. As told to Vada F. Carlson. Albuquerque, NM: University of New Mexico Press, 1964.

Rapoport, Nessa. *A Woman's Book of Grieving*. New York: William Morrow, 1994.

Ress, Mary Judith, Ute Siebert-Cuadra, and Lene Siorup, eds. *Del Cielo a la Tierra: Una Antolotia de Teologia Feminista*. Santiago, Chile: Sello Azul, 1994.

Rich, Adrienne. *The Dream of a Common Language: Poems 1974–1977*. New York: W. W. Norton, 1978.

Ruether, Rosemary Radford. *New Women, New Earth: Sexist Ideologies and Human Liberation*. New York: Seabury Press, 1975.

________. *Sexism and God-Talk: Toward a Feminist Theology*. Boston: Beacon Press, 1983.

________. *Women-Church: Theology and Practice*. San Francisco: Harper & Row, 1985.

________. *Gaia and God: An Ecofeminist Theology of Earth Healing*. San Francisco: Harper & Row, 1992.

________, ed. *Women Healing Earth: Third World Women on Ecology, Feminism and Religion*. Maryknoll, NY: Orbis Books, 1996.

Russell, Letty M. *Church in the Round: Feminist Interpretation of the Church*. Louisville: Westminster John Knox Press, 1993.

Russell, Letty M., and Shannon Clarkson, eds. *Dictionary of Feminist Theologies*. Louisville: Westminster John Knox Press, 1996.

Saint Exupery, Antoine de. *The Little Prince*. New York: Harcourt, Brace & World, 1943, 1971.

Sarton, May. *Collected Poems 1930–1993*. New York: W. W. Norton, 1974.

Sasso, Sandy Eisenberg, and Sue Levi Elwell. *Jewish Women: A Mini-course*. Denver: Alternatives in Religious Education, 1983.

Schüssler Fiorenza, Elisabeth. *In Memory of Her: A Feminist Theological Reconstruction of Christian Origins*. Reprint. New York: Crossroad, 1983, 1994.

________. *But She Said: Feminist Practices of Biblical Interpretation*. Boston: Beacon Press, 1992.

________. *Discipleship of Equals: A Critical Feminist Ekklesialogy of Liberation*. New York: Crossroad, 1993.

________. *Jesus, Miriam's Child, Sophia's Prophet*. New York: Crossroad, 1999.

Shange, Ntozake. *Sassafrass, Cypress & Indigo*. New York: St. Martin's Press, 1982.

Stevenson-Moessner, Jeanne, ed. *Through the Eyes of Women: Insights for Pastoral Care*. Minneapolis: Fortress Press, 1996.

________. *In Her Own Time*. Minneapolis: Fortress Press, 2000.

Stewart, A., and M. Lykes, eds. *Gender and Personality: Current Perspectives on Theory and Research*. Durham, NC: Duke University Press, 1985.

Taylor, Dena, and Amber Coverdale Sumrall. *Women of the 14th Moon: Writings on Menopause*. Freedom, CA: Crossing Press, 1991.

Uhlien, Gabriele, ed. *Meditations with Hildegard of Bingen*. Santa Fe, NM: Bear & Co, 1982.

Walker, Alice. *Temple of My Familiar*. New York: Simon and Schuster, 1989.

INDEX